Walking
with
the Master

Walking
with the Master

ANSWERING
THE CALL OF JESUS

ELIZABETH CLARE PROPHET
AND
STAFF OF SUMMIT UNIVERSITY

THE SUMMIT LIGHTHOUSE LIBRARY

WALKING WITH THE MASTER
Answering the Call of Jesus
by Elizabeth Clare Prophet and Staff of Summit University
Copyright © 2002 The Summit Lighthouse Library
All rights reserved

For information, please contact The Summit Lighthouse Library, PO Box 5000, Corwin Springs, MT 59030-5000.
Tel: 1-800-245-5445 or 406-848-9500.
E-mail: tslinfo@tsl.org
Web site: www.tsl.org

THE SUMMIT LIGHTHOUSE LIBRARY®
is an imprint of Summit University Press.®

Library of Congress Control Number: 2002105534
ISBN: 0-9720402-1-8

Design and production: Brad Davis
Layout: Brad Davis
Cover: James Bennett

Printed in the United States of America

07   06   05   04   03   6   5   4   3   2

*To all who would be
disciples of Jesus
and follow
in his footsteps*

Contents

About This Book

Walking with the Master is a comprehensive, yet practical course for the sincere devotee of Jesus Christ who aspires to be his disciple.

Along with selected excerpts from Jesus' discourses we have compiled additional teaching from the masters and from their messenger Elizabeth Clare Prophet to explain and expand on Jesus' Calls and his message. We have also added commentary and spiritual exercises that we hope you will find helpful in applying Jesus' teachings and answering his Calls in your daily life.

Jesus Calls us to be "fishers of men," teachers who can share his teaching with a world still hungry for his truth and comfort. If you desire to follow in the footsteps of the Lord, you will hear his voice speaking clearly to you through the pages of this book.

The Staff of Summit University

Introduction

Two thousand years ago, Jesus called his first disciples with these words: "Come, leave your nets; and I will make you fishers of men." The Call went forth to the twelve, the other seventy, and many others during Jesus' Galilean mission.

And now, at the turning of the age, Jesus opens the door to discipleship in a more than ordinary way. Jesus sends forth the Call through nineteen powerful discourses to his students around the world. These messages were delivered through Elizabeth Clare Prophet, a disciple of Jesus and a messenger for the ascended masters.

Jesus outlines here a path of discipleship that is practical and accessible in the twenty-first century. It is a path that requires a great deal of us—and yet offers something incomparable in return.

He issues twenty-eight specific Calls, which represent a spiral of initiation. The goal is outlined by Jesus himself: "He that believeth on me, the works that I do shall he do also; and greater works than these shall he do; because I go unto my Father."[1] This is a comprehensive course of spiritual instruction for those who would walk and talk with the Master today, all the way to their own reunion with the Father.

The Meaning of Discipleship

Jesus' mission in Palestine was one that changed the world. Yet, it was after only three short years that he rose from Bethany's hill. The world has known him since that time as a very real and living master, now ascended, and his departure from that scene did not close the door to discipleship. During these two millennia the ascended master Jesus has appeared to many and called them to this path. The first we have a record of is Paul, who was confronted by Jesus on the road to Damascus and who received his teaching directly from Jesus over many years.[2] Through the centuries many have heard his Call and answered. Jesus spoke to Saint Francis of Assisi from the cross of San Damiano. When Saint Catherine of Siena was a mere child of six, she had a vision of Christ the King, and from that time she knew a very personal relationship with Jesus. Saint Teresa of Avila experienced an interior call from the Master that was so powerful it set her course for the rest of her life.

The true foundation of Christianity is not so much that Jesus lived on earth two thousand years ago, but that he lives today, and we can have a direct relationship with him that the disciples and apostles and many others have known.

What does it mean to be a disciple of the master in the fullest sense?

Perhaps we will never really know until we experience it personally. We know that this relationship and the love of the Master has inspired some of the most beautiful and profound writings of the Christian mystics. They speak of a love greater than any known in this world—a mystical union of the soul with the beloved. They liken it to a marriage, perhaps finding in this the closest approximation in human experience to a bliss that cannot adequately be described in words.

Jesus himself speaks of it in metaphors. He speaks of himself as the good shepherd, the one who lays down his life for the sheep. He speaks of himself as the sower of the good seed. And he uses the image of the vine:

> I am the vine, ye are the branches: He that abideth in me, and I in him, the same bringeth forth much fruit: for without me ye can do nothing.... If ye abide in me, and my words abide in you, ye shall ask what ye will, and it shall be done unto you. Herein is my Father glorified, that ye bear much fruit; so shall ye be my disciples.[3]

This relationship of master and disciple is one that is, in some ways, understood even better in the East than in the West. In India the path of following a master, or *guru*, has been known for thousands of years, and it has long been taught that only as the disciple, or *chela*, of a true master can one achieve salvation. Jesus' message is the same. Unless we abide in him as the vine, the master, the guru, we can do nothing. Unless we come as disciple, as chela, unless we have a direct relationship with the master, we can make no real progress on the spiritual path. Knowing a teaching is not enough—we must have a real and vital bonding to the master.

Our hope in publishing this book is that you will come to know the Master personally as you walk and talk with him. We also hope that you will come to know the angels and other masters who come to support his mission of salvation for planet Earth.

As you study these Calls of the Master, may you discover how you can personally answer them and thus fulfill your own destiny and your mission in this life.

CHAPTER 1

"Come, leave your nets!
I will make you fishers of men."

"Come, Leave Your Nets—
I Will Make You Fishers of Men"

"Come now, let us reason together," saith the LORD. "Though your sins be as scarlet, I will make them white as snow."

Consider, then, the lilies of the field and the eternal whiteness of the Mother's blooming in thy heart, O child of love. Consider, then, and understand that God has called thee to a mighty purpose—not forever to be engaged in the transmutation of sin, but to do so with joy and all Godspeed, knowing that this is not the end! No, the goal that is set for thee is another.

Let us study the teaching and become it and not forever be learners, never coming to the knowledge of Truth. For this, too, is not the end—all things converging through the assimilation of the body and blood of Christ, the universality of the Father-Mother God; all things coming to the quintessence of thy being.

What is this goal of thy being—cleansed, purified, God-taught, truly the Word present? The goal, beloved, is that thou thyself be our magnet in the earth, magnetizing the little ones, the ones who are caught—caught truly in the intense tide of the temptations of the world, caught up in the magnetism of the senses. They are not fed by God. They have not the wholeness of the Holy Spirit. They seek it by outer means.

Beloved ones, you who know the temptations and the experiences of life understand full well what is this pull of which I speak. It is a counterweight and an antimagnet, consisting of the entire momentum of nihilism—the denial of God the Father, the Son, the Holy Spirit and the Mother—the entire counterweight of those who have chosen the left-handed path and stolen the light of the Mother to enshrine it as a way of death to be followed by the many.

Understand, therefore, that to rescue the souls from this pull and tide of the world and the mass consciousness requires pillars of eternity, the Polestar, the magnet of the Central Sun, as *you* (as your heart, your chakras, your soul, your spirit), that when you encounter souls on the path of life and they come into your orbit, they are drawn mightily by archangels and the I AM Presence for realignment to Reality.

This, beloved, is known as the power of conversion—the power of conversion whereby I converted Saul of Tarsus on the road to Damascus, raising him up to be the apostle Paul and thus giving to him also these teachings and this lesson whereby he became that magnet and became the LORD's instrument, a converter of souls—turning around, demagnetizing them from error and evil and maya, fastening them to God by the mighty cross of Christ. This is the goal of thy striving, thy work, thy service, thy learning, thy purification, thy preparation.

Let us not be caught up in the ritual. Let us not allow the ritual to become rote. Let us not forever dally in the process itself, but understand that we are on the highway of our God. We move on! We internalize Truth. We do so quickly, for souls are caught in the downstream current and they need to be rescued.

Therefore, I come this Thanksgiving Day 1984, and I speak to you personally, spirits of the living fire, brothers and sisters of the eternal flame of Zarathustra, Melchizedek, Helios, seraphim of God. All saints are worshipers of the sacred fire. And in this heart, I come—I come and I call you. I call you fervently as Jesus, your brother and your loved one.

I AM the Beloved and I AM the rose of Sharon, and I ensconce myself firmly, one with your messenger. Have no fear, for I shall be—and she in me shall be—the instrument for the raising up of the nations of the earth, for doing all those things that are promised. Fear not—fear not the fulfillment of my mission through this vessel. For it is come to pass and it shall be and none shall turn it. But fear this, O soul: Fear that thou mayest miss thine own calling to also be myself.

Fear, then, that in the hour of the fulfillment of God's holy purpose through this mission of the Mother of the World that thou might be set aback by the darkness rising from the mists of the unconscious. Fear, then, and know that this fear is the sense of the awe and the holiness of God in thy Presence eternally. And have the sense of the honor of God, trembling before the sacred fire of Sinai and knowing that in this hour the LORD thy God does require of thee the fulfillment of thy holy purpose. This is the reason for thy calling, for thy blessing, for our love to thee.

For angels have gone forth from the Keeper of the Scrolls, reading unto us, the ascended masters, the names of those of whom the LORD does require answer in this hour and decade and century. And to each and every one of these we have sent forth legions of light to draw them to the fount of this wisdom, this path and this teaching. For it is written in the Book of Life that the LORD thy God does require of thee in this hour the fulfillment of thy holy purpose and thy calling.

Thy choice to be here is the choice to fulfill a fiery destiny that cannot be delayed any longer, will not be set back! Thus the open door of opportunity is given to the world of lightbearers whose names are written in the Book of Life and to many others whose names are not written therein—that they might be converted, that they might be drawn back to the original Creator, to the Elohim, and repent and be saved and therefore fulfill the requirement to become God instead of the anti-God.

It is the hour of the LORD's requiring of the law of thy being. Thus, in the case of those who have deified evil as an "energy veil," the LORD God does require of them this day also that they fulfill their reason for being. Thus, there is outpictured and outplayed in their world, beloved hearts of living fire, before their very eyes, from the beginning unto the ending (as there does flash before the one drowning), the entire record of the sowing of the seeds of the flowers of evil.

And they may choose to live in the grace of God and be converted and come under the rod and the shadow of the Almighty through the I AM Presence and the LORD's anointed and the

Mother flame and the one who holds it. And if they do not accept the conversion of the Holy Ghost and the holy angels and the holy Mother, then the requirement of the Law shall be unto them as a searing fire of judgment as they and their works must stand the trial by fire and be consumed.

Understand, beloved hearts, that the opportunity of the light-bearers to be all that they truly are is an opportunity that has a cycle and a season. And to each one it is given seven days, seven months, seven years, seven centuries. But in the end of the cycle, beloved hearts, if those unto whom the LORD has required the fulfillment of Sonship deny that Sonship, its source in the Mother and in the Father, then the Law shall require of them every jot and tittle of their karma, every jot and tittle of their evil sowing.[1]

This is the law of the ages. But in the hour of its speaking through the messenger, it becomes a physical binding—a binding of the soul to God for his liberation or the binding of the soul to God for his undoing. Understand, blessed ones, that for some the binding of the soul to God is a gross inconvenience, an uncomfortability, and they lash and they thrash. And they lash out against the great light. Therefore, this resistance to the impelling force of love becomes their undoing.

Is not God the keeper of his universe? Is this not God's universe? Then does not the LORD thy God, the Holy One of Israel, have therefore the God-freedom to determine the cycles of the appearing of his sons and daughters and to require fruits of a harvest long overdue and to deliver his people from this ongoing struggle with forces of darkness beyond their ability to overcome? Is not God in his temple through Sanat Kumara and through the hearts of his own? God, therefore, the knower of all things, does call the cycles. And happy are ye who live in the fulfillment of my age and in the inauguration of the age of the seventh angel.[2]

Therefore, on this day, in the full knowledge and the profound awareness of the Law behind these words, I say to all entangled in karma, in the personality cult, and in the pull of the world: *Come, leave your nets! I will make you fishers of men.*

This is a calling directly to the heart of every student of the ascended masters. In Maitreya's name I come to teach you the way of Maitreya's path, to teach you the way of being the Mediator, as Moses is the eternal Mediator; the way of your Christ Self, as your Christ Self is the way of the eternal Mediator; the way of the Shepherd and the way of the magnet of the Central Sun—the way of being the pillar in the temple of my God[3] (which signifies the Alpha/Omega polarity of the magnet), the way of being the instrument of the Holy Ghost that through thee none may resist my presence.

I AM Jesus, the Saviour of all men. I bring opportunity for your salvation—the true elevation of the Real Self within you—that you might be the instruments of the Saviour of all men. I ask that you discontinue to separate me from my messenger but remember that heaven is much closer than this.

You may count on my Word, not upon the outer person of anyone. You may count on my Word and the Word made flesh. And you may know that as you become the Rock and reach for "the Rock," as it was said, "that is higher than I,"[4] you shall also be instruments of my love.

May you recognize the calling and know that there is a cycle to leave the nets of the world and come apart. And when the calling goes forth, those who answer receive ministering angels to assist. The world must be served notice through the messenger and through yourselves in the indomitable will of God that the hour of repentance and eternal life is at hand, that the hour of the opening of the twelve gates of the city is at hand, that the hour of Truth is come.

This dispensation is now extended to all, everywhere on earth. May they hear it through your lips and hearts, through your consciousness in stern meditation upon the Word, in unswerving concentration. May the devils tremble! And indeed, they do tremble at the sound of my footstep through ye all. And may your hearts not tremble for fear but rejoice and give a mighty shout that God shall deliver you in every instance from the tempter.

Know the Word. Know the secrets. Write them in thy heart.

And then, when the devil does assail thee in the way and in the hour of the fasting and the prayer and the service, thou wilt have the answer. It is written: "Man shall not live by bread alone, but by every word that proceedeth out of the mouth of God."[5] This is thy sacred trust: that all "these things," as bread, are as naught. For the Word is life and the Word giveth life and the Word giveth all these things to those who require them.

No other hand shall feed thee but my own. No other hand shall teach thee. No other heart shall love thee. No other mind shall confound thee, but the mind of Christ shall be with thee. It is the principle of the Law of the One.

I the LORD thy God am a jealous God.[6] I deserve and desire all of thy desiring and thy love and thy life—not half, but all. When thou givest all of thyself, I give all of myself. And the Father and the Son shall live in thy temple.[7] This means, beloved, thou shalt walk the earth no longer the Presence above thee, the Christ Self above thee; but the Father in heaven and myself, through the I AM Presence and Christ Self, shall dwell bodily within you. Until this shall occur, the Holy Spirit in the full power of the Godhead cannot come upon thee.

Thus, strive to *be* the Presence, to *be* the Christ. And listen to the inner voice that does guide thee. Before thou speakest in an ungodly manner, the Presence does warn: Refrain thy speech; it is not pleasing unto the LORD. Each act, each desiring, each contemplation of deceit or ambition as it does come from the tempter is rebuked by the Christ. Listen to the inner voice and obey, and all shall be well with thee and the bliss of God shall be upon thee. And the holy angels will see that not a hair on thy head is touched.

Be at peace in the Calling. Let those who would be tutored in the path of fishers of men fear not the Word of the LORD and fear not his Work. We have enshrined this place for the *full* appearing of that Word and Work in ye all. And I say full appearing. And when I say it, understand that the fullness of God has need of thousands upon thousands of instruments, each one showing a shining facet of the treasure of heaven. Thus, we assemble the mighty, the eagles, as well as the meek of the earth. Let the Word and the Work of God in you be a monument to the testimony of the Great White Brotherhood through the messengers and yourselves—a temple built without hands, eternal forever.

I behold you here and now as saints: saints Above and below. And I behold your destiny as ascended masters of the Great White Brotherhood.* I, Jesus, call you to become fishers of men in the full knowledge that in this thy sacred labor the requirements of thy being shall be filled. And I consecrate our messenger to tend to the hearts of those so inclined, for in this answer ye are my disciples indeed....

Come now, fishers of men, for there are many ways to catch souls into the net of God. It is a divine net. And each one must come because he savors the offering and is drawn by that special sweetness, that special preparation of your heart with my heart. We two walking together—behold, let us convert the world!

I AM with you always, even unto the end of this state of world consciousness and unrest.[8] And truly, beloved, it shall end! The question is *when*. The answer from you will determine and make the difference.

Come unto me, ye who labor and are heavy laden. My burden is light. My yoke is easy.[9]

Come, disciples of the eternal Word. Come, leave your nets.

---

*The ascended masters are our elder brothers and sisters on the path of personal Christhood. Having balanced their karma and accomplished their unique mission, they have graduated from earth's schoolroom and ascended to God.

They are a part of the Great White Brotherhood, spoken of in Revelation 7 as the great multitude of saints "clothed with white robes" who stand before the throne of God. (The term "white" refers not to race but to the aura of white light that surrounds these immortals.) The Brotherhood works with earnest seekers and public servants of every race, religion and walk of life to assist humanity in their forward evolution.

Among these saints are Gautama Buddha, Maitreya, Jesus Christ, Saint Michael the Archangel, Zarathustra, Moses, Melchizedek, Mother Mary, Saint Francis, Saint Germain, El Morya, and unnumbered and unnamed loving hearts, servants of humanity who have ascended to the I AM THAT I AM and are a part of the living God forevermore.

I will make you fishers of men. We shall convert a world!

In the name of the Mother, I AM come. In the name of the heart of the Mother, I AM come. In the name of the life, the mind, the soul and the purity of the Mother, I AM come.

November 22, 1984
Thanksgiving Day
Royal Teton Ranch North
near Livingston, Montana

And Jesus, walking by the sea of Galilee, saw two brethren,
Simon called Peter, and Andrew his brother, casting a net into
the sea: for they were fishers.
And he saith unto them, Follow me, and I will make you
fishers of men.
And they straightway left their nets, and followed him.[10]

Jesus' first Call to his disciples is recorded in these verses
from the gospel of Matthew.

In this dictation from Jesus we experience the timelessness of
his teaching. Just as he called his disciples by the sea of Galilee to
leave their nets and follow him, he comes today with the same
Call: "Come, leave your nets! I will make you fishers of men."

What if the apostles had not answered Jesus' Call? Perhaps
they would have lived out their lives as fishermen. The world
would be little different for their having lived, and their lives from
beginning to end would probably have changed little. But how
much their lives—and the world—were changed when they followed Jesus!

They had to decide whether they would answer the Call and
follow him—and we have the same choice. What will our
response be?

If we were to immediately leave our "nets" and follow Jesus,
as the apostles did, we realize that our lives might never be the
same again. It would require a leap of faith, a leap into the
unknown. Follow him—where? We do not know. The only way
to find out is to follow.

It was clear what Peter and Andrew had to do to answer
Jesus' call, and their response was immediate. But how do we
respond to this call today? What does it really mean to follow the
Master? And what are the nets we must leave behind?

Jesus tells us that these *nets* represent the entanglements in
our "karma, in the personality cult, and in the pull of the world."

Leaving these things doesn't mean that we have to close our businesses or leave our occupations or families. We may have responsibilities that are ordinate and are part of our divine plan. It does mean, however, that we must leave behind our preoccupations and *inordinate* desires for the things of this world. This requires a shift in consciousness.

He says: "When thou givest all of thyself, I give all of myself. And the Father and the Son shall live in thy temple. This means, beloved, thou shalt walk the earth no longer the Presence above thee, the Christ Self above thee; but the Father in heaven and myself, through the I AM Presence and Christ Self, shall dwell bodily within you." This means that the three figures in the Chart of Your Divine Self (see page 373) become one.

And in answering the Call, we must also look to be "fishers of men." We must find ways to share the teachings of Jesus with the world.

An Invitation to the Guru-Chela Relationship

The messenger has explained the great opportunity that Jesus has opened to us in this Call. She said: "A very powerful call went forth, as powerful as the day when Jesus called his disciples. 'Come, leave your karmic entanglements.' In the very command he is demonstrating the guru-chela relationship. He is saying, 'I will bear the burden of your karma if you will simply walk away from it.'

"Nets are nets of entanglement—human karmic entanglement. Through service to the guru, who is the embodiment of the God flame, we balance our karma because our service benefits every lifestream on the planet. Thus, tied to the heart of the guru, the guru's office holds in abeyance your karma as you balance it in service.

" 'Come, leave your nets; I will make you fishers of men.' Jesus is saying there are two paths: you can live your life going through the entanglements of karma, balancing it a little bit each day ad nauseam for the next million years—that's where we've been for the last million years—or you can join the Great White

Brotherhood; become a chela in the fullest, strictest, ancient sense of the term; attach yourself to the ascended masters; do their work…. And you can be a chela and a fisher of men working for Saint Germain [or Jesus] in almost any field of endeavor that is lawful and conducive to injecting spirituality into the world."[11]

We might imagine that if we had been there with Peter and Andrew, we would not have hesitated. We would surely have responded as eagerly as they did to the call of the Master. And yet, today, the Master is calling us, and we find that it is often not easy to surrender our worldly ties and desires in order to answer an inner calling—whether from a master, or even from our soul.

The messenger speaks of the importance of answering the Call of the Master quickly: "I love this moment in the Bible, because I do believe that the swift response to the Master is a great key in our own personal life. I would not intrude myself between you and your relationship to the Lord Jesus Christ. I can only say that it is true: 'He who hesitates is lost.' And whatever you are called to do, the Call itself contains the will of God, the impelling force, the actual dispensation from the Master himself to do those things that you must do. When one attempted to take care of family responsibilities before responding to Jesus—going home and burying a family member—Jesus responded: 'Follow me; and let the dead bury their dead.'[12"13]

We realize that the cycles of life do move on. Jesus had three short years for his mission. What if one or more of his apostles had procrastinated? What a loss for them—and for the world.

And how often do we hear of people in middle age or the later years of their lives who look back with regret on the choice not made, the opportunity not taken when it was available.

Let us take the opportunities of life while they are available, since none of us knows for certain what tomorrow may bring.

Preparation for the Calling

The pull of the world from which Jesus would cut us free often comes from our desires—whether these be for comfort or

pleasure or human companionship or any of the things that
might be a distraction from our real calling and our real desiring.
And sometimes we may have desires on the conscious level to follow the Master, to serve others—but other desires we are not
fully aware of at other levels of being, and which work at cross
purposes to our conscious choices. Gautama Buddha gives us a
key to the resolution of our desires and calls us to pray for God-
desire at all levels of our being:

"I counsel you that the thoughts you think in the outer mind
and the words you speak do not necessarily reflect the momentums of your desires in the subconscious or the momentum of the
spiritual pride or even some rebellion that does set you on a
course on which God has not set you. Therefore, beloved, it is not
the words you speak that are telling, but it is the resolution to the
very core of your being that must now take place that is telling.

"Therefore, you must pray with great fervor that what you
desire to be your desire will truly be your desire. Pray for God's
desiring for you to be implanted within you as a bulb of a beautiful flower in springtime, that the bulb be planted at all levels of
the subconscious and the unconscious that God's desiring might
occupy the totality of your being and that the flower might
spring forth and show itself as an angelic flower, an amaryllis,
blossoming in full glory at the conscious level.

"I will tell you, beloved, that joy and perpetual joy in the
Holy Spirit is the sign of the resolution of your desiring unto
God's desiring at these deeper levels of self, whereas agitation and
anger and depression and despondency at conscious levels is the
sign of inordinate desiring at the subconscious and unconscious
levels, which can never truly be fulfilled simply because it is inordinate.

"Truly, it is the joy of the spirit and of the Holy Spirit and the
perpetual love of that Holy Spirit in the heart that is the sign of
those who have that inner resolution. All of their being ripples
with the joy of desiring to do God's will. And that desiring multiplies itself and increases until the will of God, as a shaft of ray
from the Central Sun, does entirely engulf such a one until that

one is perpetually buoyant in the joy of her Lord."[14]

The Violet Flame

Along with the call, Jesus also sends the impetus of energy to cut us free from our karma and entanglements with the world. But we must also cut ourselves free, and one way we can do this is to use the violet flame to dissolve and transmute all that would tie us to a lesser path.

The messenger explains that the violet flame is a key to entering the path of Jesus: "When we meditate upon the sacred fire in the heart, we soon discover that this pulsating light that comes clearly to our consciousness accelerates to a vibration that reads as the color violet—hence, the term, *violet flame*. The violet flame has been seen by seers, by mystics and by saints. It is the flame of the Holy Spirit, and it is also the flame that is revealed in the Aquarian age. It is the seventh-ray aspect of the Holy Spirit. The time for mankind's realization and application of this flame has come. And the ascended master Saint Germain is the one who sponsors its release.

"How does your soul get to God? By your invocation of this flame, by your meditation upon the flame, by bathing your consciousness in the flame until you experience that transmutation, that change of energy and consciousness that was so often promised by the Hebrew prophets—the promise of forgiveness, the promise that 'though your sins be as scarlet, they shall be white as snow....'[15]

"How do we invoke the violet flame? Well, we can give a simple mantra where we affirm the name of God, I AM,[16] and then declare that that I AM is the violet flame right where we are. This is a mantra that I like to give to increase the manifestation of the violet flame in my aura:

I AM a being of violet fire!
I AM the purity God desires!

"This little mantra becomes a meditation and a visualization that is anchored in the physical temple by the spoken Word.

Giving words to our thoughts and our feelings through the throat chakra is the means whereby we gain a new dimension from our prayers, from our mental affirmations, because it is through the throat chakra that we bring into the physical form that which is in the mind and that which is in the heart.

"This is why when people begin to give these mantras, they experience an immediate acceleration of consciousness. The violet flame, then, is the first step on the path of initiation with the ascended masters, the first step to the point of the soul's return to the Spirit, or to the I AM Presence.

"It is interesting to note that the first miracle Jesus wrought was at the marriage feast in Cana of Galilee, where he turned the water into wine. This symbolizes the turning of the water of the human consciousness into the wine of the Spirit. Interestingly, wine itself is a purple or violet color. And this is a clue to those of you who are mystics that Jesus was using the seventh-ray aspect of the Holy Spirit."[17]

Relationships

Sometimes the nets from which Jesus would cut us free can be seen very clearly in relationships in our lives, karmic situations with people that do not seem to be healthy or nurturing to the soul. How do we know if a particular situation is one we should walk away from, or if it represents part of our mission in this life?

We can always begin with spiritual solutions. We can call for the violet flame to go into the relationship, the job, the debt, whatever the karmic situation. The violet flame will dissolve and transmute negativity and limiting conditions. Sometimes this is all that is needed to transmute the karma of a specific situation and find a new freedom. But don't neglect the practical steps: ask forgiveness if you are in the wrong, seek to balance the karma through extending love and service, seek counseling if appropriate.

Sometimes after doing all this, the karma is balanced and the whole relationship changes. It is no longer a net, confining you and holding you back. It becomes, instead, a support and a strength for your mission.

Sometimes the net of karma just dissolves, and you are suddenly free to move on.

Sometimes, however, after doing all this, things are no closer to resolution, and it may be that you need to cut the tie and move on in a higher calling.

And sometimes, even when the karma is balanced and there is no need to remain in that situation, there is still a reluctance to move on—the situation is somehow comfortable and familiar, and there is a fear of stepping out and entering an unknown territory.

These decisions and initiations are often challenging, and there may be no clear outer sign to guide us. Nevertheless, we can walk in faith and prayer, seeking the highest good and trusting that God and the masters will see us through if we have faith in them.

Practical Keys

The masters have given many spiritual keys to help us overcome the limitations of our human consciousness and everything that would hold us back from our mission. When we use these keys, we also find that they unlock the door to our Christ consciousness.

Perhaps their greatest gift to us is the science of mantra, the science of the spoken Word. Practicing this science can help spiritualize our consciousness and make us more ready to answer the call of the master.

The ascended master El Morya has dictated a series of mantras that he has called the "Heart, Head and Hand Decrees." These mantras represent different stages in the life of Jesus Christ and his path of initiation. They begin with the meditation upon the heart and drawing through the heart the energy that is the violet flame—the energy of the Holy Spirit, of the sacred fire, for transmutation and forgiveness. These initiations culminate in the Transfiguration, the Resurrection and the Ascension.

The "Heart, Head and Hand Decrees" are an effective way

to purify your chakras and connect with your Higher Self. As you give each succeeding step, you are actually ascending (transcending your lesser self) by degrees. The change is subtle but definite, because as you give the mantra and invoke the light of God, you can actually change your vibration. This decree, given in its entirety, is a formula of the steps and stages of your own union with God.

As we give our prayers and decrees, we give them for others as well as for ourselves, and this can also be the beginning of our path as "fishers of men." Beloved Helios gives us an understanding of the importance of our prayers for so many on earth who are in need: "Let the devout hear me! Understand that God has so great a need for your devotions and prayers on behalf of those who are as shorn lambs. Know, then, that your prayers may invoke the intercession of angelic hosts for the saving of many souls who at the end of an age could be lost—for they have lost their divine spark and their divine momentum, yet they are not evil, per se. And that call, that intercession for the saving of souls can result in the balancing of your karma and your victory. Heroic deeds are in order, but prayer is the greatest heroism in this day.

"Your prayers have already spared many lives across the earth and in this war of lightbearers on all sides. May you continue to keep the vigil for those who know not how to pray, who know not that the science of the spoken Word must be exercised in the physical octave else, the Law declares, those of us in heaven may not intercede, not even a fraction.

"Prayer is the key to salvation in this age. When you couple it with good works and the cosmic honor flame ablaze in you always, you will know an acceleration unprecedented."[18]

"Fishers of Men"

Having left our "nets," Jesus promises to make us "fishers of men." How will this happen?

First of all, we know that preparation will be needed. Jesus tells us of the "preparation of your heart with my heart." There is an inner preparation as we walk and talk with Jesus and seek that oneness with his heart. There is also an outer preparation of studying Jesus' message and the teachings of the ascended masters so that we will have a morsel ready to give to anyone God brings to our doorstep.

When we study the masters' words, we may also gain new awareness about ourselves. We may realize that there are specific changes we must make in our lives. If we are willing to honestly observe ourselves and to receive illumination through the masters' words, we will be ready to impart Jesus' message to others, and we may also find the keys to cutting ourselves free from all the "nets" that hold us back.

Jesus concludes his message by telling us that it is our sacred labor, our divine plan, to be fishers of men. He says: "I behold your destiny as ascended masters of the Great White Brotherhood. I, Jesus, call you to become fishers of men in the full knowledge that in this, thy sacred labor, the requirements of thy being shall be filled.... I come to work through you for the saving of every soul that is gone astray.... This is a dispensation of a moment, the hour and the decade. Work in this wise while ye have the light.... Come now, fishers of men, for there are many ways to catch souls into the net of God."

Souls are waiting for you to contact them and remind them of their true purpose for being here on earth. In fact, there are some souls that are waiting for you specifically because you have a karmic tie to them from the past, or even from a previous life. The masters have said that many times they work for years or embodiments to arrange for us to meet a particular person to whom we are intended to give the teachings. The angels plot and plan and finally get this person standing right next to us, at a bus stop or wherever, and what do we do? We ignore them.

Don't miss these opportunities, but pray to be alert and always ready to be "fishers of men." You never know when a simple word and the gift of your heart flame will be an instrument for the conversion of a soul.

| SPIRITUAL EXERCISES |

The following spiritual exercises will assist you in fulfilling this Call of Jesus:

Pray Fervently for God-Desire

In order to be free from your "nets"—entanglements of karma, the personality cult and the pull of the world—you must have the desire to be free. If you find that you lack this desire or that you have conflicting desires, you can pray for resolution. You can also pray for your desire to be purified and to become the highest it can be—which is God's desire for you from the beginning. Give the following prayer:

Prayer for God-Desire

In the name of Almighty God, in the name of the Christ, I call on the law of forgiveness for my rebellion against the law of my being, the law of my karma, and I call forth the sacred fire for the transmutation of the cause and core of the records of that rebellion.

In the name of the Christ, in the name of the Holy Spirit, I call forth the light of Almighty God. I call directly to the heart of the Father for the release of that energy into my four lower bodies, the release of the full power of the violet flame, the cosmic honor flame and the flame of cosmic worth to penetrate now and release all energies that are locked in pockets of wrong desire. I demand the shattering of the forcefields of all wrong desire of all incarnations since the day of my soul's entering into Mater.* I demand the breaking of the forcefields of wrong desire.

I demand that God-desire be the penetration of my subconscious, that only God-desire be the momentum and the motive of my life! I demand the full power of the Holy Spirit and the sacred fire to purge me now of all wrong matrices, of all wrong patterns, of all wrong grids and forcefields. And I call in the name of the Christ to Mighty Astrea to lock your cosmic circle and sword of blue flame around the

---

*Mater is the *mater*-ialization of the God flame. The term is used interchangeably with "Matter" to describe the planes of being that conform to and comprise the universal chalice, or matrix, for the descent of that light of God that is perceived as Mother.

cause and core of all momentums and globules of desire floating in the astral plane that I have ever sent forth, knowingly or unknowingly, in any of my incarnations. I demand that that energy be seized in the name of the Christ! I demand it be drawn now into the flaming Presence of the Maha Chohan.

I demand that in my consciousness, in my soul, in my heart and in all of my chakras there be released only the full momentum of God's desire to be free, to be whole, to ascend, to resurrect, to love life free, to bring forth the teaching and the Law and to be the fullness of the divine example to all mankind. In the name of the Father, of the Mother, of the Son and of the Holy Spirit, I accept it done this hour in full power, and I AM grateful for the Presence of God desiring in me now.

Write a Letter to Jesus

Do you want to answer Jesus' call and follow him? Write and let him know of your desire and your commitment to answer his Call. Let him know what entanglements of the past you are willing to leave behind in order to follow him. You can also ask him to release you from your burdens so that you can be in the best possible position to find your brothers and sisters of light and give them the teachings of the ascended masters.

When you have written this letter, make a copy to keep in order to remember your commitment to the Master. Burn one copy, and ask for the angels to take the etheric matrix of that letter to the Master.

Heart, Head and Hand Decrees

El Morya asked that we give these decrees daily. Find a quiet place where you will not be disturbed. Give your personal prayers before you begin these mantras and then give them in the power of the spoken Word.

HEART, HEAD AND HAND DECREES
by El Morya

Violet Fire

Heart
Violet fire, thou love divine,
Blaze within this heart of mine!

Thou art mercy forever true,
Keep me always in tune with you.

Head
I AM light, thou Christ in me,
Set my mind forever free;
Violet fire, forever shine
Deep within this mind of mine.

God who gives my daily bread,
With violet fire fill my head
Till thy radiance heavenlike
Makes my mind a mind of light.

Hand
I AM the hand of God in action,
Gaining victory every day;
My pure soul's great satisfaction
Is to walk the Middle Way.

Tube of Light

Beloved I AM Presence bright,
Round me seal your tube of light
From ascended master flame
Called forth now in God's own name.
Let it keep my temple free
From all discord sent to me.

I AM calling forth violet fire
To blaze and transmute all desire,
Keeping on in freedom's name
Till I AM one with the violet flame.

Forgiveness

I AM forgiveness acting here,
Casting out all doubt and fear,
Setting men forever free
With wings of cosmic victory.

I AM calling in full power
For forgiveness every hour;
To all life in every place
I flood forth forgiving grace.

Supply

I AM free from fear and doubt,
Casting want and misery out,

Knowing now all good supply
Ever comes from realms on high.

I AM the hand of God's own fortune
Flooding forth the treasures of light,
Now receiving full abundance
To supply each need of life.

Perfection

I AM life of God-direction,
Blaze thy light of truth in me.
Focus here all God's perfection,
From all discord set me free.

Make and keep me anchored ever
In the justice of thy plan—
I AM the Presence of perfection
Living the life of God in man!

Transfiguration

I AM changing all my garments,
Old ones for the bright new day;
With the sun of understanding
I AM shining all the way.

I AM light within, without;
I AM light is all about.
Fill me, free me, glorify me!
Seal me, heal me, purify me!
Until transfigured they describe me:
I AM shining like the Son,
I AM shining like the Sun!

Resurrection

I AM the flame of resurrection
Blazing God's pure light through me.
Now I AM raising every atom,
From every shadow I AM free.

I AM the light of God's full Presence,
I AM living ever free.
Now the flame of life eternal
Rises up to victory.

Ascension

I AM ascension light,
Victory flowing free,

All of good won at last
For all eternity.

I AM light, all weights are gone.
Into the air I raise;
To all I pour with full God-power
My wondrous song of praise.

All hail! I AM the living Christ,
The ever-loving One.
Ascended now with full God-power,
I AM a blazing Sun!

Take note of the changes in your life as you give these decrees regularly.

To find out more about the science of the spoken Word and how it can transform your life, see *The Creative Power of Sound* by Elizabeth Clare Prophet; *The Science of the Spoken Word* by Mark L. Prophet and Elizabeth Clare Prophet.

A Call for the Quickening of the Lost Sheep of the House of Israel

When Jesus sent his disciples out on their first missionary journey, he sent them to find the "lost sheep of the house of Israel."[19] These are a specific group of lightbearers who have a heart-tie to Jesus and who have an inner awareness of the path he came to demonstrate. Many of these souls are still lost and do not know who they are and what their mission is. We can begin our calling to be fishers of men by praying for them to be quickened to an inner awareness of the teachings of Jesus' path and the ascended masters.

Prayer for the Quickening of the 144,000

In the name of my mighty I AM Presence and Holy Christ Self, in the name of Jesus Christ, Gautama Buddha and Saint Germain, I call for the cutting free of the 144,000 and all lightbearers and ask for their memories to be quickened to their inner-plane experiences. I especially ask that I might encounter them so that I might give them a wallet-size Chart of the Presence or some portion of the teachings of the ascended masters or anything that is appropriate to which they might be drawn, that is now a part of their immediate inner awareness from inner planes.[20]

FOR YOUR JOURNAL

How Will *You* Answer Jesus' Call?

"Come, leave your nets!
I will make you fishers of men."

What does this Call mean to me?
What will I do to answer this Call?

CHAPTER 2

"Take up the sword of the Spirit and fight for my sheep ere they are lost to the clutches of the drug peddlers and the peddlers of deceit and annihilation."

The Foundation of Christendom
That I Have Laid

I AM present in you now, beloved—the resurrected Christ. Come to me, O my beloved. I come with the whispering hope of resurrection's fires. I come with the gentleness of the spiritual flame that does now gently take from you every care and burden of this life.

Blessed hearts, the way is not sorrowful; neither is it a struggle, save to those who desire not to give up the lesser self. The joy of acceleration in light is incomparable! Only witness those who have my fire upon them. Blessed ones, they cannot be known by any outer standard or classification or labeling. They are anywhere or everywhere in the sea of life. Suddenly you see that fire and you know: Truly, this man, this woman is the anointed son of God.[1]

You may look into a million faces but you will come to the one. And here where truth abounds—and the violet flame and the Spirit—it is not uncommon to see many, beloved. How true is Truth unto its own witness? For the fire cannot be denied, nor can the overlay, as a glassiness, fail to expose nondiligence in my path.

Angels read but humanity know not the sign. They have never seen the light of the eye of the ascending one. Well, I say, beloved, let us make it a familiar sight! Let them rejoice to see the alive ones—the lively stones[2] who have a testimony.

O beloved, you who have sunk back into a comfortable situation, even proposing monuments called focuses and other trappings to signify a spiritual forcefield, I say, there is no spiritual forcefield save the Sacred Heart! Desire, then, that the LORD should look upon you and call your heart sacred or immaculate or magnanimous in Spirit. Blessed ones, the sacred heart may endow surroundings with a holiness and a vibration that cannot be denied, but surroundings can never endow the individual with that which he must seek within.

Thus, modern civilization and wealth, intended to be an abundant life shared with all to the blessings ordained by God, has become a substitute for the true path of spirituality. And a dead ritual has replaced the "right-you-all" of righting the wrongs of an ancient karma and getting on with eternal life in the here and now. And a theology dead twice, thrice over, yet lives. For man and woman are too busy to examine and to know the Truth. Nor do they seek my voice within.

I speak to many, beloved. They do not hear—they *will* not hear. Then again I speak through the child who in holy innocence declares the Truth so simply. But the elders smile and say, "What can you know? You are too young."

Blessed hearts, my angels and the ascended host have truly sought and they have pursued every means to reach and contact the heart that is riveted in a rigidity of a belief system that does not allow for the resurrection presently and in an ongoing daily accretion of the fire of the rainbow rays of God.

Blessed hearts, I therefore propose a summoning of archangels in this hour—as this is my day of days and inasmuch as many have prayed to me this day in a manner seldom accomplished except at the Christ Mass. Blessed hearts, these prayers, though perhaps based on ignorance, are sincere. People are sincere in their orthodoxy. O beloved, such a tragedy of errors.

Therefore, I say, in answer to their calls, let us one and all together in this communion answer prayer by invoking the intercession of the archangels. This I propose, beloved, for it is fear, it is anger on the part of the fallen ones and their rebellion that presents to me as I knock at the door of the heart that impenetrable wall of a misused free will!

Even the Son of God may not transgress the threshold of free will! Understand that this is our Father's rule and we do not violate it.

Therefore, we are free by coaxing, by preaching, by loving and by the violet flame to attempt our conversion to change the alignment of free will as one would change, then, the alignment of molecules, ions, electrodes. Blessed hearts, alignment is a universal necessity, both in science and religion. Nothing works without alignment. Thus, let the Polestar [of the mighty I AM Presence] descend!

Know, beloved, that when you pray for another, the prayers are locked in the heart of the Holy Christ Self, who does minister unto the needs of the soul to the fullest extent that the Law will allow. Some have released the false doctrine that it is not lawful to invoke the violet flame for another. I tell you, it is indeed lawful to pray for gifts and graces unto all, for every call is adjudicated by the will of God. Every call made in the name of Christ descends only by that Christ-discrimination of the individual's I AM Presence and Christ Self.

Therefore, beloved, understand me: The momentum of prayer and graces and light is held, as it were, in a vault of safekeeping, preparing to descend as a bower of loveliness upon the soul who does at last, in desperation with the limitations of a belief system, cry out unto God, "O LORD, help me now!" And at that moment the angels come and they release the bowers of your momentum of prayer on behalf of that one.

Precious ones, there is help unto all. There is grace unto all. Criminals engaged in crime have called to Astrea and invoked the violet flame and received results. This is the guarantee of the decree itself. However, the Great Law does limit even by the matrix of a mantra itself (for the mantra is the power of the Word) the repetitive cycles of the misuse of the water of life given freely.

Therefore, my proposal in this hour, beloved, is that I give my office this day for the invocation unto the Father to send legions of angels for the binding of the Liar and the lie and these fallen ones who corrupt my children.

I would speak to you again, then, of the path of illumination—of being the world teacher with me and Kuthumi, understanding, therefore, that next to the violet flame and the Ritual of Exorcism and the power of the Divine Mother Astrea* to bind entrenched forces of limitation, there is nothing that can equal the enlightenment of the Holy Ghost or the true teachings of my heart for an absolute conversion of the soul unto life.

I would desire to read to you my teaching on the concept of sacrifice, that you would understand that you can live a life of sacrifice in abundant joy. I would desire you to know the true theology of the doctrine of the remission of sin by the blood of Christ.

Blessed one, hear me, then—you who have looked and toiled long for your Lord. I AM indeed Jesus. I AM here, beloved, as I AM a free spirit ascended. And I may choose to anoint and ordain one among you to deliver my Word, and none may deny my right. Thus, be safe and secure. Should I not, then, call Martha, who has served me in numerous lifetimes, to come now and feed you as she has fed me so well?

Blessed hearts, I AM able. I AM able to raise up in you by the Spirit Holy that instrumentation of my doctrine, if you are willing to study to show yourselves approved.[3] Perceiving, then, that some are negligent in the learning of the true theology, I shall indeed read to you from my book.

Blessed ones, understand the need and be watchful. Those beset by orthodoxy and the lies incorporated within it know not why they believe what they believe nor who was the instigator of this anti-Christ religion that passes for my own. When you meet them in the way, you must know every point of the Law, both in codified scripture and in my teachings now released.

Students you must be. I require it, beloved. For the age shall not turn or the freedom be gained unless my Church is founded upon the rock of your confession of the living Christ in me, in you, in every child of God....

[Jesus reads *Corona Class Lessons,* chapter 22.]

Beloved, this is one of a number of dictations given by Kuthumi and me under the heading of "Sin." I desire students of

---

*See chapter 12.

my life and teachings to know that this book of the Law will enable you to be experts in my divine doctrine. My soul hungers and thirsts for those who truly know me and speak of me and of my words and my teachings that I gave two thousand years ago and have not left off giving to my saints who know my voice.

This is the work of the doctrine in forty-eight lessons that will give you a corona of light when you know it, understand it, teach it and assimilate it. I desire to see the halo of illumination upon you. I desire you to be able, so gently but firmly, to simply undo the snarl of human, conceited dogma.

Blessed hearts, neglect me not. I have been neglected for two thousand years. This day I affirm: My mission shall not be aborted! It shall no longer be aborted, for I AM here in the flesh of my servant—and in your own hearts. I AM *here*. I AM resurrected as you, too, *can be,* as you *are,* and as you *shall be.*

This work of Truth shall swallow up error. And when seen as the keystone to all teachings of the ascended masters, it provides you with a foundation and an open door for speaking to people and groups as out of the Holy Spirit. For when in your heart the Truth is set, the Holy Spirit shall play upon you, as upon an aeolian harp, melodies of the Spirit and a fire for conversion— conversion away from that fear and anger and rebellion and ignorance.

O beloved, the time *is* at hand.

Some have not believed me when I said, "I came not to send peace but a sword."[4] Throughout the ages, beloved, I have loaned my sword to special initiates. The well-known legend of Arthur pulling the sword from the stone derives from an initiation of Maitreya's Mystery School. Blessed hearts, the time did indeed come when I did tell the disciples to take the sword.*

Blessed hearts, I am not an advocate of physical war. But I AM fully engaged in the slaying of demons and discarnates who

---

*"... Now, he that hath a purse, let him take it, and likewise his scrip: and he that hath no sword, let him sell his garment, and buy one.... And they said, Lord, behold, here are two swords. And he said unto them, It is enough." (Luke 22:36–38)

prey upon my own. And I AM fully willing to challenge the mighty and the kings and the potentates. I AM alive forevermore.

Therefore, beloved, seek the initiation of the sword. And understand that it is a rod of sacred fire fashioned by the Divine Mother out of your own sacred life-force rising from the base chakra to the third eye. Therefore, beloved, the sword that is taken from the stone of Matter is a spiritual fire. Legend would have it that it is a magic sword.

Beloved, the spiritual fire does dissolve on contact all unlike itself. Know, then, that as I pray, so I also act that you may do likewise. Therefore, I say:

O my Father, by thy Presence send the archangels! I command them in the Christ Spirit of every soul upon earth. I AM in this hour the fulfillment of the prayer of the righteous. Now let the sword of God descend for the binding of those who have too long taken away my own from the altar of the living Word.

My Father, in the name of my brother Saint Germain, in the name of my Mother Mary, I ask—do thou grant it—for the dispensation of legions of light to clear the way for the true teaching and the true Church to be manifest swiftly.

Let the houses of worship, O Father, be cleansed by angels and seraphim. Let billions of angels descend into America and the earth! My Father, this is my call, answering the prayers of my own.

Let it [the answer] come swiftly as the two-edged sword which I now hold. Let Excalibur be in the hand of the initiates who run quickly to receive this initiation from the Cosmic Christ. O Father, to win, to have our victory, we desperately need an action in America *now,* as Saint Germain has said.

O Father, gather those in the fields white to the harvest.[5] Gather them *now* and let them be cut free. Send forth the light, O Father!

I see thee raising now thy right hand. So I raise my own. And so it is time, told by the Mother, for the right hand of the Son to descend in the earth. I accept thy judgments, my Father. I accept them, my Mother.

I AM in the earth and on the battlefield, at the workplace, in the home, at the birth of the child and the passing of the elderly. I AM with my own, O Father—away from thee, as it were, for a time and space—fully engaged to clear a place for a victory that would be denied. It shall not be, O Father, for faithful hearts have arisen.

Thou knowest the secret prayer of my heart for each and every one on earth who calls to me and even those who do not. Let recording angels and the Holy Ghost deliberate and give unto me thy graces for their fulfillment....

You must know, beloved Keepers of the Flame, that I have dedicated my Easter address 1987 to this cause of the rescuing of souls from dead-letter doctrines and all manner of self-indulgence *because there is a war.* It is ongoing and continuing. And the devils would tear them limb from limb until they sense themselves insane and have no more heart for the struggle.

I AM here and I have summoned Archangel Michael. I summon all the archangels in the command of God and Michael, thou Prince of the Church.

O holy ones of God, I command you from the heart of the Father—Go to! Cut free them in the seven planes of being. Cut free them throughout the quadrants of Matter. Blaze the light of this dispensation of cosmos. And let them come to the marriage supper of the Lamb.[6] For I hold court in heaven this night. And I invite the beggars and the waifs and the orphans to my table. I invite all that have not been dealt with justly by the rich, the prosperous and the proud.

Blessed hearts, come to the marriage supper of the Lamb. Come, then, all among you who need this sealing of your heart to my sacred heart. Come, then, and make yourself an elder brother, an elder sister of these almost lost ones.

Blessed hearts, long ago I said, "Feed my sheep."[7] And this you will also do. But in this hour, I say, take up the sword of the Spirit and fight for my sheep ere they are lost to the clutches of the drug peddlers and the peddlers of deceit and annihilation. This is my cry and my plea.

Angels of the Resurrection, angels of Archangel Uriel, Spirit of the Resurrection, descend where I have placed my Electronic Presence twenty-four hours a day for the rescue of souls! Wrap them in the swaddling garment, mother-of-pearl, warmth and comforting presence of the resurrection flame.

This is my decree, O God. I thank thee that thou hast heard my Call and answered—even the answer forthcoming through these, my beloved.

I send you as sunbeams of my sacred heart to brighten a world and to tell all the world we are not defeated but shod with sandals—winged sandals of light. And we shall be and are Victory's legions now and forever: It is done. 🍇

April 19, 1987
Easter Sunday
Dallas, Texas

Understand this, beloved—that the power of my Word comes forth through you, each and every one of my disciples. And that Word is a two-edged sword.

JESUS

Having called us to be fishers of men, Jesus speaks to us in this dictation of the tools we will need to fulfill this Call. Most important is the "sword of the Spirit" that cuts free the children of the light from all that binds them and all that separates them from God. Jesus' second Call is his cry and plea to "Take up the sword of the Spirit and fight for my sheep ere they are lost to the clutches of the drug-peddlers and the peddlers of deceit and annihilation."

This sword of the Spirit is a sword of Truth that exposes the false doctrines that have kept the people in ignorance. Jesus, therefore, calls us to be students of his teaching—the true teachings of his Galilean mission as well as his teachings released at the dawn of the Aquarian age. He directs us especially to his book *Corona Class Lessons,* and asks us to become experts in the true understanding of the doctrines of Christ that it conveys.

The *sword* is the sacred *Word.* This Word is the truth of the teaching and also the spoken Word of the prayer, decree and mantra. The sword is spiritual fire that we invoke in our decrees and send forth as a sword of living truth that divides the Real from the unreal. We can become that living sword as we stand, one with Christ, and send God's energy forth as blue lightning to cut free souls—especially our children and youth—who are caught in the drug culture and in all manner of illusion.

We see many souls burdened and depressed by the return of personal and planetary karma. Some of these are Jesus' lost sheep. They have not been reawakened to either the knowledge of karma and reincarnation or the violet flame, the flame of transmutation and freedom.

Lacking the spiritual understanding and resources to cope

with the pain and the challenges of life, they turn to alcohol or drugs for a temporary escape, to numb the pain of their souls. They feel better for a while, but the fundamental problems have not been dealt with, and some become caught in a web of illusion and addiction. Without an understanding of the spiritual path and the true teachings of Jesus, people have neither a higher perspective nor the tools to deal with the challenges of life, and many lose hope.

Two thousand years ago Jesus came to earth with a two-edged sword of sacred fire for the judgment of all that is unreal. He said: "Do not suppose that I have come to bring peace to the earth: it is not peace I have come to bring, but a sword."[8] Today he tells us: "Seek the initiation of the sword. And understand that it is a rod of sacred fire fashioned by the Divine Mother out of your own sacred life-force rising from the base chakra to the third eye. Therefore, beloved, the sword that is taken from the stone of Matter is a spiritual fire.... The spiritual fire does dissolve on contact all unlike itself. Know, then, that as I pray, so I also act that you may do likewise."

The science of the spoken Word is the most powerful spiritual tool we have to deal with the challenges we face in our lives and in the world. Through the spoken Word, we can call forth light, and the darkness can be consumed. One reason it is important to speak the Word aloud is that karma is returning physically to the planet. We see diseases, incurable viruses, earthquakes, wars and famines—signs of an ancient karma coming due. When we stand in the physical plane and invoke the Word of God, a spiritual fire descends to challenge and consume darkness. God needs an intensity of the spoken Word in the physical octave to do battle with the manifestations of Antichrist.

The ascended masters have pleaded with us to take action and "make the call" to command legions of angels to enter into this battle, which we know as the battle of Armageddon. The sons and daughters of God have been given authority for what happens in the earth,[9] and by cosmic law the angels and masters cannot enter the physical octave without our invitation. When we truly understand this, we realize what a great responsibility we have to daily invoke the light and call for the intercession of the masters and the angels. The Elohim Astrea tells us:

"We must have those in physical embodiment to speak the decree in the power of the spoken Word.... If *you* do not do it, we are not authorized to enter this octave. This is *your* octave, this physical octave, and what happens in it is up to you and the call you will make. God has given you two things—free will and planet Earth. He will not take back that free will by entering in to do for you those things that you are ordained of him to do."[10]

How to Make a Call
on Personal and Planetary Situations

How do we invite the angels and masters to intercede in specific situations on planet Earth? The mantras and decrees they have given us are specifically for this purpose. The masters recommend that we keep up to date with world and local affairs so we can know exactly where the intercession of the angels is needed. It can be helpful to keep a notebook for specific calls and issues we would like to focus on when giving our prayers and decrees.

The following is an outline of how to make a call for a specific situation, whether personal or in your city or nation:

1. Decide exactly into what situation you would like to direct the light of God. According to your best and highest understanding, formulate what action needs to be taken by the angels and masters to see resolution of the situation. If God's will in the situation is not clear, simply ask for the angels and the masters to enter in and implement the will of God. The more specific you make your worded statement, the more specific your answer will be.

2. Always begin your call by addressing your mighty I AM Presence and Holy Christ Self. It is by this Presence of God with us that we make the call and the light of God responds.

3. Your call can be short and simple, or you can add more details,

such as specific names of people and situations. For example, if you wanted to pray for healing for an individual, you could say:

> **In the name of my mighty I AM Presence and Holy Christ Self, I call to beloved Mother Mary and the healing angels to send your light and Presence for the perfect healing of <u>(name of person)</u> and their condition of <u>(specific disease or condition)</u>. Guide and direct all doctors and medical personnel who are assisting in this case.**
> **Let this healing be according to God's will.**

If you wanted to make a short call for the children and youth, you could say:

> **In the name of my mighty I AM Presence and Holy Christ Self, I call to Archangel Michael to cut free our children and youth from drugs and all involvement in gangs and violence. I call for the protection of teachers and all who are working with youth.**
> **Beloved angels, take command of this entire situation and bring forth the divine solution to every human problem that is currently burdening me and/or my loved ones. In the name of God's holy will, let it be done.**

4. Always ask that your call be adjusted and answered according to the will of God. This gives the angels and the masters the authority to implement your call according to the highest good, even when you do not have a complete understanding of the situation and what the highest good would be. Then you know that you have put the entire matter in God's hands, and he will take the light you invoke in your mantras and decrees and direct it into the situation in his own time and in his own way.

5. Follow this call with your decrees to Archangel Michael, to the violet flame, or whatever action is most needed in that particular situation.

6. Watch for results! Watch how the angels lovingly answer your

calls. They are eager to assist and are always waiting for us to give them an assignment!

7. Be on the lookout for situations that need your calls. The ascended masters have told us that we are responsible for directing the light of our decrees into the issues that we are aware of in our cities and nations. When you direct God's light through your prayers and invocations, you can see yourself as the hands and feet and mouthpiece of the LORD, the masters and the angels.

Archangel Michael and His Sword of Blue Flame

Just as Jesus has a sword, so Archangel Michael has his sword of blue flame, which he uses in his fight against the forces of darkness in the world. Sometimes the problems we have to deal with—such as the problem of drugs—seem so large as to be almost beyond solution. Archangel Michael tells us to call to him and his sword of blue flame, to call for the victory, even when things seem overwhelming.

He tells us: "I come forth to stress again the high and holy calling. I come forth to make clear that the battle between the forces of light—Archangel Michael and my legions of light—and the dragon and the fallen ones is in full sway. Thus, when we come to address this assembly, we really must perforce leave the battlefield for a moment to address you, to encourage you, to give you the word of light and victory and to say: *Charge! Charge! Charge* into the fray! And release the light of Almighty God, and you will win.

"As I stood with Joan of Arc in the campaigns against the forces of darkness, I gave her the strength and the courage and the determination to go forward when all seemed lost, when all on the side of right were ready to give up, were ready to turn back. It is then that I whispered in her ear, 'Charge! Charge! Charge!' And so she repeated the sound and the command, and the very power of my flame of faith summoned the forces of France in defense of the flame of liberty. So, then, I give you that same inspiration, that same byword. When all seems wrong and all seems heavy and all seems to go to naught, that is the time to remember to *charge! charge! charge* with light and manifest the victory of mighty Victory and his legions.

"I raise my sword of blue flame. I hold it on high! And I show you at inner levels, through the power of your soul and your third eye, the flaming brilliance of Archangel Michael's sword, the precipitated substance of the sacred Word. I impel you this day to cling to that sword and to use it. Do you think that the hosts of light, who have direct access to the consciousness of God, would use a sword if it were not effective, if they did not need it? I say to you, you need the armour, and you need the sword of Archangel Michael."[11]

SPIRITUAL EXERCISES

Study Corona Class Lessons

Jesus calls us to take up the study of his book *Corona Class Lessons*. Written with the ascended master Kuthumi, who we also know as Saint Francis, it provides a profound understanding of the true teachings of Christianity. Uncomplicated by centuries of misinterpretation, we find a living faith that liberates the spirit of man. It is a handbook for ministering servants and all who would deliver Jesus' message to the world.

Jesus explains how we can enter into this book and its teachings most fully: "I trust you will read this book as well as my *Lost Teachings*[12] in order, for the chapters form a spiral of conversion of the chakras when read in order. Once you have read the books from beginning to end and understand them well, they become scripture wherein you open the book and read what is directed and take it in as a part of a spiral, a point of quickening again of that specific instruction."[13]

"Read a paragraph a day from *Prayer and Meditation*,[14] from *Corona Class Lessons*, from my dictations or those of my beloved brother Kuthumi—a morsel of Truth that you can slowly assimilate until it becomes all of you and you become all of it and suddenly you see the whole world through that lens of Truth."[15]

" 'We have no time to study, Lord.' I say, rise fifteen minutes early, and with full concentration upon my teaching, take one of my books. Read for fifteen minutes. Carry that book with you and remind yourself of what you read. Embody it for the day. A morsel will suffice for the divine alchemy. Where there is no morsel, I, then, have nothing to multiply, no wavelength of meditation whereby to enter.... The tools are before you. Let them not rust upon the bench."[16]

Try this for two weeks. Take *Corona Class Lessons* or one of Jesus' books and read from it for fifteen minutes each morning. Carry the book with you throughout the day. Think periodically about what you read and ask Jesus to help you assimilate his words and embody the teaching. You may not be able to follow Jesus around physically and listen to his teaching today as the apostles did, but, wherever your life calls you, you can keep your consciousness attuned to him throughout your day. As you do this, see what alchemy Jesus will work in your life.

Give the Decree to Archangel Michael

LORD MICHAEL

In the name of the beloved mighty victorious Presence of God, I AM in me, my very own beloved Holy Christ Self, Holy Christ Selves of all mankind, beloved Archangel Michael, beloved Lanello, the entire Spirit of the Great White Brotherhood and the World Mother, elemental life—fire, air, water, and earth! I decree:

[Here give your prayer for Archangel Michael's intercession in specific personal or world situations.]

1. Lord Michael, Lord Michael,
I call unto thee—
Wield thy sword of blue flame
And now cut me free!

Refrain: Blaze God-power, protection
Now into my world,
Thy banner of faith
Above me unfurl!

Transcendent blue lightning
Now flash through my soul,
I AM by God's mercy
Made radiant and whole!

2. Lord Michael, Lord Michael,
   I love thee, I do—
   With all thy great faith
   My being imbue!

3. Lord Michael, Lord Michael
   And legions of blue—
   Come seal me, now keep me
   Faithful and true!

Coda: I AM with thy blue flame
      Now full-charged and blest,
      I AM now in Michael's
      Blue-flame armor dressed! (3x)

[Give this section of the decree as many times as you wish, then give the sealing of the decree:]

And in full faith I consciously accept this manifest, manifest, manifest! (3x) right here and now with full power, eternally sustained, all-powerfully active, ever expanding, and world enfolding until all are wholly ascended in the light and free!
Beloved I AM! I AM! I AM!

You can also give calls to Archangel Michael throughout the day. When you think of a situation or see something in the news that needs Archangel Michael's intercession, make the call right then:

Archangel Michael, take command of that entire situation!
Archangel Michael, bind the forces of death and hell moving against our children and youth!
Archangel Michael, cut free all those who are meant to be disciples of Jesus!
Archangel Michael, Help me! Help me! Help me!

Quick fiats are a great way to balance karma and put an unemployed angel to work!

FOR YOUR JOURNAL

How Will *You* Answer Jesus' Call?

"Take up the sword of the Spirit and fight for my sheep ere they are lost to the clutches of the drug peddlers and the peddlers of deceit and annihilation."

What does this Call mean to me?

What will I do to answer this Call?

CHAPTER 3

The Call to the path of the ascension.

"I Call you to be world teachers."

*The Call for ten thousand
Keepers of the Flame.*

From Temples of Love
The Call to the Path of the Ascension

Keepers of the Flame of My Life on Earth,
I salute you in this hour of my victory. It is a renewed victory of the life everlasting now increasing its light upon the altar of your heart.

Beloved, not only have I called you but I AM the Call. Not only am I the living Christ but I AM in the Christ of all.

Therefore, O people of light, receive me in this hour as I have received you, as I am receiving you, as I am indeed entering your life if you will respond to my Call in a more than ordinary way. For I am sent by the Father for the quickening now of ten thousand saints in the City Foursquare that I mark as North America.

Blessed hearts, it is to these states and nations of the lost tribes regathered that I come, even as I sent my apostles to the lost sheep of the house of Israel.

You have descended from [the] All that is Real. Now *defend* [the] All that is Real. For this place, North America, is a land promised to you long ago, which through my heart, called the sacred heart by certain of the Christian devotees, has been consecrated unto the path of the ascension.

Therefore, it is altogether fitting that in this city, where some disciples of mine have invited this messenger to speak, I should tell you in this moment of the quickening of your own ascension through my own that the path unto the seed of light, the path that is initiatic in nature, is one that can be fulfilled upon this continent *because,* beloved, there are certain retreats in the heaven-world, called the etheric octave, where there is a consecration of that ascension flame and path, which can be entered into only by love.

Therefore, consider the love of John, my beloved, for the

light that I bore. Not John alone but the celebration of this love betwixt thee and me, beloved, is taking place daily if you will only appreciate and contain the sense of self-worth whereby truly the gold of the Divine Image and the soul ascending is worthy of the intimate relationship with my heart.

Beloved, there have been many approaches to Christianity and to religion, but it is only by the path of love that thou mayest enter in. When to this love there is added wisdom and the joy in self-givingness unto the self-emptying unto the Self, infilling and fulfilling—blessed ones, this love that intensifies as the burning of the heart, consuming the dross and nonsensical non-self-awareness, does expand and expand until the whole of self and being is enveloped and engulfed with the living presence of love!

And in this love tryst, beloved, can you determine who is thy Christ and my Christ? Beloved, I and my Father are one, I and my disciple are one. When you merge with that Christ, lo, I AM with you alway, even unto the end of this age and all ages to come.[1]

Thus, beloved, very near to this city, encompassing a large area, is the retreat of the mighty archangels of love, Chamuel and Charity. O beloved, their retreat over St. Louis expands in a very wide dimension.

The archangels are teachers of Christhood par excellence. And when you have done visiting even the retreats of the lords of the seven rays, may you perchance be invited to a series of studies in the retreats of the archangels. This, beloved, is my prayer unto the Father, who has responded by saying, "My Son, let them prove themselves with thy brothers, the seven masters of light, and then they shall truly know the divine interchange with archangels."

So, beloved, rejoice that not alone Archangel Michael, who has called you in his service, but all of the seven may one day host you in their retreats for the accelerated initiations of life unto eternity. This retreat, then, of Chamuel and Charity is one of a number of retreats in the etheric octave over North America....

Thus, my beloved, there is a focus of Paul the Venetian, the

Lord of the Third Ray, anchored firmly over the city of Washington, D.C. There is the great retreat of Heros and Amora, Elohim of the Third Ray, over Canada at Winnipeg. Blessed hearts, these are mighty temples. Many of you here have already journeyed there while your bodies have slept.

Blessed hearts, because you are ongoing students of the inner mysteries, you have brought back from this inner temple experience an awareness of what it means to say, "Love is the fulfilling of the Law."[2] It is the whole Law, beloved. But even the heart chakra must be purified, for human love does reside there. And divine love little by little does displace it until such divine love appears, O beloved, that the white fire must also descend.

Angels of the cosmic cross of white fire, I, Jesus, mark the sign of the cross over this North America, that by the ruby ray and by the white fire my body and my blood might infuse the lightbearers for the protection of a path that is to be forged and won and for the peace of the heart.

Blessed ones, over the state of Arizona there is a temple of Eriel of the Light and there is the retreat of my beloved John. These retreats are ancient; they have not suddenly appeared. There are retreats all over the world, but I have chosen to speak to you on this day of the commemoration of my ascension of those retreats in North America that facilitate a path that some must win, a path of divine love.

Love, then, is most misunderstood and misqualified. For when the love of God comes upon an individual who has not yet pursued a path, that love may become qualified with human emotion and concepts of love that are not the fullness of the cup that I offer.

Greater love than this hath no man, that a man lay down his life for his friends.[3] Blessed ones, this is not speaking of death but of a vibrant life lived—lived truly to convey the fire of my heart to all. This is the meaning of being a disciple who is called apostle, instrument and messenger of light, conveyer of that light, beloved.

So too, beloved, learn the mystery of love. Even the sign of the Statue of Liberty points to a temple of light of a divine mother, a being who has embodied and ensouled the flame of liberty and out of love does keep that flame for all who make their way to this continent.

For, beloved, you must understand that to enter this land is to enter a path that can culminate in the soul's ascension. Even the concepts of freedom and of free enterprise, all of these, beloved, bespeak the initiations of the abundant life whereby each individual with maximum independence and freedom may prove himself in God, and in Christ reprove the lesser self and learn daily the wisdom of the heart.

Therefore, beloved, understand that though the Royal Teton Retreat at the site of the Grand Teton is celebrated as a temple of wisdom, truly all who have ascended have ascended through love, serve the seven rays in love, teach in love, give in love, initiate in love. Love may be a chastening fire that does hasten the soul's departure from error and illusion.

Thus, without love as a chastening, there is no true compassion. Let the teacher be firm yet yielding, tolerant yet stern when pointing to the immutable Law, which is the true and only salvation. Salvation through the Law of God, beloved, may be achieved by entering into and embracing the mercy as well as the justice of that Law.

Thus, you understand the great need of humanity for the Mediator, the Intercessor, the Advocate. This Person of God who does defend those who have gone out of the Way, who does plead before the courts of heaven for mercy unto the ignorant, this Person, beloved, is the Universal Christ that I AM, that you are or shall become, whose Presence just above you may descend as your vibrations are elevated, resurrected, accelerated by the great science of the spoken Word, which we teach.

Understand, beloved, that the meaning of the office of World Teacher, which I bear and share with my beloved Francis, is to be that intercessor, to bring enlightenment as well as comfort, that those who are in darkness may see a light, and a great light, and walk in it.

I call to you to be world teachers. I call to you to understand—because you have understanding, because you have an inner gnosis, because you have walked with me for centuries—the Reality, beloved, that this is the hour to claim the mantle of mediator, to claim the mantle here below of your Holy Christ Self and to take your stand through prayer and invocation, through dynamic decrees to the Father, for grace and mercy and light to flood this North America and the entire earth to contact those of greatest light and to transfer to them even the sacred fire of the Word, that there might be here below an increased manifestation of light to hold the balance for the darkness that shall surely come upon this earth unless a people swiftly turn to the inner light and unless millions, beloved, come to the realization of the God who is within as well as the God who is in his heaven.

Blessed hearts, I have come, then, to make a plea to you and to send my messenger abroad across this continent for the gathering of ten thousand who will call themselves Keepers of the Flame of Life and who will understand that I, Jesus, have called them. For I was called by the Father, by the servant-Sons, by Saint Germain and the hosts of heaven to establish a teaching, a path and even the Keepers of the Flame Fraternity, that these lessons might be studied, that the daily decrees might be given, that the light might be anchored and the light itself be the Mediator to stand between a people, a world, a continent and their own returning karma.

You have heard it said that the Son of God is come to bear the sins of the world. I AM that avatar for this two-thousand-year cycle, beloved. But the hour is come, beloved, as you have understood it and seen it abroad in the land, when inasmuch as I have borne the sins of the world, or world karma, that the transfer of that karma back to those for whom I have borne it should come to pass.

Understand this law, beloved, and heed this teaching. Forgiveness is the setting aside of karma, or sin, and that setting aside is a period of opportunity. Two thousand years, beloved, has this planet had the opportunity to recognize the Christ of me and of many saints and Masters of East and West who have gone before me.

For I am not alone in heaven as some have thought. But many have ascended by the very same law whereby I was taken down from the cross and did enter the tomb to prove the initiation of the resurrection, that you might also prove this great law of the Spirit of the Resurrection.

Therefore, beloved, understand that in this hour many have internalized greater and lesser measures of my Christhood and their own. And many have turned a deaf ear to the message.

Thus, beloved, the day of reckoning that is referred to by the prophets as the day of vengeance of our God is the day when that opportunity comes to a conclusion and every man must bear his own burden.[4] (And these words, too, are in scripture.) Thus, the burden of karma is daily being placed, individual by individual, upon the just and the unjust, beloved.

But the grace and the mercy of the Law and of all heavenly hosts and of the Father has been the gift of the Holy Spirit, the gift of the violet flame whereby through the invocation of that violet flame, intensely and daily, that karma descending at a personal and a planetary level may indeed be transmuted, or balanced. This process is by the all-consuming sacred fire of God through the Person of the Holy Spirit. It is, if you will, a baptism by fire.

This purging, beloved, does therefore enable the sons of God in the earth—and all who will heed the message of my brother and friend Saint Germain on the use and application of the violet flame—to accelerate on the path of the ascension by love, for the violet flame is love's all-consuming forgiveness.

This beloved brother who was with me as my father Joseph (for so I called him, beloved) has been an adept of the seventh ray and of the use of the violet flame for tens of thousands of years and beyond. This has been his calling in God. This is his gift from the Father and his gift to the Father's children.

Understand, then, that in the ongoing cycles of two-thousand-year dispensations, it is the age of Aquarius and of the seventh ray that has descended upon earth, meshing, then, with the final decades of Pisces.

Therefore, you will see at this altar our oneness, our oneness as we together assist earth's evolutions to make the transition into an era of freedom, that by freedom's flame that is called the violet flame, souls who yet have karma to balance may not be overcome, may not be struck down by that karma, nor a world itself be destroyed or come to an end. For there be few and then many in this planet who shall hear my voice and His, know the Truth and confirm it in their hearts and call to that violet flame, beloved, unto the victory of individual Christhood and planetary Cosmic Christ-awareness!

I, Jesus, preach this message to *you*, beloved. It is an urgent message. You who have an inner awareness, do not deny the signs of the times, do not deny the rumblings in the earth or my own prophecies written in scriptures already in your hands.

It is the end of an age when there must be an entering in of a new vibration, a new opportunity. And the question is, beloved: Will enough of the lightbearers in the earth recognize this vibration of the seventh ray and realize that it is the key to the conclusion of this two-thousand-year cycle?

Blessed ones, this North America, a place consecrated by love to the reunion of souls with God, is a place where if the lightbearers would respond and *make the Call*, even as I call you this night, there should be established even the white light over a continent to protect it from those calamities of the Four Horsemen, which could indeed appear for want of mediators in the earth.

Understand, beloved, that the mediators who must stand between a people and a planet and their karma must be in physical embodiment. If you will read my words you will find that they say, *"As long as I AM in the world, I AM the light of the world."*[5]

"As long as I AM in the world..." Beloved, I AM in the ascended octaves of light; I AM the *Ascended Master* Jesus Christ. And I AM in the world only when I AM [the I AM Presence of me, the Christ of me is] in my own, when the temple is

prepared, when the Christ Self has been invoked, and when the violet flame has cleansed the four lower bodies to prepare a highway [a tunnel of light] for our God's descent into form.

I desire to come into your temple, beloved, and be in the world. And therefore, when you feel me entering into your house in that Second Coming, understand that you in me and I in you as we are one make the same declaration: "As long as I AM in the world, I AM the light of the world."

Blessed hearts, recognize the Call. Your souls are ancient. It is your hour and the moment of your destiny. Recognize, then, that the Call to be the Divine Mediator must be answered ere the earth changes that must come about take their toll in a cataclysmic way or perhaps in war, even that war prophesied by my Mother at Fátima.

Blessed hearts, the choice is yet to free hearts and free thinkers who will know the winds of Aquarius and be the Keeper of the Flame of Life on earth. Thus, do not fall prey to a sense of predestination or of psychic prognostication wherein you believe all that must happen will happen and there is nothing that you can do to change it. You have not been taught the true meaning of prophecy, which is to show you upon the screen of life what *could* take place *if* you do not intercede.

Blessed hearts, what you see in the mind's eye can be canceled out by decision and free will. You do not need to fulfill any thought, feeling or idea that is negative. But, beloved, when you see the projection upon the world screen of that which can easily be calculated by the signs of the times, this, then, must be transmuted because you are seeing a prophecy of karma returning.

Therefore, take the violet flame; invoke it. Call to me and all saints of heaven and all powers of angels to intercede, that the sacred fire might consume planetary karma and Archangel Michael and his legions do battle and bind the fallen angels and evil spirits that would possess, destroy and defile even the souls who are on the path of overcoming.

Blessed ones, some of you have been taught that evil is not real. And indeed it is not real in God. But you cannot deny that there are spoilers in the earth who have wreaked their holocausts upon millions. You cannot deny that in the hearts of some there is a will to do evil.

You must understand that this malintent must be checked by those who know the science of the spoken Word. For the Word itself will swallow up the appearance of evil. Take heed, then, that the appearance and the illusion does not swallow up souls ere they have realized the Truth that you know—that in the absolute sense of the scientific affirmation of being, *evil is not real.*

Armageddon is yet to be fought by the archangels and the legions of light and the Faithful and True and the armies in heaven. Yet, it is your hour to make the Call. He who understands the Call made in the earth unto heaven and the Call of heaven made unto earth will arrive at the nexus where heaven and earth meet in the divine Call and the Calling.

Beloved, I leave you, then, with this charge: Make your calling and election sure. For millions who yet dwell in ignorance *need your intercession.* In the name I AM THAT I AM, in the name of Christ of you, I say, *Keep* the flame!

May 28, 1987
Ascension Thursday
Regency Park Conference Center
Overland Park, Kansas

Greater love hath no man than this, that a man lay down his life for his friends.
JESUS[6]

" I AM the Call. Not only am I the living Christ, but I AM the Christ of all." As we ponder these words of the Master and understand that he is one with our own Holy Christ Self, we realize anew what the Second Coming of Christ truly means.

Jesus is a master alchemist. He tells us, "This is my body, which is broken for you."[7] We see the miracle of the loaves and the fishes. He breaks the bread of his Christ consciousness and multiplies himself in each one of us through our own Holy Christ Self. This is Jesus' greatest miracle! But, for his alchemy to be fully realized, we must do our part. He is counting on us to receive him in this hour and to allow that Christ to descend into our being. This is the miracle we are intended to manifest in this age—to walk the earth as Christed ones.

Archangel Gabriel, in a dictation given through the messenger, told us of the great power our Christ Self has to displace darkness in the earth. He said: "The single anointed one who will claim his Christhood and call forth the Father and the Son to take up their abode in his temple, that one may displace the darkness of ten thousand-times-ten thousand individuals."[8]

From Jesus' statement: "All power is given unto me in heaven and in earth,"[9] we have a sense of the power of God that is focused in one Christed one. And in this age, Jesus calls many to walk the earth as Christed ones.

Soul Travel to the Retreats of the Brotherhood

Jesus speaks of the retreats of the Great White Brotherhood in North America and throughout the world. These are great temples of light located in the heaven-world, or the etheric plane.

As our body rests in sleep, the ascended masters invite us to travel to their etheric retreats in the vehicle of our soul and our soul consciousness. There we attend classes at the universities of the Spirit and receive teaching for our spiritual path. Sometimes people return from sleep with vivid memories of having been instructed by the masters. Most often, however, there is no outer memory of these experiences except a prompting, a feeling or inner direction about decisions to be made in life.

On January 1, 1986, Gautama Buddha announced that he and the Lords of Karma had granted the petition of the seven chohans to open universities of the Spirit in their etheric retreats for tens of thousands of students to pursue the path of self-mastery on the seven rays. Gautama Buddha outlines the course of study that students may pursue at these etheric retreats.

"The plan, therefore, is for students to spend fourteen days in Darjeeling and fourteen days with Saint Germain at the Royal Teton Retreat and to alternate these fourteen days as they weave a balance and restore themselves to the commitment of the beginning [the first ray] and the ending [the seventh ray] of the cycles of life.

"Having successfully passed certain levels, albeit beginning levels, nevertheless strong levels of accomplishment in the use of these rays, they will have a turn also with Lord Lanto [chohan of the second ray of divine wisdom] and Confucius here at the Royal Teton and Paul the Venetian [chohan of the third ray of love], who prefers to use in this hour the Temple of the Sun of the Goddess of Liberty, who is the Divine Mother of beloved Paul, and to anchor that action in the Washington Monument, as it has already had anchored there a focus of the threefold flame from the Château de Liberté.[10]

"Beloved ones, this training, then, will be for the rounding out of the threefold flame in the wisdom of the Path and especially in the development of the path of the sacred heart, the expansion of love that they might rid themselves of fear and hardness of heart and records of death surrounding that heart.

"Then, you see, comes the path of ministration and service [the sixth ray], which is the logical manifestation of love and a balanced threefold flame. Through ministration and service in the retreat of Nada in Arabia, they will find, then, a place where they can give the same dynamic decrees you give here for all those untoward conditions in the area of the Middle East. And this shall be their assignment at inner levels even as they study the true path of Jesus Christ on that sixth ray as it has never been taught to them before.

"Having come through these retreats, they are now ready to be washed in the purity of the sacred fires of the ascension temple [the fourth ray] for a beginner's course and for the first baptism by water of the Divine Mother. Then, they proceed to Crete with Paul the Apostle, and there Hilarion [chohan of the fifth ray] shows them the Truth of all ages, and the science of Being is unfolded layer upon layer.

"Thus, having completed a round in all of these retreats—cycling fourteen-day cycles, some repeated in the same retreat, some interchanging—they will come again to second and third levels of training on those seven rays."[11]

In the Spiritual Exercises section there is a short prayer you can give before you go to sleep to ask to be taken to the retreats of the chohans for these two-week training sessions. Make this call nightly, and see how the angels will swiftly take you, clothed in your finer bodies, to the ascended masters' classroom to learn important soul lessons.

The Path of the Ascension

Jesus gives us three specific Calls in this dictation. The first is to the path of the ascension. The ascension is the ultimate goal of our life. In the beginning, we came forth as a soul from the heart of God in our I AM Presence, and, in the ending, it is our destiny to return to the Presence once again. This is the path Jesus walked, and he calls us to walk in his footsteps *all the way.*

The ascension is an attainable goal. It is a scientific and practical path, a daily road before us of aspiration and opportunity. Saint Paul told us, "I die daily."[12] As we walk the Path each day, we, too, can put a portion of our unreal self into the flame. At the same time, each day we can enrobe ourselves with another portion of our Real Self. The ascended master Lanello gives us a wonderful vision on how we can do this: "You ascend daily! It is like mounting a flight of steps. You know not the count, for the steps represent each step that must be taken in life. How to ascend is to arrive at the top step at the end of this embodiment."[13]

He then gives us the following practical tips:

1. **Embrace each day as a cycle of initiation.** "You must take a step a day, a day being a cycle of an initiation that might endure for weeks or months. But if you do not take the appropriate measures each day, those that you know so well, in terms of maintaining your harmony, the fire of your dedication, your decrees intertwined with meditation upon God, even as you invoke and meditate, visualize and affirm the Word simultaneously—if you do not fulfill in a day's cycle the requirement of a certain step, it will be much more difficult to fulfill it later."

2. **Make a chart to check off tasks accomplished in the hours of your day.** "Your daily tasks and obligations and responsibilities have everything to do with your initiations on this staircase of life."

3. **Take control of your day, and use your time wisely.** "Guard your time!... For time is indeed an element of eternity, as eternity has compartments of measurement.... Score a victory each day!"

4. **Plan for the next day the night before.** Take the end of the day "to organize what you will do: when you will arise, who you will see and who you cannot see. Set goals and achieve them, no matter what!"

5. **Be a compassionate one.** "The compassionate ones manage to achieve their victory and also accomplish their daily assignments."

6. **Have a sense of joy.** "Neglect not the hours. Fill them with joy. Joy is the very first principle of the ascension.... Joy is the key

to healing! Joy is *movement!* Joy is *life!* Joy is self-attention to the needs of the four lower bodies but not over-self-concern. Joy is the sense of committing oneself to God and letting God flush out the nonjoy by that descending cascade of the mighty river of life."

7. **Use Archangel Michael's sword.** Use the sword of Archangel Michael each day to cut yourself free from all burdens and all that would hinder your joy and your victory.

8. **Take hold of your desires.** "Go after your wrong desires, beloved, and devour them by the sacred fire! For if you do not, they will only grow, even at the subconscious level, and soon they will devour *you.*

"This is the single factor that takes people from the path of initiation. It is wrong desire. Pray to your Holy Christ Self that you might know what is wrong desire and the idleness of the mind and the misuse of time and space. Pray to know it. Pray to have that Christ mind. Pray to have the Presence of The Lord Our Righteousness.

"Right desire can be known, beloved, in every circumstance. Therefore, seek ye first the kingdom of God and his righteousness, and all these things shall be added unto you.[14]"[15] (See Prayer for God-Desire in Spiritual Exercises, chapter 1.)

Serapis Bey, hierarch of the Ascension Temple at Luxor, dispels any doubts about making our ascension if we desire it and are willing to strive for it. He says:

"I, Serapis, keep my notebook. I have your names, beloved, for some of you are candidates for the ascension, and some of you are precandidates, preparing to be accepted as candidates. Some of you know how much preparation is needed to get into the finest schools and universities of learning in this earth. Thus, beloved, you also prepare as candidates for our retreat and for this victory.

"I tell you that the ascension is possible for many more than those who attain it. Those who do not try are those who think that they are still too human, too possessed or obsessed with their human creation. Beloved, it is not so! You must know and understand that all of you can make your ascension, if you will it so. You may begin this day with your resolutions according to the priorities set.

"Beloved, the highest priority is the ascension. The assignment at hand is the means—the means for the preparation of all faculties. To accomplish, therefore, this current assignment and not to see it as the means to the end is a pity. This preparation is not an end in itself....

"The possibilities are almost without limit as to what you may accomplish in this lifetime. Many more of you than think you are even on this track can make it. But I kid you not! It does take all of your striving and your love and your trust. It is a trust that says, 'I know my God will do the very best for me if I have the courage to face my karma and to do my duty.'

"Blessed ones, there is a saying at our retreat among the wise ones who have had ample experience with me: 'If we do our best, Serapis will do the rest.' There is a great confidence in this commitment of the guru to the chela and the chela to the guru. And those who have proven this Law again and again do not fear to give their most and their all, knowing that the reward will come as surely as the pendulum of life does swing." [16]

You may wish to write down what these wise ones say about Serapis and post it on your mirror as a reminder: "If I do my best, Serapis will do the rest!"

The messengers have outlined the requirements to attain the ascension: "The ritual of the ascension is the goal for everyone who understands his reason for being. This initiation can and will come to anyone—even to a little child—when he is ready: when he has balanced his threefold flame; when his four lower bodies are aligned and functioning as pure chalices for the flame of the Holy Spirit in the world of form; when a balance of mastery has been achieved on all of the rays; when he has attained mastery over sin, sickness and death and over every outer condition; when he has fulfilled his divine plan through service rendered to God and man; when he has balanced at least 51 percent of his karma (that is, when 51 percent of the energy given to him in all of his embodiments has either been constructively qualified or transmuted); and when his heart is just toward both God and man and he aspires to rise into the never-failing light of God's eternally ascending Presence."[17]

Become World Teachers

Jesus' second Call is truly a vehicle for us to fulfill our mission: "I Call you to be world teachers."

You might be wondering, "What does it mean to be a world teacher? How can I be a world teacher?"

Jesus and Kuthumi share the office in hierarchy of World Teacher, and they are in search of disciples to serve under their office. As we serve with them, we can be their representatives and take the true teachings of Christ to the world. This is the real meaning of Jesus' Call to "feed my sheep."[18]

Perhaps you are also thinking: "Surely this calling is beyond what I am capable of accomplishing." Well, in truth, it is God *in you* who is capable, not the little you—the ego.

Jesus tells us that he is calling us to be world teachers "because you have understanding, because you have an inner gnosis, because you have walked with me for centuries." We sometimes forget that our souls are ancient and we have known the masters and their teachings before. Now is the hour to bring all of this past experience and attainment to the fore, to claim the mantle of Mediator.

Our true reality is that we are great spiritual beings. As we realize this and become more of this in manifestation, we realize that God is the doer. As we allow our divine reality to enter in, we find that with God all things are possible!

We can use the words of Jesus' Call as an affirmation of our willingness to answer the Call:

> In the name of my mighty I AM Presence and Holy Christ Self, I say with Jesus:
> I claim the mantle of the Mediator. I claim the mantle here below of my Holy Christ Self. I take my stand

through prayer and invocation, through dynamic decree
to the Father for grace and mercy and light to flood this
North America and the entire earth to contact those of
greatest light and to transfer to them even the sacred fire
of the Word.

For many years the ascended masters have asked us to take
up the calling to deliver the Word. Archangels Jophiel and Uriel
have said: "Beloved hearts, know this: that if people are to be
God-taught, we must have teachers.... You cannot neglect the
calling to transmit the knowledge that you have of who and
what you are and the knowledge of this earth and what has
turned it aside....

"Blessed ones, the responsibility is great that has been
entrusted to this community. There will not be world enlightenment without world teachers. We are not about to leave crumbs
of bread in the forest as markers for Hansel and Gretel. The evolutions of the planet deserve more. And *you* deserve to have
more of your divinity functioning through you. Thus, let each
one unite with each and every other one to exchange the teaching. One teaches the other, the other teaches the friend. And
thus, you share the resources and your research, and you bring
together what is absolutely essential to rescue the nations."[19]

The Goddess Sarasvati also calls us to teach: "It is the
requirement of every disciple of the Divine Mother to pass on his
talent to the next generation ere he take his leave from this
octave.

"So, beloved, before the day and the hour of your transi-
tioning to other planes, remember to deposit in many hearts
your skill, your creativity, your art, your science, the melody of
your soul, the preciousness of your heart. And do not think for
one moment that you do not have anything to teach! If you have
nothing you have learned, beloved, then teach compassion, teach
love, teach joy, teach gratitude, teach all children of all ages how
to magnify the Lord in their hearts."[20]

Each one of us has a unique God flame, unlike any other person on the planet. We all have a gift we can pass on to another,

even if it is as simple and sweet as the quality of God-gratitude.
And we know that the best teacher is the one who teaches by
example.

What happens to us when we teach? As representatives of the
World Teachers, we seek not just to convey an intellectual knowl-
edge of their teachings, but to transfer the *Word* as a living flame.
As that flame and that light passes through us, we find that we
ourselves are transformed. As we empty ourselves and allow the
Holy Spirit to work through us, we are filled again by his grace.

Lanello points to Saint Francis, our beloved Kuthumi, as
one who was a teacher of the Word by his example: "Let us walk
together in the footsteps of Saint Francis and our dear Lord and
realize that you and I and we are drawn together in this hour of
the victory of our love sublime to become teachers of the Word
by example. When you are called upon to teach the Word, there
is no need to fear or to have some trepidation that you are not
able to stand before a group and give the teachings of the World
Teachers. For, beloved, the best teacher among you is the best
example.

"How, then, to best teach the Word? Become the fullness of
that Christ who dwelt bodily in Saint Francis and in so many of
us who have walked the Path before you. Let others know of him
by the light-emanation of your heart, by sweet and consoling
words and by firmness 'gainst those who would encroach upon
the letters of living fire burned in your very hearts, I AM THAT
I AM."[21]

When we make the commitment to be world teachers, the
angels and the masters will come to help us and strengthen us.
Heaven is waiting to help, but we must make the commitment to
do our part. Jesus tells us of the commitment he makes to those
who will prepare and respond to his Call:

"This vow I make before you and before Almighty God:
When you stand before the world to give the fullness of my
flame and my teaching, in the moment when you open your
mouth to speak, then the Holy Spirit will come upon you until
you have delivered the fullness of that light ordained for that
transfer of my Sacred Heart."[22]

Ten Thousand Keepers of the Flame

Jesus' final request in this dictation is the Call for ten thousand Keepers of the Flame. Jesus says: "I have come to make a plea to you and to send my messenger abroad across this continent for the gathering of ten thousand who will call themselves Keepers of the Flame of Life and who will understand that I, Jesus, have called them."

El Morya speaks of the purposes of the fraternity of the Keepers of the Flame and the opportunities available to those who wish to be a part of this endeavor, sponsored and founded by Saint Germain:

"The Keepers of the Flame Fraternity is a universal spiritual order dedicated to eternal faith, unwavering constancy and infinite harmony with the love of God that is forever the radiant flame called life. Keepers of the Flame live for the flame of life, and Keepers of the Flame are the lively stones in the temple of our God.[23] They uphold the flame of life as the threefold flame ablaze within their hearts, a focus of overcoming victory to negate personal and planetary spirals of death, disintegration and decay....

"Keepers of the Flame are responsible to the spiritual board of the fraternity, which is headed by the Maha Chohan, the Keeper of the Flame, and the Knight Commander, Saint Germain. The board of directors is composed of the seven chohans, who direct various aspects of the unfoldment of the Law both through the printed instruction and through the individual training that Keepers of the Flame are given in the etheric retreats of the Great White Brotherhood. A special Committee for Child Guidance formed for the preparation of parents of incoming souls and for the proper education of children is headed by the World Teachers, Jesus and Kuthumi, together with Mother Mary....

"Upon the founding of the fraternity, the spiritual board, with the assistance of the entire Great White Brotherhood, ordained and dedicated the Keepers of the Flame Lessons as an official channel that should serve to further enlighten mankind and to vanquish ignorance by the light and power of the God flame. And it was determined at the Darjeeling Council table that the sacred knowledge of the flame that the masters are pledged to release in these lessons should provide a safe platform for ascending souls—a path so well-lighted that none who examine the teachings and pursue them with an objective heart should ever hesitate to cross the threshold into eternal life and the truth that shall make all mankind free.[24]

"Those who have faithfully served the cause of the Brotherhood through their support of the Keepers of the Flame Fraternity have been amply rewarded with countless blessings. One and all, though sometimes unbeknownst to their outer consciousness, have had the opportunity to attend closed classes in the retreats of the masters as well as at our quarterly conferences and to balance an extraordinary amount of karma through their application to the violet flame multiplied by the sponsors of the fraternity (the members of the spiritual board), who enter into a direct and intimate relationship with each chela who is willing to make the commitment that is required."[25]

The Violet Flame

In this dictation, Jesus speaks of the importance of the use of the violet flame in this time of earth's history. It is the end of an age and a time when karma from past cycles comes due for resolution.

The messenger explains how the violet flame works on the substance of karma: "How does the violet flame work? Let me use an analogy. As experts in the ancient Oriental art of Feng Shui know, clutter and the arrangement of your physical environment determine the flow of energy in your surroundings. And that flow of energy powerfully affects your health, your abundance, your relationships—the very course of your life. In the same way, karmic clutter is in your body, mind and emotions. It can cause the energy within and around you to stagnate.

"We all have some karmic clutter. While we have done much good in our lifetimes, we have also created negative energy. This energy has collected and then calcified in our physical body, our mental body, our desire body and even at the level of the etheric octave. As a result of this karma, we don't feel as light, free, happy, vibrant and spiritual as we could. The violet flame can literally consume the debris within and between the atoms of your being.

"Each morning an angel brings us our karma for the day. That means our untransmuted karma of the past. It could be the karma of yesterday or it could be the karma of five hundred years ago or ten thousand years ago or eleven thousand years ago on Atlantis or Lemuria.... If you give violet-flame decrees first thing in the morning, as many like to do at five a.m., your day will go much more smoothly. You'll be more successful because you will already have transmuted the karma of the day.... The violet flame lets you transmute the negatives and capitalize on the positives."[26]

SPIRITUAL EXERCISES

The Universities of the Spirit

If you would like to find out more about the chohans of the rays, their retreats and the teachings they deliver in the Universities of the Spirit, read *Lords of the Seven Rays,* by Mark L. Prophet and Elizabeth Clare Prophet. As you attune to the masters and their retreats, you will find it easier to travel there as you sleep.

Avoiding heavy foods in the few hours before sleep is recommended so that the functions of the body can be at rest and the soul more easily ascend to higher octaves. It is also best to avoid violent or negative movies or television shows in the hours before sleep. These can magnetize the soul to lower levels of consciousness instead of the highest levels of the etheric. A period of spiritual attunement before sleep, perhaps reading the words of the master, helps attune your consciousness with the intended destination. Where we are in consciousness before we sleep will often determine where we go.

You can give the following prayer as you go to sleep:

Father, into thy hands I commend my spirit.

Mighty I AM Presence and Holy Christ Self, I call to Archangel Michael and his legions of blue lightning angels to protect and transport my soul clothed in her finer bodies to the retreat of the ascended master _____ at _____ this night. Escort me, instruct me, guide and protect me as I work to set free all life on earth. I ask this be done in accordance with the holy will of God.

Keep a notebook by your bed, and write down any impressions or ideas that come to you on awakening.

Reflect on What You Can Teach

Jesus has called us to be world teachers. What do we have to teach in this hour? Sarasvati explained that even if we have nothing else, we can teach love, joy, compassion, gratitude. We all have unique gifts and something we can teach.

1. Take a moment to reflect on your skills, talents and your personal qualities. What do you have that you can pass on to another?
2. If you are coming up short, ask a good friend. You may be surprised at the feedback you receive!
3. Make a list.
4. Watch for opportunities to teach these things to others.

Ten Thousand Keepers of the Flame

If you are not already a member of the Keepers of the Flame Fraternity, consider joining. You may yourself be one of the ten thousand Keepers of the Flame that Jesus called for. If you would like to find out more about the fraternity, write to: Keepers of the Flame Fraternity, PO Box 5000, Corwin Springs, MT 59030, USA.

If you are already a member of the fraternity, consider what you can do to answer Jesus' Call. There are many people who understand what it means to keep the flame spiritually for the earth and yet have not heard of the fraternity. What can you do to help them find out about it?

One thing we can always do is to pray for them. You may wish to include the following prayer in your daily rituals:

> **In the name of my mighty I AM Presence and Holy Christ Self, beloved Jesus and Kuthumi, beloved Saint Germain and Portia, beloved Mighty Astrea, beloved Archangel Michael and the seven beloved archangels: by the power of the light of God that never fails, cut free ten thousand Keepers of the Flame of Life for Saint Germain. Protect and seal them in the blue lightning of the mind of God and give them the vision of their God-reality manifest in their own beloved Holy Christ Self.**

And then, do not forget the practical steps to let people know about the Keepers of the Flame Fraternity.

Violet Flame °

The masters who serve on the seventh ray, the violet ray, have given many mantras that we can use to invoke that light. The messenger explains one aspect of this science: "When the ray descends from the heart of the Great Central Sun or from the heart of your I AM Presence, it comes forth as a ray through the plane of Spirit until it reaches the place where it is invoked— the plane of invocation. When the ray descends and contacts that plane, it springs up as a flame.

"When you call forth the violet flame from the heart of God, it comes forth as a ray of light. When it reaches this point of the nexus—the point in the center of the cross where Spirit and Matter meet, the point of the Christ consciousness—the ray becomes the flame."[27]

Give the following violet flame decree, and visualize the violet light descending as a ray, igniting a flame that blazes all around you or wherever in the world you direct that light.

I AM THE VIOLET FLAME

In the name of the beloved mighty victorious Presence of God, I AM in me, my very own beloved Holy Christ Self, Holy Christ Selves of all mankind, beloved Lanello, the entire Spirit of the Great White Brotherhood and the World Mother, elemental life—fire, air, water, and earth! I decree:

> I AM the violet flame
> In action in me now
> I AM the violet flame
> To light alone I bow
> I AM the violet flame
> In mighty cosmic power
> I AM the light of God
> Shining every hour
> I AM the violet flame
> Blazing like a sun
> I AM God's sacred power
> Freeing every one

And in full faith I consciously accept this manifest, manifest, manifest! (3x) right here and now with full power, eternally sustained, all-powerfully active, ever expanding, and world enfolding until all are wholly ascended in the light and free! Beloved I AM! Beloved I AM! Beloved I AM!

FOR YOUR JOURNAL

How Will *You* Answer Jesus' Calls?

The Call to the path of the ascension.

"I Call you to be world teachers."

The Call for ten thousand Keepers of the Flame.

What do these Calls mean to me?

What will I do to answer these Calls?

CHAPTER 4

"I call you to be my disciples."

"I ask that you renew your commitment to giving my Watch, my 'Vigil of the Hours.' "

The Call of the Cosmic Christ
Discipleship unto the Ascended Master Jesus Christ

Into the fullness of the light I would draw you, my beloved—not into the partial light, not into the uncertainty between the darkness and the daylight. I AM come to this city very personally to claim my own disciples.

My heart is open, opened by the Father once again to call my own to a path whereby they shall embody my Word, my teaching, my flesh and my blood.

Discipleship in this age is the Call of the Cosmic Christ.

O souls mounting the spiral staircase unto heaven where thy Christ does await thee, I AM Jesus and I call you to be now the embodiment of all that I AM and to receive me that you might have with me henceforth the most direct relationship.

I call for a purpose and it is the step-by-step containment of the light. I call you to my fold not in the general sense but in the specific sense of knowing that a teaching, a way of life, a spirit of the resurrection cannot endure upon earth unless, truly, ten thousand determine in this hour of my appearing to embody the fullness of myself. Truly, I have answered the call of the child and the teenager who have asked to be my disciple.

Blessed hearts, with ten thousand I will show you and Saint Germain what we together can do for the turning of the tide. Our God has decreed and the Trinity does embody his will, but here below, if that kingdom is to come into manifestation, truly there must be those who can be pillars to hold up the new city, the Holy City, the etheric octave of light come down to earth. Let the New Jerusalem be seen and shared, be partaken of by my own.[1]

I would receive you, then, in my retreat in Arabia[2] [on the etheric plane] to tutor you as I did tutor my apostles Paul and John and countless others through the ages who have come to be initiated in the secret rites given to those who are able to enter the inner circle.

Blessed ones, that door is open to all who qualify. Therefore, it is not an apartness but the saving of a divine grace until ye are able to drink this strong wine of the Spirit.

Blessed hearts, the inner circle consists of the five secret-ray rings of light that surround my sacred heart and do exist in pattern as prototype around your own heart chakra. These spheres of light have been occupied by your human creation. Therefore, the invitation to be my disciples is given to one and to all—all who will understand the self-emptying by love in order that you might be filled anew with these five frequencies of spherical lights that must be present round the heart chakra if the fullness of my sacred heart is to abide in you.

Let there be a recognition, then, that it is I who have called you to bring ten thousand Keepers of the Flame to the heart of Saint Germain. To be a Keeper of the Flame—of light in the Lighthouse of Being—is the first step toward discipleship.

Having so fulfilled the basic requirements of these lessons, you then come to that time, beloved, when you desire to study the mysteries under Maitreya. And the World Teachers approach you, that you might know that we give a path of initiation step-by-step to his heart. It is the hour when the fulfillment of all promises is come.

If the cumulative light of all ages and avatars is to be brought to the fore and to the physical octave in the new age, then the forerunners of the age—those who have lived on earth (and continue to live on earth) bearing with them the signs of previous dispensations—must be willing to enter this age in the fullness of my Christhood and their own [Christhood] appearing within them. Wherefore shall there be, then, a path of the ascension or of saving grace except ye are the light of the world and the city that is set on an hill that cannot be hid?[3]

Let it be known, then, forever—let it be known that in this

hour of maximum karma descending, ten thousand have heard my voice and understood that wherever there is the Anointed One [The Lord Our Righteousness,[4] the Holy Christ Self raised up within the individual], I AM in that heart and the Father with me. We do take up our abode in those who are in harmony with love, never an offense to the light itself. Thus Father and Son dwell in thy temple and in this my own.

Know, then, the meaning of the expansion of the fire of the heart as almost with pain the increase of sacred fire creates the burning [sensation], the expanding, even of the chalice [heart chakra] until the fullness of the Christ is come.

Therefore, in this body, [become] my body, I AM.

I AM in every disciple who knows the path of the inner mysteries. And to those who desire them I come to teach. Receive, then, all that I have offered, all that is written and spoken. And be ready at any hour; for the Bridegroom, thy Christ Self, cometh to take the soul by the hand into the secret place. And there I come to initiate.

In this moment, beloved, angels of the Holy Spirit and of our Lord, the Maha Chohan,[5] are with me. By the Holy Spirit and the intense love of angelic hosts there is this day a quickening of the twelve petals of the heart, as though new life were blossoming: and the green stalk and the green shoot are quickened.

And the fountain of the Divine Mother rises up within you that you might perform a work for our blessed Saint Joseph in his day. Called Saint Germain in this hour, my father and your own does reappear to go before my Mother Mary, my brothers and sisters, each and every one of you.

Blessed hearts, it is sometimes true, though prosaic, that the greatest light compels the greatest darkness. And therefore by our light in the earth the darkness is forced out into the sacred fires and altars of transmutation that you have erected by violet-flame invocation.

Consequently, beloved, the presence of the greater darkness in the earth does compel you by love to externalize the greatest light. Therefore there are those who need to see and know human suffering, that the desire to be healed and to be the instrument of healing might be kindled to a white-hot fervor that does magnetize the Holy Spirit in the fullness of his divine appearing.

Know, then, beloved, that when all is well in a level of mediocrity in the earth, there is no goad to spiritual progress. And in past ages when the conquest of the earth itself—eking out an existence, forging new civilizations—was the demand, again, only the very few sought the interior life.

But in this hour, beloved, you who are "my disciples in deed"[6] have drunk the cup, even the dregs of all activities of the sine waves of the rise and fall of civilizations, continents and planetary cycles again and again. There is no new thing under the sun[7] on this earth for you, for the cumulative experience of karma and the world has seen it all. And you yourself look to new worlds to conquer. Yet without wings how does the soul fly to the Source and to her God?

I AM come, then, to give you wings, to teach you to fly to the heart of the Father. I AM come ready to place upon you a crown of everlasting life[8] when you shall have triumphed over the lesser nature and out of love and purest love magnetized the infilling of the Word, of the Holy Ghost, of the water of life and the blood that is my Being, my Self.[9]

Blessed hearts, it is a path of love that I bring, love illumined by wisdom and illumining wisdom in the way. The burning in the heart for none other than to be in the very Presence of the I AM THAT I AM—this burning is a fire that does propel the soul as nothing else can.

Therefore, with all thy getting[10] on the path of self-mastery and knowledge, I counsel you, my own, that to love one another profoundly as I have loved you[11] in the secret places of the Most High[12] is the key to an accelerated path whereby adeptship is a by-product of love and good works and inner purity and divine motives rather than the goal.

To seek to be master, then, or disciple without great concern for those things that are upon the earth and coming upon the earth makes no sense and does not balance in the equation of life.

Love, then, is that sacred fire that does lay down its life for the friend and take it again.[13] And each time in the givingness of life you increase in Christhood. There is no sense of loss as former garments are laid aside and the robe of Christhood descends. Therefore, with each leaving off of the familiar, one becomes acquainted with the outer court of the kingdom and successive spheres of divine awareness where new friends and new angels abide who attend thy coming.

O blessed one, is it not true that "The Hymn of the Pearl"[14] does awaken the divine memory of other years and lost spheres and a song that the soul has sung and a hymn of choirs that have not recently rung? Therefore, let the bell that tolls be not for death but for eternal life.

And in the process of the inner conviction and knowing "I AM ascending unto my God and your God,"[15] let there be a certain abandonment unto the service of our God, our LORD, our Saviour. Let there be the sense in all thy waking hours that, but for thy ministration, some poor soul may be lost. Bypass the "blank ones" whom the Father himself has no desire to convert, but go to the "little ones of my heart." Go to the simple ones rather than those of pomp and story and majesty who mix with the princes of this world and desire not to commune with me one hour.

I ask, then, that you renew your commitment to giving my Watch, my "Vigil of the Hours." So it shall be to you that I shall be in your midst, beloved, as you give this prayer service in my name weekly. You may give it alone, all-one with me, with the recording provided.

And, therefore, know that there is no limit to the expansion of the five spheres of the five secret rays around your heart. And when I AM near and nearest to you in vibration—for you have called me by the magnet of your love and prayerful devotions— I promise you that all who commit to be my disciple as a Keeper of the Flame shall have my spheres of light and my sacred heart superimposed upon him or her throughout this Watch each week.

It is my desire, then, that in fifty-two sessions with you, which I would like to be of ninety-minute duration (or more), you might experience such renewal and such self-transcendence at the conclusion of a single year's Watch with me that you shall indeed know that I AM come into the earth to take my own in the grand ritual of the resurrection and the ascension.

Blessed hearts, I come with a simple call and a plan. And yet I remain mindful of the accelerated and complex requirements that the Law does place upon you as you invoke the archangels to engage in Armageddon to defeat those who would devour souls in the earth.

Therefore, the Watch itself is for the opening of the heart that a door might exist where I might enter and thence release to the earth renewed light and Presence, beloved, that you might understand that through you I desire—I, Jesus, your brother, desire—to increase the Christ consciousness in the earth, that upon this foundation all other servant-sons of heaven and heavenly hosts might indeed build the new age, magnetize the little children and devour the darkness abroad.

Blessed hearts, the greatest persecution of my life in this age is the persecution of my message and of those who speak the Truth in the true teachings that I have given. Therefore, as in the days of Jeremiah, it is the false prophets of peace, the false shepherds of Christ,[16] who are the betrayers of my Word—those who speak of me and yet do not have my Presence in their hearts—it is their message and their example that do belie the true path of discipleship.

And, therefore, to remedy this I choose to enter in—at a renewed level of calling and dispensation from my Father—to a most intimate relationship with all who will not only call to me with their lips but will also enter my heart by embracing Saint Germain's teaching of the violet flame and acquaint themselves with my Mother Mary and not shun her. Further, I choose to enter into this relationship with all who will call upon Saint Michael the Archangel to defend both Church and State and to exorcise these domains of Alpha and Omega of all fallen angels who have come to steal away the best of the hearts of men.

Blessed ones, realize that this path of discipleship has its

foundation in my earthly mission and its culmination in the fullness of my teaching of the New Age.

I would speak, then, of my messenger Mark who did write
down the Gospel bearing his name and reincarnate as my messenger[17] in this age to found this organization from which you
now abundantly receive our graces and gifts. The calling of this
one, and his response in his aloneness as he did respond to my
heart, has meant for all hosts of heaven an open door in this
activity that is absolutely essential to the survival of the lightbearers in this century.

I desire you to understand that my persecution is [the persecution of my Christhood is carried out in] the limitation of my
Presence, my Word and life wherever there are those who have
limited my own to commune with me and to receive my progressive revelation by the Holy Spirit. Therefore, few there be
who have retained the integrity of our message and brought
forth in detail a divine mosaic of all that I have taught.

Therefore, beloved, as a single individual may be the key to
unlock a door through which all humanity may pass, such being
the case with my disciple Mark, so I say to you it is no less the
case with yourself. It is the hour to decide if in your aloneness, all-
oneness with me and the Father, you shall then be a key for millions of souls who will step through the door that you have
opened.

Let it be, then, that you embrace my teaching and that you
recognize that the persecution of the sacred mysteries and those
who bear them in this age does require that all who catch the
spirit of the message here stated therefore band together and
present themselves as a movement of light that may not be set
aside—whose members apart might have been put down or
persecuted, but as one fervent heart, one sacred heart dedicated
to my mother through me, might then be a magnet to magnetize
a world, to literally pull it up and away from the old magnetism
of the lower levels of orthodoxy that truly have entombed me
and left me upon the cross crucified and therefore left my sons
and daughters and my children crucified on a cross of iron and

steel and a Cain civilization with all of its burdens.

How can those who are truly Christians or followers of Christ in any world religion cease for a moment their concern and their activism to defend life that is unborn, life that must reincarnate that souls and a world might move on? How can any who know the true path sit back while the world may be devoured in flames of World Communism and by the betrayal of all those of the West who have made this possible?

Blessed hearts, this is why I have spoken of the fervor of the heart. For those who love do not stand by while youth and children are destroyed and civilizations crumble. They walk out from their pulpits and into the streets and they rescue life, not in a humanistic sense but because they have received that power from on high and, therefore, by the empowerment of the Trinity may act in our name to stand between a nation, a people, a family, a single soul and a returning karma too hard to bear.

This is why and to this end I call you to be my disciples in the most serious effort, of all of your incarnations, to recognize that in thy flesh thou shalt see God and be my Self.[18] And only thus shall this world be endowed with a sufficiency and Presence [of my Christhood] in the physical to stay the hand of oncoming darkness.

The lambs have been shorn not only of their identity but of a teaching that could enable them to realize that identity. They have been turned aside by every false prophet, false pastor and false guru. Blessed hearts, for every vice there is a false prophet that has embodied it. For every false teaching, whether in the economy or the arts or the sciences, there are the fallen ones who do embody it....

Let it be understood that every area of life must have my disciple standing there holding the key that does unlock the mystery of the Word and the Path whereby every branch of service and knowledge and endeavor might be once again endued with the flame of Gautama Buddha, Padma Sambhava, Sanat Kumara, Lord Maitreya, my brothers, my friends, my cohorts of light.

Heaven is filled with the witness of the glory not alone of my coming but of His appearing. Therefore, beloved, I seek no preeminence in the hierarchical chain of being, for I AM WHO I AM, I AM Alpha and Omega, the beginning and the ending. And my speaking is of the eternal Logos, who I AM, who you also can be and are. For in the highest planes of thy being, O beloved, I, Jesus, affirm it: Thou art the living Christ!

Now I speak to your soul, sometimes fully awake and sometimes not so, and I implore you, my soul, my bride, come now and determine and desire with all of your desiring to be that Christ whom thou art—here in flesh, here in form. This world hath need of thee. Thou dost occupy the heavens and the stars. Now occupy earth till I come in the full glory of the physical manifestation long attended by many. Occupy till I come, beloved.[19]

And when you stand in my place, being my Self in form and embodying my light, then I do come to you, Jesus, your teacher, and I sponsor you, beloved. And you shall know a sponsorship never known before. For my legions of angels are ready and waiting for the ten thousand and more who shall hear me because I come pleading the cause of Saint Germain and world freedom.

Without this victory, then, of a spiritual and physical defense for the nations, there shall not be seen in the earth nor a new age, nor a new day. Therefore, act swiftly and make haste, for I have called. I have called. ❦

October 4, 1987
Penta Hotel
New York City

I Call you to be my disciples in the most serious effort of all of your incarnations, to recognize that in thy flesh thou shalt see God and be my Self.

JESUS

There are many followers and students of Jesus in the world, but in this dictation, Jesus calls us to a new kind of relationship—to be his disciple. This is an important difference and a key step on the Path. The messenger explains that as a student, "the individual studies and becomes a student of the writings and the teachings of the master. He is free to come and go in his community, enjoying fellowship with his followers and the fruits of their dedication but has declared no particular responsibility to the person of the master. He has taken no vows, made no commitment, but may be studying to 'show himself approved'[20] in order to be accepted as a servant, or co-server (otherwise known as 'chela'), sharing the joy of the master's world mission."[21]

In the relationship of disciple, however, "the individual desires to enter into a bond with the master—to be taught directly by the master rather than through his published writings alone.... The disciple receives the initiations of the Cosmic Christ in the course of his service to the master. His heart, mind and soul have begun to unfold a greater love as appreciation and gratitude for the teachings received in the previous level of student. This love is translated into action as self-sacrifice, selflessness, service and surrender to the Person of the Christ, the Sun behind the Son of man of the master."[22]

What will it mean to be a disciple, or chela, of Jesus? The ascended master El Morya explains the Eastern understanding of this relationship, and from this we can gain a new understanding of what it means to be a disciple of the Master:

"*Chela* is a term meaning student or disciple of a religious teacher. It is derived from the Hindi *celā,* which is taken from the

Sanskrit *ceta,* meaning slave. In the Eastern tradition of chelaship, recognized for thousands of years as the way of self-mastery
and enlightenment, one desiring to have the mysteries of universal law imparted to him applies to the teacher, known as the
guru, considered to be a master (through the ages the real gurus
have included both ascended and unascended masters), to serve
that teacher until he is found worthy to receive the keys to his
own inner reality....

   "In the Eastern tradition, the chela is the slave of his master
for a good reason—not for the loss of his true identity, but for the
replacement of the pseudoimage with the Real Image of selfhood.
The chela, by submission, day by day is weaving into consciousness the threads of the garment of his master. The master's garment (as the much sought-after robe of the Christ) is synonymous
with the master's consciousness.

   "In return for illumined obedience and self-sacrificing love,
the chela receives increments of the master's attainment—of the
master's own realization of his Real Self. Through the acceptance
of the word of the master as inviolate, the chela has imparted to
him the Christ consciousness of his master, which in turn is the
means whereby the base elements of the chela's subconscious and
the momentums of his untransmuted karma are melted by the
fervent heat of the sacred fire that comprises the master's consciousness.

   "Thus, by freely and willingly setting aside the momentums
of his human consciousness, the chela discovers that these are
soon replaced by his teacher's mastery, which, when he makes it
his own, serves as the magnet to magnetize his own higher consciousness and attainment."[23]

   Jesus and Kuthumi include six chapters on the subject of discipleship in their book *Corona Class Lessons.* They explain that
the purpose of their instruction on this topic "is to address those
who would learn to teach others the Way and find thereby
greater illumination and avenues of service for their own mission....

   "A disciple is one who is disciplined and whose course is parallel to my own. Each such a one I lovingly call brother—sister. Welcome into the family of those who consciously present themselves to the eternal will and purpose, saying with Isaiah, 'Here I AM, send me!'[24]"[25]

In this dictation, Jesus lets us know that he expects his disciples to be more than those who accept his teachings and assist to spread them. He says, "I AM Jesus and I call you to be now the embodiment of all that I AM and to receive me that you might have with me henceforth the most direct relationship."

The messenger has explained that the guru-chela relationship is fundamental, not only to the spiritual path, but also to life itself. "The guru-chela relationship actually sustains the entire Matter cosmos. Without that interchange from heart to heart of the teacher and the disciples, the world, the stars, the galaxies, would not exist, because all is the interaction of Alpha and Omega down the universal chain of being, a universal chain of hierarchy."[26]

In this dictation, Jesus reveals something of this chain of hierarchy that connects us all the way back to the Great Central Sun of the cosmos. He introduces us to his guru, the ascended master Maitreya, who holds the office in the spiritual hierarchy of this planet of Cosmic Christ.

Jesus explains that his guru, Lord Maitreya, was very present with him in his Galilean mission: "I, then, came into this world sent by the One who has sent me, and when I said, 'I and my Father are one,'[27] I spake of the All-Father and the living I AM Presence and of his representative, the One who should wear the mantle of guru. Thus, the One who did send me in the chain of hierarchy of the ancients was none other than Maitreya....

"Blessed hearts, the continuity of the message of Maitreya come again is in this hour in you, not in one individual chosen apart, but through you and through that Holy Christ flame....

"Come unto my heart and know me, then, as the Son, the 'sonshine' of Maitreya. Know, then, that my mission, going before him, even as John the Baptist went before me, was to clear the way for the coming of this Universal Christ in all sons of God upon earth."²⁸

Although Jesus did not reveal the name of his guru to the apostles—at least not in the scriptures that have survived to this day—his relationship to the guru is clear in the Bible. The messenger explains: "As recorded in the New Testament, Jesus often spoke of the Father who had sent him. Of note are his words following his triumphal entry into Jerusalem on Palm Sunday, only days before his celebration of the last Passover supper. In this appeal we hear Jesus crying out, almost in desperation, for his disciples to know him as messenger of the Cosmic Christ, his beloved guru Maitreya.

Jesus cried and said, He that believeth on me, believeth not on me, but on him that sent me.

And he that seeth me seeth him that sent me....

For I have not spoken of myself; but the Father which sent me, he gave me a commandment, what I should say, and what I should speak.

And I know that his commandment is life everlasting: whatsoever I speak therefore, even as the Father said unto me, so I speak.²⁹

"Jesus wanted his apostles to know the one he called Father as the ascended master Maitreya, who had overshadowed him as his guru throughout his final incarnation. And he wanted them to know himself as the one sent by Maitreya. For thereby they would not worship his flesh and blood but they would worship the continuity of the Word Incarnate, which was in the beginning with God and had been in Lord Maitreya and his predecessors, the Lord Gautama Buddha and the Lord Sanat Kumara, as it was now in Jesus Christ.

"Furthermore, the master wanted his own to know the Word Incarnate in him as the same 'Light' that, he told John, 'was the true Light, which lighteth every man that cometh into the world.'³⁰"³¹

Jesus wanted them to know him as the avatar of the Piscean Age and a link in the chain of hierarchy of the Buddhas and the Cosmic Christs. The messenger explains the inner meaning of his words and his statement of his mission: "Thus, the Master would have said to his own:

" 'If you have seen me, you have seen Lord Maitreya, you have seen Gautama Buddha, you have seen Sanat Kumara—for each one in his turn and time has embodied the Father. And not only have you seen the personages of the Father in those who have sponsored my Christhood and my mission, but you have also seen the Father as the mighty I AM Presence overshadowing me and entering my temple:

" *'For I and my Father are one.'*[32]

" 'The indwelling Father—as the I AM Presence and the living guru—dictates the words that I speak and the works that I do....

" 'And because "I ascend unto my Father and your Father, and to my God and your God,"[33] I will sponsor you on this path of the disciples of the Cosmic Christ becoming the bodhisattvas of the Buddha Maitreya. As I AM, so you may also become. If you do not choose this calling sent to you from your Father and your God through my messengership, then I will have failed in my mission and you will have failed in yours.'

"Jesus then explained to his disciples the all-power of the Father that is vested in his name. He promised to transfer this power to his disciples by doing 'whatsoever ye shall ask in my name,' that the Father may be glorified in the Son.[34]"[35]

Thus, we understand that to fulfill our mission and be victorious, we must also become a part of this chain of hierarchy. We must take up Jesus' calling to become his disciples—the disciplined ones.

"I and My Father Are One"

One of the keys that Maitreya gave to Jesus when he was in the East[36] was the use of the mantra, "I and my Father are one." Maitreya explains:

" 'I and my Father are one' is the mantra of the protection of the guru-chela relationship that I gave to him, the Son of man. I and my Father are one! When you speak these words, the lineage of your ascended masters is with you, the Electronic Presence of Jesus is upon you, your own I AM Presence and Christ Self are there, and I AM instantly there....

"Thus, you see, the 'I and my Father are one' mantra is actually a call. It is a call you may give in time of danger, chaos, confusion or accident or illness or any need, as long as you have the perception that the Call cannot and will not fail as long as you have the understanding of who is Father. The LORD God Almighty is Father and his emissaries to whom he has given the mantle of his I AM Presence to teach mankind are Father. Thus the 'I and my Father are one' mantra uses the I AM name to confirm the bond of our oneness.

"By cosmic law I cannot fail to answer the call of this mantra. The only variation in my answer is in your vibration. For though I may be with you, you may not feel it until you have quelled the turbulence of your emotions."[37]

"I and my Father are one" is a mantra you can say throughout the day. You can put it on your desk or on your mirror to remind you of your oneness with Jesus as his disciple and as a reminder to give the mantra frequently.

Jesus' Retreat in Arabia

In this dictation, Jesus invites us to journey to his retreat located in the etheric octave over the Saudi Arabian desert, northeast of the Red Sea.[38] He promises that if we come to his retreat, he will tutor us in the secret mysteries, face-to-face, just as he tutored his apostles Paul and John.

In Galatians 1:17, Paul speaks of his journey to Arabia: "Neither went I up to Jerusalem to them which were apostles before me; but I went into Arabia, and returned again unto Damascus."

The messenger explains the significance of this passage: "He took three years in Saudi Arabia in the desert where he communed with Christ. Many do not know what he did then, but we know that the etheric retreat of the ascended master Jesus Christ is over Saudi Arabia in the etheric octave. So we can see the apos-

tle came as close to that retreat as he could and communed with
Jesus, who gave to him the mysteries—mysteries which Paul said
it was not lawful for a man to utter.[39] Jesus gave him the inner
keys to life—teachings that are being unveiled only today, teachings far ahead of his time, teachings that were a gnosis, or a self-
knowledge.

"And so, Paul had the inner mysteries as well as the outer rituals. And he set up a rule and an order and, through his epistles,
admonishment for the running of the churches. But he also had
for initiates those sacred mysteries and a path of initiation."[40]

Spiritual Exercises, chapter 3, includes a prayer to be taken
to the etheric retreats. You can use this prayer or compose your
own and ask to be taken by the angels to the retreat of Jesus
while you sleep.

Mother Mary

In this dictation, Jesus calls his disciples to "acquaint themselves with my Mother, Mary, and not shun her." One way in
which we can do this is through the recitation of her prayer, the
"Hail Mary," and the recitation of the rosary.

The messenger has explained that the "Hail Mary" is not
only a prayer to Mary, but it is a universal prayer to the Divine
Mother: "[Mary] gave me a new rosary and a new meditation
upon the Mother flame. She explained to me that the name *Mary*
means 'Ma-ray' and that all people, men and women alike, must
meditate upon this Mother ray, this Mother flame, which is a
fountain of living fire within us. It is a fountain of purity. It must
be quickened, raised and released.

"When the Mother comes into prominence and into domi-
nance within the temple of our being, she quickens God the
Father, God the Son and God the Holy Spirit. We see, then, that
the Mother on earth is the one who helps us to understand the
Father and teaches us his laws. She enables us to understand
the wisdom of the Son and shows us how the love of God is
the action of the sacred labor in the Holy Spirit.

"And so Mother Mary said to me that the rosary is not an

idolatrous adoration of her person. It is simply the giving of one's energy through the science of the spoken Word to the Mother of the universe, the Mother of cosmos and the Mother force, the life-force that is in oneself. The quickening of this energy leads to the soul's reunion with the Father.

"Mother Mary... desires that we should understand that the term *Mother of God* means one who will nourish the flame of God on earth and in heaven by sponsoring life, by taking care of children and of creative projects and of the work that is needed here. And so she gave me the 'Hail Mary' for all who are moving into the New Age and realize that the Aquarian age is the age when the Mother unlocks the key to the Holy Spirit:

Hail Mary

Hail, Mary, full of grace
the Lord is with thee.
Blessed art thou among women
and blessed is the fruit of thy womb, Jesus.

Holy Mary, Mother of God,
Pray for us, sons and daughters of God,
Now and at the hour of our victory
Over sin, disease and death.

"Mother Mary wants us to understand that God does not hold us in a death grip of sin and the sense of sin, but he holds us in the immaculate vision of his All-Seeing Eye as the son and the daughter who are the fruit of the union of the Father-Mother God."[41]

"Watch with Me One Hour"

The next request that Jesus makes is: "I ask that you renew your commitment to giving my Watch, my 'Vigil of the Hours.' "

This service of prayers, songs and decrees commemorates the vigil Jesus kept in the Garden of Gethsemane while his disciples fell asleep. He says to us today as he said to his disciples then, "Could ye not watch with me one hour?"[42]

Jesus is present as we give this prayer service in his name weekly. He also promises that all who commit to being his disciple as a Keeper of the Flame will have his spheres of light and his

Sacred Heart superimposed upon them throughout the Watch each week.

The messenger described her experience with the presence of Jesus as she gave this service one evening: "I felt Jesus place his Electronic Presence over me. It was so physical that I could see the beautiful golden color of his hair and his skin and his entire Presence." She said that "in order to sustain his Presence, it takes a great deal of concentration and meditation. As his Presence is over us he is weaving a filigree light around us, which takes place as Jesus comes to mesh his light body with ours. He is weaving his body to our own by way of assisting us to heal the holes and tears in our own garment and to heal the burdens of our souls and of our four lower bodies."[43]

It is for this reason, when you give this weekly service, that you should find a place where you will not be disturbed. The Master said it is during the singing of the opening song that he places his Electronic Presence over those who are in attendance at what he refers to as his "Wednesday Evening Mass." At the conclusion of this song, you should seal your room and go into meditation and concentrate fully upon the service and Jesus' Presence with you.

The messenger goes on to say, "Jesus revealed to me that once he builds a forcefield with the angels and all whom we invoke around us during the one-hour 'Watch with Me' service, it is the moment of our greatest receptivity to his Mother Mary.... During the first hour we are saturated in the Sacred Heart of Jesus, in the filigree energy he builds in our forcefield, which is multiplied each week as we regularly give the Watch. At that moment we can drink in the fullness of the blessed Mother. As we give the rosary, Mother Mary anchors her great love and then merges her Electronic Presence with our Presence, and we put on the flame of the Mother as the polarity to Jesus' flame....

"Our 'Watch With Me' Jesus' Vigil of the Hours is a very holy occasion. Remember to meditate deeply when you give the Watch, not just saying the words but by really entering in and profoundly meditating with your eyes closed as you memorize the readings, songs and decrees. When we participate in this ritual we are sealed as though we were in the Upper Room with Jesus and his disciples. The doors are sealed shut and Jesus enters."⁴⁴

SPIRITUAL EXERCISES

Write Jesus a Letter and ask Him to Accept You as His Disciple

You may wish to write Jesus a letter asking him to accept you as his disciple. The masters have told us that we may write to them and then consign our letter to the physical fire.

Calls to Invite Jesus to Enter Your Body Temple

"As I have said to you, 'Occupy till I come,' so I say to you now, allow me to occupy. For I must have your assent, your consent, beloved, to enter any secret, sacred part of your being that you have kept most private—compartments of shame or self-glory or self-deprecation. Whatever they be, beloved, I ask you (for your free will must have its day) to simply say:

Jesus, I bid you enter my whole temple now!
By my free will, by my God-dominion, I welcome you!
And I let go of everything, my Lord.

"So be it. It is done, and I am entering, beloved. If you give this fiat regularly, then each time your being passes through the cleansing fires of my heart and is washed by the waters of the Word incarnate, you shall find again and again the opportunity to receive me.... Thus, each time I return, even as you enter in to the 'Watch With Me,' the Vigil of the Hours, you may say this, and I may come unto you at deeper levels and to accomplish other purifications."⁴⁵

"I and My Father Are One"

Remember to give Jesus' mantra, which he received from his guru, Maitreya. As you give this mantra, you affirm your own place in the great chain of hierarchy.

I and my Father are One.

Meditate Weekly with Jesus by Giving his "Watch with Me" Vigil of the Hours Service.

Wherever you are, you can fulfill this Call of the Master. All you need is the "Watch With Me" booklet and a place where you will not be disturbed. If you have the tape recording of the service, you can give this beautiful healing service right in your own home, accompanied by the messenger and many other disciples.

FOR YOUR JOURNAL

How Will *You* Answer Jesus' Calls?

"I call you to be my disciples."

"I ask that you renew your commitment to giving my Watch, my 'Vigil of the Hours.' "

What do these Calls mean to me?
What will I do to answer these Calls?

CHAPTER 5

"Become that Christ!... It is time for you to be true shepherds and ministers."

The Day of Thy Christhood
Keep the Flame of Eternal Life

Out of the light I AM come, never absent but only making you aware, beloved, of my entrance, that you might realize that your own proximity to the Universal Christ does indeed have to do with the preparation of the bride. As you daily invoke this wedding garment by the science of sound, know that this is the vessel I require [that I may] enter into your heart and being, to dwell with you, to walk with you, to be a part of the great overcoming in this era.

Let my disciples, then, fulfill the Word of light and the Law of the One. For I, Jesus, as the Bridegroom, desire my perfect love [to be] in you to give unto you that union of Christos for which your souls have longed and hungered.

Blessed hearts, there must be a sustaining, a continuum of light. Let discipleship, then, be thy reason for being and thy goal the attainment of the All.

Our desiring, as the ascended hosts of light, is to work with you daily [in order] that this soul within you be formed and reformed by the sacred fires of the Holy Spirit....

Blessed hearts, it is the hour and this is the day of the marking of the hour, November 1st, 1987.[1] Mark it well, beloved, for it is a date written in the Book of Life. And for this reason and on this date I have come to these Twin Cities [Minneapolis and Saint Paul] to celebrate our twin flames, each and every one of you as Alpha and Omega.

I have come to bring to you, then, the Word of our Father, and it is this: The hour has come for you to understand, beloved, that nothing less than becoming the Christ will suffice as fulfillment or requirement of the Law. Too long and long enough have you been blessed and fed by other anointed ones, too long

have you come to receive in your church services, in your syna-
gogues and temples and mosques.

Realize, then, that those who have received a light, a witness,
a testimony of the ascended hosts, those who know now the true
path of the geometry of God, those whose internalization of the
Word is long due are given the sign in this hour. And it is the sign
of the Holy Spirit. This is the day that the path of thy Christhood
must begin in earnest. Not [postponed] till tomorrow but today,
my Christ, thy Christ One.

Counting this day as the first day, if you will, of an earnest
discipleship unto my flame and heart, I draw you if you will be
drawn. I receive you if you will indeed be received. Therefore,
beloved, know that I, Jesus, declare this day, formally with my
Father, as the commencement of a path for lightbearers of the
world who know that in my mantle and in my momentum there
is a gift to be received—to be earned and won.

I, Jesus, come to you, beloved, in this hour to impel you forward. For I will not leave thee except by your own request. And
therefore I will be as the "hound of heaven."[2]

Too many yet sleep, having been awakened yet preferring
sleep. Be quickened, beloved, and know that the accountability
is upon you from this day forward and that the Law does require
it for thy salvation, for the very survival of the soul herself.

Cosmic cycles have turned. And in their turning, even the
days and the hours of thy life now numbered must be filled with
light and the cup filled daily. For, beloved, if you heed me not,
you will find yourself at the conclusion of this life wanting in the
light necessary to make the transition to higher octaves.

Foreseeing the world as I foresee it, I do not recommend in all
cosmic honor that you plan on reembodying again on this earth.

**The hour of your fulfillment is come! Your Christhood is
nigh and has been knocking at the door for many years and lifetimes. And some who have known this path and received, as it
were, a mouth-to-mouth resuscitation by the chakras of the messenger have retained the light and yet not sought the mastery of
the light, the self-perfecting in the light, the protection of the light
and the will to be as GOD IS.**

Thus, we minister unto you. Now we say, Become that Christ! Receive your Lord and your God into your temple. And I, Jesus, as your brother, will walk at your side, will talk with you, will counsel you. And you will know me in the love that I shared with John, my beloved. You will know the intimacy of love's communion and love's initiation.

Take to your hearts, then, the lessons given by Saint Germain. Resolve to keep the flame of life that is your own Christhood, for only in that Christ flame do you have with you eternal life.

Blessed ones, your eternal life is not something to be set aside as a garment or to be left in heaven. You need a lamp in which a flame of eternal life is burning continually. For in the day or the hour of the coming of the dark night of the Spirit or even the dark night of the soul, it is this light that shall light thy way and be a light unto all thy house.

One and several, many and thousands will depend upon this light. And in the day of your appearing in this Christ, you will be grateful unto God that you have heard me and heeded my word. For so shall you see that ten thousand may be saved because the flame of eternal life is burning brightly in the temple of being.

Feel it now, beloved, for I place my sacred heart one with your own, one for the impetus of the balance of the threefold flame, for the impetus of the twelve petals of the heart chakra to provide you now, one by one, with the initiations of the twelve gates of the temple, even the seven chakras and the eighth and the five secret-ray chakras. Thus the thirteenth is the deliverance of the All unto the all of you. By the path of the sacred heart, by the path of the ruby ray, so triumph in grace and in good works, so triumph in graciousness and selflessness.

I, then, predict your future. For this day I have studied the record of the Book of Life for each and every lifestream who has come to this seminar and for all individuals who are called Keepers of the Flame worldwide. My prediction, then, given coming events, given your own karma, is that the only way out of the dilemma of the human equation is to act now.

Hear me, beloved! I have never been more in earnest. I have cried unto the LORD for you. And God's emissaries have brought abundant light and teaching.

Hear me, beloved! For even my plea is a measured one. For the Father has said to me, "How many times will you plead for their own cause of eternal life, my Son?" Therefore, the Law and the dispensation of karma does allow it, but not forever.

Therefore, hear my cry to your soul! Hear my cry to pick yourself up, to wax hot in your devotion and fervor, to know the inner life, to desire to feel the flow of sacred fire in your being and to desire this until by your very imploring, as in the parable of the unjust judge,[3] so God does respond.

For the soul that does trouble the LORD does truly receive her recompense. If your desiring is sincere and you implore God daily, I tell you, beloved, the Father will not withhold from you every test and initiation, every teaching and interior correction, every leading you require to the fount of knowledge, even Gnosis, even my own lost teachings.

Beloved, hear, then, the Word of the Son of God and live! I AM your brother of light. I come to you in such reality with my angels in this hour. I come for your rescue. And I come for that rescue that you might in turn rescue others. It is time for you to be true shepherds and ministers, ministering unto the Word at the altar and ministering unto souls who have need of that light....

Be it known, beloved, that to leave off the keeping of the flame of eternal life is the very first act of suicide. Let it not be said of this generation that they have lost the Word so ready to descend into their temples to save a planet and a people. I cannot speak otherwise, for the messianic mission is yours! The word *messiah* means simply "leader." Some must rise up and lead.

Here is the One, the Divine Mother, who leads up the spiral staircase. Follow, then, the Divine Mother all the way to your own crown of life. Follow, then. For as you set the pace, as fads go in this world, many will follow. It seems a folly in itself that people will follow others in doing almost anything, even if it is most obviously ludicrous or a desecration of life.

The example set of the light in you must be a quickening. I direct you, then, to the example of my messenger Mark who is ascended with me now. This one who lived in your midst did truly have the charisma of the Holy Spirit, which is the presence in the aura of the magnetism of love. That presence became a profile of Christhood impressed upon the ethers of the earth. There are many who walk following that profile today, though they know not that they follow him.

Realize, beloved, that all souls of earth take a reading on your footsteps. And those of light who desire to know the Great White Brotherhood and to enter in, they follow those who call themselves disciples. Therefore, no longer be disciples but anointed ones. I, Jesus, declare it! I summon you and I command you as my own. Take up the lead. For many must follow, and that quickly, ere the age draw the curtain on my dispensation.

I AM Jesus of Nazareth. I AM your own. Receive me now and receive the serving of holy Communion as a sign and a promise that I give you of my life essence, my spiritual fire, my Mother body.

My Alpha and my Omega be unto you the quickening. Then return it unto me multiplied and with good fruit. Such is the requirement of the Great Law and the Great Guru, our God.

I see now you and your twin flame in heaven. And my inner eye is fixed upon you and your beloved complement in your inner white-fire bodies. I hold this in my inner sight until you should reject my path, my counsel or comfort.

I AM your Jesus. Now I say to you, Be my Christ!

With the sign of our Oneness and the Law of the Word, I AM with you alway—to the end of your tribulation in this age.

AUM AUM AUM

In the Oneness of the All, I AM thy True Self. 🍇

November 1, 1987
All Saints Day
Minneapolis Hilton Hotel
Minneapolis, Minnesota

*Realize, beloved, that all souls of earth take a reading on
your footsteps. And those of light who desire to know the Great
White Brotherhood and to enter in, they follow those who call
themselves disciples.*
                                                        JESUS

In this dictation Jesus steps up his Call to a command:
"Become that Christ!" And he tells us if we will receive the
Lord into our temple, he will walk by our side as a brother, talk
with us and counsel us.

He tells us: "Blessed hearts, it is the hour and this is the day
of the marking of the hour, November 1, 1987. Mark it well,
beloved, for it is a date written in the Book of Life.... I have come
to bring you the Word of our Father, and it is this: The hour has
come for you to understand, beloved, that nothing less than
becoming the Christ will suffice as fulfillment or requirement of
the Law. This is the day that the path of thy Christhood must
begin in earnest."

The messenger has explained the significance of this Call for
all of us, whether we were present for the dictation or not.
"Whatever day you hear this dictation or read it, on that day it
becomes a reality for you, and you know that this is the day that
your path of Christhood begins in earnest. You should mark that
day and date.

"Earnestness in that path means acceleration. It is a burning
desire in your heart and a cosmos responds and you are truly
engaged in personal Christhood. There is a difference between
engaging and not engaging just as there is a difference between
assimilation, the total digestion of the Word until it lives in every
cell of your four lower bodies, and accommodation, where you
make room for it in your life but do not allow it to enter in.

"People who accommodate the Word are those who follow
the rituals of the Church and affirm their belief in a certain doctrine and dogma but never really assimilate the Word that was

incarnate in Jesus Christ. So they make room for that in their lives but not in their consciousness and inner being.

"The engaging is a certain fixing of the mind on God, and one's mind never leaves God, never leaves the mind of God, and one's inner ear is always listening for the call from God or the call from those in need on earth. One is perpetually available to God when one is on the path of Christhood. One sees every experience as the ritual of the perfecting of the Word within, its assimilation. And only then, of course, can we have the perfecting of the outer work, which is the result of the inner Word and its assimilation."[4]

The date of your receiving this Call from the Master can be a key date in your life. As the messenger explains: "I am certain Jesus emphasized this date because he wanted us to mark it on the cosmic clock[5] and to study the astrology of that date, the juxtaposition of forces of light and darkness whereby in that moment our Lord called us because he needed us, and he needs us every day the rest of our lives just as we need him. And so, that moment, as it configures in your own chart, will tell you the profile of your Christhood that you will outpicture in this life if you will put your mind and heart and soul to it. Nothing in this world can stop you from realizing your Christhood except yourself....

"You may have a number of goals in your life today and one central goal that is all-consuming. I urge you to pray as to how you can make all of your goals converge at the point of the path of Christhood. For you, becoming that Christ may be being a householder and having a family and children or being a professional or doing all kinds of things that are necessary to fulfill positive momentums of karma and to balance negative karma. All these things can converge.

"You don't have to let go of anything except it comes under the headings of such things as incorrect livelihood [or other activities that are not compatible with the Eightfold Path of the Buddha]. Whatever is lawful in the purity of the Christ and the Holy Christ Self, whatever is lawful for the Buddhic manifestation within you, which is love and joy and the givingness of self— whatever that is can become a part of your Christhood. And whatever else you are doing that is not a part of your Christhood, let go of it. Just let it drop....

"You don't need to have a part of yourself in the astral plane to be happy. You may think you do because you've become dependent upon the vibrations of the astral plane and people who are a part of the astral plane or the weight of your own karma and your own emotional body.

"But if you really desire to be free, you need to know that real sacrifice is when you keep all that garbage and all that baggage. That's a sacrifice because you are sacrificing your Christhood to that mess of pottage that will mean nothing to you as far as the ongoing journey of eternal life is concerned. It is no sacrifice to be the Christ. It is the greatest joy and the greatest gift of God to us....

"So let us recognize that when we talk about a path of surrender and sacrifice and selflessness and service, it is not a path of self-denial. It is a path of the affirmation of True Being and the letting go of all that is unreal about ourselves. This is such an important and intense elixir that I give to you in this moment, to forever let go of those things that you keep looking back to and that you can't let go of when all of the things that are really important in life are yours in abundance, in joy, in happiness, in glory.

"There is no path of the sorrowful way. There is no path of burden. Don't be burdened about persecution. It happens to come with the whole package. So what? Have compassion for those who in their ignorance know not what they do. And when you know of such ones, send powerful love from your heart. Either the love ray and the ray of the ruby ray work, or they don't work. And we know that they work. Let them consume the hate and hate creation, the misunderstanding.

"When you learn of these things, don't be jarred from the centeredness of your being in your Christhood. Don't be moved. Don't be upset. Don't get into vortices of fear.... Don't let the devils shock you. Don't let them amaze you. Don't let them unhorse you. Don't let them get you confused and feeling bad and depressed about yourself. Just know that where that light is raised up, darkness will come in, and it comes for transmutation. And so, you have to stop what you're doing and for five minutes give tremendous fiats unto the LORD, and then go on with what you're doing. Don't be moved. Every problem in your life can and will be solved as long as you don't get out of alignment with the living Christ."[6]

Weaving the Wedding Garment

In the first paragraph of this dictation, Jesus refers to our souls as his brides and says we must strive to prepare ourselves to be that bride of Christ. The soul is the feminine potential of being of both man and woman in the sense that it is the part of us that has descended from the Father, the I AM Presence, to evolve in the planes of Mother, or Mater/Matter. Thus, as we approach our Christ Self, or Jesus as the representative of that Christ, we do come as the "bride," the feminine polarity. And this is true whether we happen to wear a masculine or feminine physical body in this life.

Jesus also speaks of the "wedding garment" that we must invoke daily by the science of the spoken Word. This is the term we find in the Bible, in Jesus' parable of the wedding feast.[7] The masters also refer to this wedding garment as the "seamless garment" or the "deathless solar body." We weave this garment of light around ourselves as we invoke the light through our decrees each day. This vessel of light becomes the chalice that Jesus may use to enter into our hearts, and it is also the garment of pure light that clothes our souls at the hour of our ascension.

How Do We Become the Christ?

The ascended lady master Portia says, "Do not accept that it takes so many years or lifetimes to achieve your Christhood, neither entertain the folly that the achievement of Christhood is easily won. It is not easily won, beloved, or you should have long ago won it, for many of you are devotees of great ardor."[8]

Becoming the Christ is a process, something that we must

engage in day by day. The messenger tells us: "El Morya says that before becoming the Christ, the disciple does become, on occasion or often, the vessel of his Christ Self.[9] So, first, we are the vessel, and in the process of being the vessel of the love of Christ, the truth of Christ and the qualities of Christ, we are putting on that oil of truth, that oil of love. We are becoming saturated with it, and we are beginning to take on its characteristics. We are beginning to think as Jesus thinks. And when we say, 'What would Jesus do?' we know exactly what he would do—and, therefore, what we would do. It is a very gradual process. It doesn't happen overnight, and that is why you have to be attentive day by day, weaving the wedding garment."[10]

Archangel Jophiel and Christine give us a key to assessing our progress on the path of putting on our Christhood: "When you hear yourself saying things that you know your Holy Christ Self would not say, then you know that that Holy Christ Self has ascended far above you and cannot enter in. When you say things with a tone of voice of condescension, with criticism, with burden or depression, sarcasm or the vibration of gossip, then you will know your Holy Christ Self cannot enter; for it is the Law of God.

"Therefore, pursue the path of the imitation of Christ. Speak as you know or believe Christ would speak, with love but firmness, sternness where required, mercy when it is due, soft-spoken when needed, in the intensity of the sacred fire when you would awake a soul who will not be awakened. Blessed ones, speak as Christ would speak, and Christ will speak through you....

"Think as Christ would think, and Christ will think through you, and the mind of God will become congruent with the physical vessel. And there shall be no separation, as things equal to the same things are equal to each other—*one* Christ, *one* Lord, *one* manifestation within your temple!....

"When you have feelings that are not the feelings of the compassionate Christ, then you know Christ is not in you. Hasten, hasten to your altar! Call, then. Affirm. Replace. Practice sweet thoughts, sweet feelings, sweet words, and soon they will come naturally. Demonstrate them to your children, to one another, and others will speak as you speak; for all humans are imitators.... Finally, beloved, perform deeds that you know Christ would perform, and shun those that Christ would not engage in."[11]

Listening for the Inner Voice of God

Obedience to the inner voice of God is the first precept of the path of Christhood. It is a skill we have to develop as we pursue this path. The messenger explains: "If you are going to obey the inner voice of God, what do you have to do? Listen. Some people don't listen because they don't want to hear. Some people actually become physically deaf because lifetime after lifetime they have refused to listen to the voice of God, and so God has taken away their outer hearing as karma that they might learn to seek him and desire to have that hearing again.

"Jesus told the disciples, 'If ye love me, keep my commandments.'[12] The ascended master Jesus says, 'Listen to the inner voice that does guide thee.... Listen to the inner voice and obey, and all shall be well with thee.'[13]"[14]

How do we learn to discern the inner voice, the voice of our Holy Christ Self? There is all the din of the world, all the messages from the media, as well as the thoughts of other people and the mass consciousness that impinge on our own. There is also the chatter of the outer mind.

The messenger explains how we can learn to recognize the inner voice and how to avoid the mistake of not following when we do hear it: "You may have had the experience of hearing the inner voice but ignoring it.... I know that experience, and I know how it happens. It happens because the inner voice is subjective. It is quiet. It is subtle. It tells you to do something, and you think it's your own mind. You think that it's a decision to obey or not to obey, to do this thing or not to do this thing, because it is an idea that popped into your head that may or may not be right.

"Well, there are circumstances and ideas popping into your head, and you are expected to test them with all that you know about the Law. But when you really come to know the inner voice, the inner flame, it is unmistakable. You feel it in the seat-of-the-soul chakra. And when you try to go against it, you feel pain in your soul chakra.

"Now that is how sensitive you must become. And you measure the rightness or the wrongness of your action by whether or not your soul is actually experiencing pain because you are acting in conflict with the inner voice of the Christ Self. The soul hears this voice and wants to obey, but you sometimes allow your outer mind or your outer feelings to come into a period of rationalization…. The soul will give you an accurate reading of whether or not you are following the directive of your Christ Self."[15]

SPIRITUAL EXERCISES

Discerning the Inner Voice

Learning to discern the inner voice is a process. It takes practice and experience. We can accelerate our learning if we do it consciously and are aware of our successes and failures. Here are some steps that may help you in this:

1. At the end of your day, take out your journal and write down any occasions when you heard an inner voice speak to you. When did it happen? Where were you at the time? Where were your thoughts at the time? How did the voice come to you?

2. What was the direction you received? Was it consistent with the teachings of the masters? Was it practical? What was the vibration of the communication? How did you feel about it at the time?

3. Did you follow the direction? Why did you follow or decide not to?

4. What happened as a result?

5. What did you learn from this experience? Was this communication from the masters or your Higher Self, or was it from your human self or another source?

6. What would you do differently next time?

Here is another key from the messenger on listening to the inner voice: "Do you listen to the direction of your Christ Self? Are you obedient to the voice within, or are you always arguing back and saying, 'This is more logical,' and so are you in that little sense of a slight bit of friction with your inner being or your inner voice? When you have that, you see, you haven't passed your tests of attunement or obedience, so your light is correspondingly limited."[16]

Meditation to Draw Forth Your Own Christ-Radiance

There is a simple exercise given to us by the ascended master Kuthumi that may assist you in answering the Call to "Become that Christ!" Kuthumi says, "By meditating on the luminous aura of a saint, an ascended master or a cosmic being and visualizing that light around you with focused concentration, you may draw forth the intensity of your own Christ-radiance stored in your causal body."[17]

Take five minutes to give this meditation.

1. Sit in a meditative posture, with spine erect. This can be either in a chair, with feet flat on the floor, or seated in the lotus posture.
2. Close your eyes, and consciously center your attention in your heart.
3. Choose an ascended master or cosmic being with whom you have an affinity, and concentrate upon that one.
4. Visualize the master's aura around you, surrounding you and enveloping you in a radiance of light. (If you have trouble visualizing, just think about this master and hold the thought of white light.)

After completing your period of meditation, write about your experience in your journal.

FOR YOUR JOURNAL

How Will *You* Answer Jesus' Call?

*"Become that Christ!... It is time for you
to be true shepherds and ministers."*

What does this Call mean to me?
What will I do to answer this Call?

CHAPTER 6

*The Call to be true shepherds
of the children of God.*

The Call to the True Shepherds to Move among the People and to Shepherd Them
The Restoration of Your Divine Inheritance

Lo, I AM come into your midst, O people of great faith. O my sons and daughters of the living flame of cosmic Truth, I am in your midst in this hour out of the profound love of the Father and the Son for your devotion to the Blessed Mother, for your devotion to life and truth, upon whatever course it [your devotion] has taken you.

Know, then, that in the fullness of the joy of angels I come to gather my own unto the victory of life everlasting, to call you and to call you again to return to my heart and to see me as I truly AM in the victory of the ascension—one who walks midst those who are of the light and does not necessarily enter those paths of organized religion and orthodoxy [whose hierarchs] have closed out my heart and my teaching behind their garrisoned walls where they render themselves impervious to the cries of the people or to their proper role of challenging the evildoer.

What has happened to the "Church Militant"[1] on earth that does defend life when death and hell move against the souls of a people? Where, then, are today's saints? They are outside of its walls, I tell you, for the true saints have long ago recognized that these walls cannot contain nor house my great causal body.[2]

And therefore, I must in protest come again to overturn the money changers in the temple.[3] These are they who conspire with world movements of totalitarianism, who enter into compromise, and challenge and deny the true path of individual soul

freedom and the rightful inheritance of every son of God to walk
and talk with me and to commune with me as I walked and
talked with my disciples for many years, even many years after
my resurrection. For I did remain upon earth and the Gnostic
text *Pistis Sophia* does bear witness to this even as does the
Church Father Irenaeus, commenting that I was teaching well
into the [fiftieth year. And it was so.]⁴

Blessed ones, the mysteries I have taught have been banned
and denounced as heresy, and therefore you are as shorn lambs
today, having accepted the orthodox lie of sin and condemnation.

Therefore, upon the hour and the brink of an age of destiny
when the dark powers of this world are determined to make war
and to destroy and to take this entire continent, I say to you,
because they have not passed on to you the great teaching of my
heart, therefore the true shepherds are not raised up. Thus, the
wolves in sheep's clothing⁵ in Church and State have effectively
taken from my own the great Truth of the ages.

**But I AM your brother and I come to your side in this hour
of need and world crisis. I call you not only to be my disciples,
[but] I call you [also] to be shepherds and to feed my sheep, to
quickly devour by the Holy Spirit the teaching that is already set
forth and therefore to put on and receive the mantle of apostleship—that you might know yourselves as shepherds and feed the
children of God mouthful by mouthful that morsel of bread, that
cup of cold water in my name that does return to them the inner
resource of light, the fount of that holy Christhood and the Presence of the I AM THAT I AM.**

This must be done quickly, beloved, for the fallen angels
know that they have but a short time, but a narrow few years in
which to move against the world that is about to deliver* the
mandate of the Universal Christ nation by nation.

Blessed ones, it is an hour of great danger to the nations of
Europe, and you must understand that it is because of the
absence of the Christs. Each one who does follow me does
become that Christ and this is the message written down by my

---

*a world in which the lightbearers are about to deliver

apostles, such as Thomas and Philip and Mary Magdalene,[6] that has either been lost or suppressed. Know, then, beloved, that the need of the hour is for those anointed ones, anointed of the light, who are called *Christs,* to move among the people and to shepherd them.

Let it be said, therefore, that this nation that has received so great a gift as my Mother's Fátima visitations shall also receive me in this hour and know that my appearance to you is every whit as personal and as present and as seeable and knowable as was the visitation at Fátima.

Blessed ones, know this, therefore, that I come to this nation to minister to the poor in spirit that they might receive fully the fruits of my being, that they might truly know that the Spirit of God is upon them and therefore that they are equal to the task of challenging those false hierarchy impostors of my name both in Church and State.

The hour is late! And so many have become accustomed to the oppressions of these false hierarchies that they take for granted the controls that are leveled upon them.

Blessed hearts, when you expand the fire of God that is already within you, when you have the restoration of your divine inheritance, you will know that not the human but I with you and in you, God in you and with you is the deliverer of nations. Thus, it is to become a transparency for the One who sends you that is the goal of this path rather than to make the fatal error of believing that one's human self is the anointed one.

The soul is anointed and you therefore become instruments of God. Forever the instrument, you shall not fail. But should you consider yourself as the originator of the light, you will also go the way of pride, the spiritual pride of the fallen angels that has taken root on this continent from ancient times.

Blessed hearts, this my dictation, then, is spoken to the world. I am therefore calling shepherds to arise quickly and understand the great dearth of true teaching and true teachers, the dearth of leaders and leadership. Understand, beloved, that the people need in you an example, an example of one who is positive in the walk of the teaching and does serve the LORD at that altar and does go out, therefore, and challenge conditions in society.

Blessed ones, I am here to challenge also the false teaching out of the East that those who are spiritual do not soil their hands [or their garments] by entering into the arena of politics or government. I tell you, it is the withdrawal of the lightbearers from these areas that has given complete reign to the fallen angels to take over your nations, your destinies and your monetary systems.

Thus, it is certainly an area of a low vibration and power struggles. But it is entirely possible for those of the light to enter these fields and to make their statement once again as the great prophets of old, [just] as those who have sought to be statesmen in every nation have risen and therefore dedicated their empires and their nations and civilizations to a higher cause....

Know this, beloved, that the judgments are already descending upon the fallen ones, but it is the false leaders in Church and State who are preventing that judgment from descending, who take more light [as God's energy] and more money of the people to shore up their crumbling systems.

Know, then, beloved ones, that it is the true shepherds, yourselves, to whom I call this day to enter in and to establish yourselves where you ought to be, where fallen angels have stolen your seats of authority from you, and to stand for a people who need you in this hour. Thus, let this dictation go down as the call to the true shepherds of the children of God.

I am calling you as these true shepherds out of every nation throughout the world and I say, it is high time that you recognize that you may no longer allow the fallen ones to encroach upon and to abuse and oppress the children of God! Hear me, beloved! Those who have been these shepherds in the past, many of them have ascended and some are yet with you.

Understand that there is such corruption across the governments of the nations that where to begin becomes the challenge of the hour, but I will tell you where to begin. That beginning is in the raising up of the true light [as the threefold flame] in your heart. That beginning is to know me, to know my Word and to become it—and to fear not to assimilate my Body and my Blood, the fullness of the Omega-Alpha consciousness of the Father-Mother God. Fear not, therefore, to set aside the former things and to enter into the newness of the Spirit.

The second thing, therefore, is to stand before the altar of God that you erect in your own home and to daily, hourly invoke the power and intercession of God and to ask to be his instrument and to call upon those seven archangels and lords of the seven rays. Call upon all of us in heaven and we will come to your side and we will open the way for you to serve your nations and your communities. The hour is late, yet everyone must give his all to this calling....

Therefore understand, beloved, that upon the decision of the true lightbearers of Aquarius, those who understand my true coming, and upon your becoming a Christ and not merely a Christian, as Philip wrote down, upon this, beloved, does the thread of the future hang. Therefore, I say: May you be the LORD's compensation for those who have neglected so great a salvation, [for] those who do have a divine spark and do not act and do not serve and do not see and would rather follow the fallen ones than finally make an about-face and turn to the light and walk toward the Sun.

I give you now my Body and my Blood. I give you the wine and the bread of my being. I bless the Communion offering, beloved, and therefore know that I, Jesus, have come to you, as in the ritual of the sacrament of the Last Supper I did take the loaf of bread and I did break it, teaching all, "This is my body of universal Light-substance,* which is broken for you."

Therefore, that portion of my universal Christhood I give again this day, not alone to twelve but to twelve million and more. For I call my souls of light out of every nation and the call is strong, it is persistent and it is day by day; and as long as the Father does give me leave, I, the Son, shall pursue my own.

Therefore, feel the intensity of the love of my Sacred Heart that I give you in this hour and drink the wine of my Blood, the

*Christ-essence

essential light of my Being, which is surely shed for you in this hour as it was shed two thousand years ago.

My beloved, I can come to you and I can speak to you and no orthodoxy shall prevent me from communing with my own, for this is the communion of the saints. And I AM at the center of the true Church Universal and Triumphant in heaven and I AM in the center of your heart, and I will not be denied the oneness with my little ones. And therefore, no amount of doctrines and dogma will ever change the immortal Truth that thou art a son of God: this day has the LORD begotten thee, and this day shalt thou make thy decision to fulfill thy true reason for being.

Come unto me, all ye who labor, then, with the burden of orthodoxy and the laws of mortality, for in the light of my Presence I will give you life. Remember, I AM your brother always. Call to me and I will answer. Knock upon the door of my heart and I shall open. And promise me this, beloved, that when I knock upon the door of your heart you will also open and allow me to enter in and to use you in a moment of personal or national crisis in your nation, in your planet, for I need your hands and heart. I need your temples for the deliverance of souls and I need your voice to speak to them the word of comfort.

Receive me now, beloved, even as I receive you. Therefore, we are one and we are one in the beautiful prayer that has descended through the Messenger Mark, "Drink me while I am drinking thee"; and this is the divine interchange taught to me by Maitreya. Therefore, as Above, so below, as the disciple self-empties, the master enters in and the master and the disciple are one and the disciple does declare, "I and my Father are one." And therefore, there is the divine interchange, and as in heaven, so on earth we experience God through one another's vehicles.

I seal you and bless you for the victory of your whole life day by day, and the recording angels have outlined for you what is that just and perfect and holy calling for thy life in this hour. Day by day to the finish, to the end of mortality, to the soul's immortality! Day by day, thus the LORD calls you! Answer, answer and be free!

O shepherd of souls, thou Universal Christ, descend now and be unto them their divine Reality. 🍇

February 28, 1988
Cine Alvalade
Lisbon, Portugal

*Call to me and I will answer. Knock upon the door of my
heart and I shall open.*

JESUS

Jesus delivers a strong message to rise and claim our rightful
places as true shepherds of the people. He calls us to challenge those in Church and State who have denied the true path
of individual soul freedom and "enslaved and imprisoned the
children of the light in their institutions and organizations." He
speaks to us with a great sense of urgency in this call: "I Call you
not only to be my disciples, but I Call you also to be true shepherds and to feed my sheep."

Who are Jesus' sheep? They are the children of God who
have accepted the limitations of orthodoxy because they have not
had shepherds to give them the true teachings. They have not had
true leaders to tell them it is their rightful inheritance to walk and
talk with Jesus and commune with him.

We who have received these true teachings of the Master are
called to take up our role as shepherds and move among the people. Our mission: to find our brothers and sisters and remind
them of the divine spark in their hearts—that Christ flame that
connects them to the heart of Jesus.

Who are those who have denied the people the true teachings? Jesus spoke of them as wolves in sheep's clothing. The
ascended masters have exposed them as the fallen angels and
those who have followed them.

The fallen angels' strategy has been to lead the children of
God into paths of sinfulness in order to convince them that they
are "sinners" and hence unworthy to follow in the footsteps of
Jesus Christ. They have kept from the children of God the true
understanding that God has made each of them in the Divine
Image. Instead, they have taught them that they are forever
stained by "original sin" and can never become Christlike or realize their own Christ potential.

The fallen angels have thus promulgated the false doctrine that because the children of God are sinners, they can only be saved by grace, thereby denying the necessity for each one to "work the works of him that sent me," as Jesus declared of his own mission.[7]

Jesus calls us to quickly put on the mantle of apostleship and take up the calling to be shepherds of the people. The role of the shepherd is to feed the sheep, to "feed the children of God mouthful by mouthful the morsel of bread, that cup of cold water in my name." If we are to give these teachings to others, we must first learn them ourselves, and our learning has to be more than an intellectual study of the teachings. Jesus tells us we must "devour" them by the Holy Spirit.

The Master's call to us to be shepherds is urgent, because he sees the agenda of the fallen angels and their plots and plans to destroy the earth as a platform for the lightbearers to balance their karma, fulfill their dharma and ascend back to God. They know there is only a short time before the lightbearers rise up and "deliver the mandate of the Universal Christ." When this occurs, the fallen ones will no longer be able to control and manipulate the people, and their judgment will be upon them.

What Prevents Us from Becoming Shepherds?

Why is there a dearth of true shepherds in the earth? Many who have previously been called have not answered that call. Why is this so?

One reason may be fear. Fear of the unknown, fear of death, fear of persecution, fear of change, fear of loss of a way of life to which we have become accustomed—all these fears can prevent us from taking the next step and answering the call of Christ.

We have to overcome our fear, and there is an ascended master who can help us to embody the flame of fearlessness. His name is Ray-O-Light, and he gives us a key to deal with fear that might overcome us or prevent us from answering the call of the Master.

"Here is the key, then, to overcoming that fear that stiffens the corpse itself, that fear that stiffens the flow of life—the fear that ultimately is the death of self-awareness. The key is to *keep on moving!*

"When you find yourself in a snowstorm or a blizzard, you will not curl up on the side of the road, for you know instinctively you will freeze to death. You *keep moving.* This is the key to the conquering of all fear. *Keep moving!* Keep active! Move through the elements, move through the mirage of fear! *Pierce!* it with your sword and discover the island in the sun, the place of light, the Garden of Eden."[8]

If we simply keep moving forward, a step at a time, a step each day, we can overcome our own fear and the projections of fear that might come upon us. At the same time, we can do the spiritual work on our own momentums of fear, including the giving of the decree "Strip Us of All Doubt and Fear." (See Spiritual Exercises.)

Healing the Soul

Some of those who should be shepherds have resisted their calling through limitations in their psychology. Some feel unworthy. Some lack faith in God and in the power of the Holy Spirit to speak through them.

If we find that there is a missing element of self, some unresolved issue from the past or in our psychology that hinders us from fully answering our calling, healing is needed. The masters can help us. It is important for the soul to be healed at every stage of development, from conception to the present, and Jesus has offered to help us in this delicate process:

"You may call to me in the steps and stages of the unfoldment of my God-free being, from the Manchild in the womb unto the Son of God, from the infant Christ newborn to the child of seven and twelve. In all of these steps you may call to me, for each step of my initiation corresponds to a step of your own.... Some of the steps have been skipped as a result of karma wherein, because of your own actions or inactions, you have not been allowed to receive those initiations. Others have been skipped because of the ignorance or the malice of dark souls, individuals in your life who denied you the bread of life, the water and the wine. As you transmute karma, each of these steps is made possible to you."⁹

Jesus is asking us to call for his Presence with us at whatever age in our soul development needs healing. The messenger explains how we can answer this Call. "What is he saying? Did you have a traumatic experience at age four-and-a-half? 'Call for the Presence of myself when I was age four-and-a-half over your soul, your inner child. And my Presence, as I AM the image and likeness of God, will be transformed, and you will heal the inner pattern and restore the inner pattern of the age of innocence and the innocence of your own inner child.' If you don't know what age you were exactly, say to Jesus, 'Go to my inner child when I experienced thus and such.' Jesus knows when it was."¹⁰

Jesus continues: "As you attain to each level of your development, call to me at that level. Call for my correspondence! Call for my Alpha unto your Omega!... I will take you at inner levels through the steps of development from your physical body's conception in the womb. I will take you through those skipped steps until your soul is satisfied that you have fulfilled each step that God has ordained for you as your inalienable right. Know that my love is sufficient unto you to resolve every unresolved problem."¹¹

The ascended master Krishna has also offered to help us in this process of healing our soul. The messenger explains: "Krishna also promises that wherever the development of your inner child was arrested by some problem or trauma, he will heal you of that wound. He says that you should try to remember the approximate age you were when the problem occurred. Then, call for the Electronic Presence of Krishna as a little boy of that same age to be placed over your inner child.

"You can do this systematically. You can ask for the Electronic Presence of Krishna as an embryo, as a baby forming in the womb through each trimester, to be placed over you. Step-by-step, day by day, from your conception to your present age, Lord Krishna will enter your temple at every stage of your development to heal you.

"Our souls have not reflected the true image of God but the

;e of imperfect parents or the image of our karma or the image of our tyrant ego dweller-on-the-threshold from many past embodiments. As you work to resolve psychological problems, you are actually performing surgery on yourself. And until you come to resolution, you can go through a lot of pain. While you are going through this process, Krishna can enter your temple to heal you. The strength and love of Lord Krishna are bigger than the dweller-on-the-threshold, the conglomerate of the not-self of all past lives. God is greater than all of the burdens of your soul. God is still greater than these."[12]

Jesus has also likened the process of healing the soul to repairing a damaged fabric: "That which is lost and incomplete and fragmented, as ye are, must understand that life is the process of the cosmic weaver weaving day by day, repairing, weaving, pulling out the wrong threads, inserting new threads until the garment is perfected once again and the mending is without flaw. And the garment, good as new, sewn by angels using threads of your own Kundalini fire, does appear again as a seamless garment."[13]

Life is a process of removing the old and replacing it with the new. As we work on our psychology, we can use this spiritual exercise to bring healing to the soul and a new wholeness to life, and as we resolve our psychology and identify more each day with the Christ flame, we are able to feel confident about stepping into the role of shepherd.

Jesus says that there is such corruption in the governments of the nations that it is difficult even to see where to begin this assignment. But he does give two keys. The first is to know him and to become his Word, to assimilate his Body and Blood. The second is the work at the altar of prayer and invocation. We can study and learn and develop a strategy of how we will bring about change in the nations, and especially how we will bring the knowledge of the teachings to those who are waiting for them.

Jesus tells us that the thread of the future hangs on our decision.

SPIRITUAL EXERCISES

Give the Decree to Consume Fear

Call to Jesus each day and ask him to help gain your mastery over the negative momentums of fear, doubt, death and anxiety that would prevent you from answering the call to be a shepherd. The decree "Strip Us of All Doubt and Fear" is specifically to help free us from these negative energies:

STRIP US OF ALL DOUBT AND FEAR

Beloved mighty victorious Presence of God, I AM in me, O thou beloved immortal victorious threefold flame of eternal truth within my heart, Holy Christ Selves of all mankind, beloved Saint German, beloved El Morya, beloved Jesus the Christ, beloved Mother Mary, beloved great God Obedience, beloved Archangel Michael, beloved Cyclopea, Great Silent Watcher, beloved Amerissis, Goddess of Light, beloved Great Divine Director, mighty Hercules and Arcturus, Ascended Master Cuzco, beloved Ray-O-Light, beloved mighty Astrea, the cosmic being Victory, beloved Lanello, the entire Spirit of the Great White Brotherhood and the World Mother, elemental life—fire, air, water, and earth!

In the name of the Presence of God which I AM and through the magnetic power of the sacred fire vested in me, which I am consciously qualifying with the fearlessness flame, I decree:

Strip us of all doubt and fear, (3x)
Beloved great I AM.
Strip us of all doubt and fear, (3x)
Flood us with oceans of fearlessness flame.
Strip us of all doubt and fear, (3x)
Remove each human cause and core.
Strip us of all doubt and fear, (3x)
Give us faith never known before.
Strip us of all doubt and fear, (3x)
Give violet-ray freedom to all today.
Strip us of all doubt and fear, (3x)
In Victory's light sustain our might.
Strip us of all doubt and fear, (3x)
By cosmic I AM fire, manifest thy desire.

> Strip us of all doubt and fear, (3x)
> Command the earth now free.
> Strip us of all doubt and fear, (3x)
> Ascend us all to thee.

And in full faith...

Note: Whenever appropriate, you may replace the word "doubt" in this decree with "death."

An Exercise for Healing the Inner Child

Jesus and Krishna have offered to help heal our inner child and fill in the gaps in our soul development in this lifetime, from birth to the present. Take some clean sheets of paper, and on them write down significant events in your life, starting from birth. In particular, write down painful or difficult events or circumstances, anything that you feel may have left a scar or a sense of incompleteness.

Have this list in front of you as you play the tape of Krishna bhajans.[14] The bhajans are recorded in order on the tape from Krishna's birth onward, each bhajan celebrating a different attribute or element of his being and a different stage of his life. As you give the bhajans with the tape, ask Krishna and Jesus to place their Electronic Presence over you, particularly at those ages where there are elements in your being that need healing.

"Drink Me While I AM Drinking Thee"

Jesus tells us that we are one with him in the beautiful prayer "Beams of Essential Light." As we give it, we experience the divine interchange between the master and the disciple. As the disciple self-empties, the master enters in, and the master and the disciple are one.

The messenger has given a meditation and visualization we can use in conjunction with this decree. "When we give this mantra, it is a call to the Cosmic Christ and to the indwelling Christ to rise in intensity, to come into physical awareness. The absorption of Christ physically is not only possible, but it is a part of the ascension process—the absorption of light within the cells because the cells are a perfect mirror of the Person of Christ and of the causal body. This comes through harmony. And the flame of resurrection restores God-harmony. We see the opalescent mother-of-pearl light that we invoke filling millions of cells within the physical body."[15]

Visualize this light filling your body as you give this decree:

BEAMS OF ESSENTIAL LIGHT

Beloved mighty victorious Presence of God, I AM in me, my very own beloved Holy Christ Self and Holy Christ Selves of all mankind: By and through the magnetic power of the immortal, victorious three-fold flame of love, wisdom and power anchored within my heart, I AM invoking the flame of resurrection from the heart of God in the Great Central Sun, from beloved Helios and Vesta, beloved Ascended Lady Master Nada, beloved Kuan Yin, beloved Lord the Maha Chohan, beloved Jesus the Christ, beloved Mother Mary, Archangel Uriel, Archangel Gabriel and all who serve resurrection's flame, beloved Lanello, the entire Spirit of the Great White Brotherhood and the World Mother, elemental life—fire, air, water, and earth! I lovingly accept your full-gathered momentum of the resurrection flame consciously expanded without limit throughout the earth, infinitely, presently, and forever:

1. Blessed flame of resurrection,
   Flame of white and rainbow substance,
   Restore in me the fullness of my heavenly portion.

Refrain: O Unifying Spirit of the Great White Brotherhood,
   Opalescent mother-of-pearl,
   Milk and honey of resurrection's happiness,
   Drink me while I AM drinking thee.

2. Blessed flame of resurrection,
   Splendor shining through me like a mist solidified,
   Comfort me with the Christ-reality of thy blazing.

3. Blessed flame of resurrection's glory,
   Beaming hope and splendid future joys appearing bright,
   I AM filled with thy beams of essential light.

4. Mother Mary, blessed Jesus dear,
   Hold me in the whiteness of thy heavenly glory.
   Let earth's shadows fade: O living light of God appear!

And in full faith...

FOR YOUR JOURNAL

How Will *You* Answer Jesus' Call?

The Call to be true shepherds of the children of God.

What does this Call mean to me?
What will I do to answer this Call?

CHAPTER 7

*"I Call you to the House of the LORD,
your mighty I AM Presence."*

The Zeal of My House
Keep the Flame of the Ark of the Covenant Blazing upon This Altar

Hail to the light of the holy ones of God here below who do reflect the Holy One of God above! O Thou I AM THAT I AM, reveal thyself now in this form. Reveal thyself that all might know that the LORD God [the mighty I AM Presence] has shone upon his own in this hour and he will not leave his people comfortless. For I send my messenger before my face, saith the LORD.[1] And therefore, behold the messenger of God and know that even as the Holy One of God above is of too pure eyes to behold iniquity,[2] so, beloved, your eyes cannot yet look, as they are of the flesh, upon the pure image of sacred fire of the I AM THAT I AM in this octave.[3]

Therefore, we send a messenger of God to earth to proclaim the coming of that Presence in ye all. Therefore, while ye have that one with you, may you know the inner accord of the harmony of that divinity that is the Real Self above and recognize that it is a sign, even a signet unto the people of God that God does also dwell in your midst in this hour when, beloved, you must fulfill all things, all things of the Great Law, all things of the karmic condition and [when] all does come to bear upon the center of self as the coils of cause and effect infold, recoil and bring back to every point upon the aura, the electromagnetic field, [and] the four lower bodies that which has been sent forth.

Thus, people speak of pressure and they speak of stress. Let it be known, beloved, that this is returning personal karma though you may identify it as condition and circumstance or the result of another's hand.

Let it be known this day, beloved, that the violet flame raised up within you by love and by adoration is able to give you that sheath and armour, purple vein wherewith to consume that which comes from without and that which would erupt from within. Thus, the insulation of the violet flame as the additional skin of self, as an armour of substance as though metallic, impervious, out of the heaven-world, does give to you the soothing comfort of perpetual transmutation.

But, beloved, only that violet flame that is called forth in utter adoration and obedience to the inner Christ, to the Universal One, to the Holy One of God, the I AM THAT I AM, can afford you the living presence of the swaddling garment, as it were, of the God of the seventh ray.

Blessed ones, let love endow every word and syllable. Let the attention flow to the heart of your I AM Presence and to my beloved Saint Germain, to Portia, to the entire Spirit of the Great White Brotherhood....

So Maitreya does live and so he does walk in your midst. Fear not, grumble not, worry not. Do not enter into a doomsday consciousness but recognize there has never been a moment in your personal history, and I speak to everyone here, to all light-bearers of the world, to all Keepers of the Flame, when *you* could so intensify the inner coil of being!

I cry to you, beloved, that you do not perceive [the jeopardy] in the hour of the descent of your karma and the dark night of the soul! And therefore I come with a light to lighten the very cave of your world that you might see and know that that karma shall pass but not without heroic effort and heroic measures.

Blessed ones, the door is cracked. I, Jesus, may open it to you. Therefore, be long-suffering with your own soul, but do not allow your soul to suffer or to be surfeited whether in pleasure or pain. Mount up as with eagle wings.[4] Mount the fiery coil of being and desire more light than you have and know that it is that light that will quench the darkness.

Let the zeal of my house, then, come upon you in this hour! Let the zeal of the Holy Spirit come upon you![5]

I, Jesus, tell you that that zeal which I give to you is of the fire of the Sun. And though you may not have noticed, beloved, I have journeyed to the very Central Sun this week, there to fetch that fire of the LORD God that my own in the earth might have from me and from my own heart even a quickening, even a fervor—even seeing in my Presence and aura this day something you have never seen before, even the fires dripping from the altars of that very center of a spiritual cosmos.

I, therefore, bring you tidings of Alpha and Omega. I bring you the presence of ring upon ring of seraphim of God to *shake you awake!* O I would to God you would understand how so great a salvation is at hand, how it is offered to you and how the darkness that does descend does allow you to again and again and again so indulge these worn-out grooves of karmic consciousness!

Therefore, I say again of you, beloved: "Father, Mother, forgive them, for they know not what they do."⁶ Yet, beloved, how long may I say this prayer of the enlightened ones who have been told and told again and yet in the hour of the descent of the very density of karma are enveloped by it and do enter even its degradation and, beloved, [this] after so long, so long being a part of this holy communion [the dictations of the ascended masters by the Holy Spirit] that we share.

Thus, my beloved, let it be known unto you this day that I, Jesus, have implored before Alpha and Omega [that they might] give me that fire whereby in the zeal of the LORD [the mighty I AM Presence] and by the fire of that Presence with you, you should come to know the means and the wherewithal to endure spiritually and to be endued and empowered from on high⁷ as our messenger has been by my hand in this very week.

Blessed ones, so know the LORD. So know that some must qualify. And, beloved, thank God—thank God that one called is yet here; for I tell you, the hour of the dark night of the soul for you, each one, must be met: and that hour is now! And you may either weep and wail and depart and be divided and allow all of the venting of the anger in the subconscious or you may come and bend the knee and kneel before the altar and fasten yourself to the flame of sacred fire burning thereon.

Blessed ones, that dark night of the descent of karma must come, for if it come not you cannot endure nor the light [of the Universal Christ consciousness] nor the dark night of the Spirit, [i.e., the absence of the light], that shall come upon this planet ere the new day shall appear.

And for the record, may you understand that the dark night of the soul is the period when the soul does groan in travail with her own karma, and it is meet. And in that hour you have reinforcement of angels and saints, myself and ascended masters and cosmic beings. It is an hour when you keep tethered to the Law; and if you do, beloved, you may be saved by the very Law that does demand [that] you right all wrong against that Law.

Thus, beloved, this path is known, the path of karma balanced by fervent hearts who have willed, *who have determined* to slay inordinate desire. For by this and this alone shall you suffer calamity.

Thus, beloved, take to heart the teachings of the Buddha, of Maitreya. And let all of thy desiring be this: to pass beyond those karmic conditions that at any moment by the condition of planetary, solar and galactic karma could sweep you from the very center of your first and best love.

So having passed this dark night of the soul, as ye all have observed the messenger pass through in the long years of this service, so you come to the hour when you must have internalized that Christ and you must be able to sustain that momentum of Christhood. [This initiation of the Cosmic Christ is called the dark night of the Spirit.] And this is the eclipse of the Sun of the I AM Presence. And it does come about, beloved, precisely under the conditions in which you find yourselves upon this planet: the astral sea rising, the outpouring [from the pit that is opened[8]] and the spewing of the astral consciousness, and you here below in physical embodiment.

And therefore, the astral plane does present that separation between the externalized self-mastery and the I AM Presence. And if there be no self-mastery for want of love of Christ and of me, your own Beloved, then in the dark night of the Spirit, beloved, you are cut off and it is the dark night when none may extend that hand, for your opportunity has been given to manifest a light that never shone on land or sea.[9]

Thus understand, beloved, work while ye have the light.[10] Work on your karma! Work on your zeal! Be not satisfied with your mediocrity! Work while you have a physical hand extended to you and know that that hand is the best hand we can offer you. And therefore, by that sustaining love you may receive that imparting and that reigniting of the Word....

There be some among you who since your entering this path have indeed kindled a divine spark when you had it not. All things are possible. But when you hear of the possibility of failure, you sink back into that sense of failure instead of realizing that the possibility of victory is present whenever it is possible to fail.

Why, then, enter the negative assessment of oneself? Why not perceive with the inner sight? Why do you see with a flesh-and-blood consciousness and therefore curse yourself to that consciousness ad infinitum?

Let the holy ones of God truly be more holy. For those who do have that flame must make more rather than less effort until the light so shine in you that your eyes are as stars and your aura so powerful that none can deny that truly a path of Christhood is won; and therefore the lesser endowed take hope to follow in your footsteps.

Cast down the idols of your flesh-and-blood consciousness, for those whom you worship are not the living Christ. Blessed ones, worship not but adore the light. Adore the light and do not set on a pedestal any human being. Ye do err, not knowing the scriptures.[11] Ye do err, sustaining the idolatry of self.

I come for the breaking of the pitchers.[12] I come for the breaking of the vessels that no longer serve you. I raise my staff and I say, let them be broken by the rod of fire! I, Jesus, decree it that you might come forth and stand God-free sons and daughters.

Blessed ones, *be pillars of fire in the earth!* Be pillars of fire in the earth, beloved, and *heed* the Call! Heed the Call of light....

I, Jesus, speak to you and you know of whom and whereof I speak. And therefore, there are some who should be ashamed to stand in my Presence and there are others who have kept the flame as saints of God.

Thus, I call you to the House of the LORD [your mighty I AM Presence]. May you know now that Communion of my heart. May you know it, beloved....

Keep my flame in this community, beloved, for I have given more of myself than you will ever know to the very presence of my Church in this place. And it shall not be bestowed upon me that I may start anew or begin again. With Almighty God [and] all saints of heaven who have gone before you, I say: *in this community we must not fail.*

Let there be not fragmentation or division, but know that your loyalty is to the flame that burns upon the altar because the LORD God has sent to you a messenger who is able, by his grace, to keep that flame. And as you sustain your devotions the flame is kept in this octave. It is a light unto the world, beloved, and that sacred fire is your salvation in this octave....

Beloved, when the Law does require that I should withdraw from you for a little while that you in your aloneness might choose to be all that I AM, then remember, *O remember*, that my fervor and my love is waiting, waiting for your decision, that I might come close again.

For you see, beloved, there are some tests that you must pass in the aloneness of the aura and the electromagnetic field that you yourself have created. In that hour, then, I say, trust. Trust and do not forsake. Trust and remember, I AM thy brother.

I AM Jesus, thy love, thy perfect love. And I AM watching from afar your victory. O snatch it from the very teeth of the defeat of death and hell. Snatch your victory, beloved! *Tear it!* from these fallen ones who would steal [in] in the night and steal it from you.

Blessed, all is in divine order for you to fulfill all things.

Do it, I say. Do it for the sake of our love.

November 24, 1988
Thanksgiving Day
Royal Teton Ranch
Park County, Montana

*In my Father's house there are many mansions: if it were
not so, I would have told you. I go to prepare a place for you.*

JESUS[13]

In this dictation Jesus Calls us "to the House of the LORD,
your mighty I AM Presence." He also calls us to "know
that communion of my heart."

Jesus says that he is speaking to all lightbearers of the world.
His Call is not just to Christians, but to all who would become
the Christ. That Christ existed long before Christianity, as Jesus
affirms: "Before Abraham was, I AM."[14] And the mission of
Jesus is a universal one, as he opens the door for all who would
find that Christ in themselves.

The ascended master El Morya gives us an insight into this
mission: "Some still think they can skip making their peace with
Jesus. I tell you it is not so. He is the Son of God whom God has
sent. God has sent him for the resolution of all souls on earth
with God the Father and God the Mother. It is through his heart,
the heart of this Son of God, that you find that resolution. This
does not mean that you must worship Jesus exclusively, but it
does mean that you must recognize his office whereby he restores
to you the bonding of your soul to the heart of your Holy Christ
Self and thence to his own heart.

"Some of you have so much karma between the seat-of-the-
soul chakra and the heart chakra that without the intercession of
Jesus, you could not be bonded to the heart of your own Holy
Christ Self, though you may think you have so bonded to that
heart. Please know, beloved, that it is unrealistic to think so
while you yet have anger in your heart and while you have non-
resolution in your being and in your heart vis-à-vis your Creator
and his creation.

"Thus, Jesus holds the office of the one who restores the soul
to the level where marriage to the Bridegroom is an option. Let

none take for granted that this bonding has already taken place, for, beloved, when it does take place, it can never be undone. It is the first step of the ascension. It signifies that the one so blessed now walks the earth as a Christed one. Therefore, you will not receive this bonding until you attain resolution of the heart with the Sacred Heart of Jesus. And because many of you have not done so, many areas of your inner life still need tending.

"Therefore, have remorse this day. Have humility. Enter in and know that those who have not secured that oneness with Jesus may pursue it through Padma Sambhava, the great devotee of Jesus Christ and of Gautama Buddha. And they may begin by letting their hearts sing the Golden Mantra as they go about their tasks—taking care to listen as the mantra echoes back to them from the secret chamber of the heart."[15] (See Spiritual Exercises.)

The Most Important Assignment of Our Lifetime

The masters have told us that the most important assignment of our lifetime is bonding with the heart of Jesus Christ and our own Holy Christ Self.

The messenger has told us that all of us are at various levels of achieving that goal. She said, "It is more than having a three-fold flame. It is the establishment of trust—trust between you and El Morya, the guru who has sponsored you. El Morya leads you to the feet of Jesus Christ. He is your tutor, your confessor. He brings you to that place where you may be acceptable to enter into that bonding....

"We find this concept of bonding in the decree, 'Drink Me while I AM Drinking Thee.' It is the divine interchange of the Alpha/Omega. This is the same teaching that Jesus gives, 'Except ye eat the flesh of the Son of man, and drink his blood, ye have no life in you.'[16]

"God sent the Christ, the only begotten Son, in the person of his Son Jesus Christ into the world to give us the life everlasting, the ultimate life of the I AM THAT I AM, because we are not at this moment carrying a sufficiency of that life on our own. We cannot yet solo. We are not yet independent. We are dependent on that Lord and Saviour, on our gurus, on the ascended masters, on our mighty I AM Presence.... Because we understand this, we have to understand that we are not entirely in a zone of safety. Not until we receive that bonding are we safe."[17]

To answer this Call to come to the House of the LORD, your mighty I AM Presence, you must pursue this bonding to your Holy Christ Self and your mighty I AM Presence, and recognize the need to come to terms with all that separates you from the heart of God—all nonresolution. If you have an anger problem, are prideful, become irritated with others or allow darkness to come through you, you can break the delicate thread of contact and the delicate presence of the threefold flame.

The Dark Night of the Soul
and the Dark Night of the Spirit

Jesus speaks in this dictation of two initiations on the path of Christhood: the dark night of the soul and the dark night of the Spirit. Our understanding of these and our preparation for them can make the difference in our victory. The messenger explains the dynamics of these two initiations:

"The dark night of the soul is the test of the soul's encounter with the return of personal karma, which, if she has not kept her lamps (chakras) trimmed with light,[18] may eclipse the Light (Christ consciousness) of the soul and, therefore, its discipleship under the Son of God. It precedes the dark night of the Spirit, the supreme test of Christhood, when the soul is, as it were, cut off from the I AM Presence and must survive solely on the Light (Christ consciousness) garnered in the heart, while holding the balance for planetary karma."[19]

"Jesus had already passed through the dark night of the soul when he came to the cross. And the dark night of the Spirit was that experience when all of God was removed from him except that portion of God that he had realized as the flame within his heart. But the contact with Father, the contact with hierarchy, for a brief moment was cut off as part of the plan, part of the initiation. Because the culmination of all of your testing is so that, for a brief moment, without any support, you can stand alone and still choose light and still choose God."[20]

We see Jesus' experience of passing through this initiation recorded in scripture: "And at the ninth hour Jesus cried with a loud voice, saying, Eloi, Eloi, lama sabachthani? which is, being interpreted, My God, my God, why hast thou forsaken me?"[21]

"Through the purging that comes with the dark night of the Spirit the soul is at last ready to enter into the bridal chamber. The mystics' description of their love pact with the Beloved has produced some of the most exalted expressions of love ever written."[22]

Jesus gives us keys for passing through the first dark night: the fervor of the heart, the slaying of inordinate desire, remaining tethered to the Law. The internalization of the Christ is the requirement for passing through the dark night of the Spirit.

SPIRITUAL EXERCISES

Give the Golden Mantra and Pursue Oneness with the Heart of Jesus

According to tradition, Padma Sambhava taught that his Golden Mantra should be used in a coming time of troubles, during which warfare, disease and poverty would increase. He said the mantra would be an antidote to the confusion and frustration of that dark age. Beloved Durga has told us: "How very close to you and this messenger is Padma Sambhava. Therefore, do not neglect his mantra....

Om Ah Hum Vajra Guru Padma Siddhi Hum.

"It is your key at this level of service for the entering in to the hearts of all those Buddhas and Bodhisattvas whose lineage goes back to the Great Central Sun, back to the heart of the Godhead."[23]

Listen to *The Living Flame of Love* Album

Saint John of the Cross gave profound teachings on the dark night of the soul, the dark night of the Spirit and the ultimate fulfillment of the alchemical marriage with the Lord. To learn about this path and understand the process of bonding to the heart of Jesus, listen to the teachings by Elizabeth Clare Prophet on the masterpiece of the mystic Saint John of the Cross, *The Living Flame of Love.*[24]

FOR YOUR JOURNAL

How Will *You* Answer Jesus' Call?

"I Call you to the House of the LORD, your mighty I AM Presence."

What does this Call mean to me?
What will I do to answer this Call?

CHAPTER 8

"I command you to allow that Christ to descend into your temple."

The Second Coming of Christ
"Receive Me and Become Who You Are"

I AM Christ, thy Lord. I come to receive my brides.

O my souls, thou who art the mirror of the Divine Image of my Self and thy Christ Self to all the world, know, then, that all the world does see that Christ Image as at inner levels I touch everyone.

And every eye does see me face to face and in the mirror of thy souls—thou who hast prepared and truly polished the mirror of self [so] that the weary traveler or the doubter or the one gone astray or even those who champion the cause of evil might look into your soul, beloved, and see the true image, the Divine Image out of which all sons and daughters of light were made. Take thee to thy self this solar image. Take to thy self my Self.

I come, then, in the appearance prophesied[1] and I come again and again and again, my beloved, for the so-called Second Coming has occurred and recurred. So understand, beloved, that I am in the earth as foretold and I am here to fulfill the prophecy that every eye shall see me.

Blessed hearts, I have called you to be my own, my disciples, my apostles. I have called you to be the Christ. I have called, beloved, that the multiplication of my Body, which is broken for you,[2] might be that my Electronic Presence should move in the earth through you and that my Sacred Heart upon your sacred heart might amplify that threefold flame and that open door of the heart whereby through us, one upon one, my Self superimposed upon [your self], the souls of earth might enter into the path of discipleship unto the same fulfillment of the Law that you yourselves are realizing and have realized in some measure.

The hour is come, beloved, when the dead shall hear the voice of the Son of God, and they that hear my voice and they that see me shall live.³ For to see the true image of Christ, even with the inner eye, is truly the quickening, the resurrection. It is to take unto oneself that image; for what the eye beholds of me, beloved, is instantaneously stamped upon every cell and atom of being.

Let it be so, beloved, for all must choose to receive the Christ of the heart—Jesus of the Sacred Heart—and to live, else in seeing [him] they may choose to deny that Christ and [thereby] instantaneously commit their souls to outer darkness.⁴

Beloved, the denial of the Christ in oneself, when that Christ does come as I AM come to enter the temple, is sudden death to that soul.⁵ [For] though the body may continue to [have life and to] move about [until the life force is spent and death does overtake it], the soul that has [with finality] denied Christ has denied its own immortality, its everlasting life and, alas, its reason for being, [hence any possibility for continued existence].

This is why the Second Coming of Christ is an apocalyptic event, beloved. For in the first coming [of the avatar of the age] the opportunity to choose to be or not to be is given: to embrace the light or not to embrace it. And two thousand years, beloved, [and, in truth, many aeons prior to my advent] were given to all inhabitants of these several worlds to choose to be in Christ the fullness of everlasting life and the fountain of youth and of resurrection's flame to all. Therefore in the end [of the age of Pisces] that Second Coming does denote for many final choices, [even for the fallen angels whose time is up].⁶

Blessed ones, they pay me lip service. They pretend to look to the coming kingdom and [to] their entering in as the goal of life, but inwardly they are ravening wolves.⁷ They are the seed of Satan sown⁸ in the body of Christ and in the churches of the world. When they see me, beloved, face to face, they reject that Christ and that light. They deny [my Second] Coming [though they have trumpeted it loud and long; they deny my] Person and, above all, [they deny] the Divine Image that our Father-Mother God has placed in you all.

[It is because the Second Coming is also for the judgment of the seed of the Wicked One that it is written: "Behold, he cometh with clouds; and every eye shall see him, and they also which pierced him: *and all kindreds of the earth shall wail because of him. Even so, Amen.*"⁹]

Now, therefore, as the seed of Satan move up and down the earth, so I come. And I come until spring and beyond, up to the moment of the prophesied end of the age of Pisces. And from now unto that hour, beloved, I assure you that I shall have appeared to everyone on every plane of this Matter house and on other worlds whose time has also come for my Second Appearing.

This, then, must precede, even as some consider it must follow, that moment [and that hour] when there is the dividing of the way on a planetary scale, where such light does become incarnate in all who choose to be that Christ and [to] enter the ritual of the alchemical union, and where such darkness [does] descend [so] as to result in the second death of souls.

There, beloved, is alchemy. There, beloved, is world chemicalization. There, beloved, happy are ye, centered in the violet flame, centered in the Holy Spirit, making your abode in the heart of the earth that the darkness may pass over and the dawn of light may come....

Be it known, beloved hearts, that every step of the way you must see the Call as that which knits together the hearts of the lightbearers with the hearts of those ascended and with our God in the Great Central Sun, with our God, who is your I AM Presence with you every hour. Yet the momentums of this world come between you and your mighty I AM Presence more often than not, more often than they should.

Do you see, beloved? Keeping the light in a world that will get darker before it gets brighter is a full-time calling. It is a rejoicing. It is a love-emanation in your hearts as you love and love and love your God and his own, as you pray for them and beseech him and the Divine Mother to perpetually hold open [a passageway to the etheric plane], at least at this place on earth, where there may be no interference from the physical octave to the highest realms of light....

The astral sea is rising. See that your tube of light does keep it out. See that you, then, tackle your own astral body [as you challenge your dweller-on-the-threshold, the patterns of your electronic belt and the archetypes of Absolute Evil in the unconscious] that there might not be [found therein] a point of resonance with the astral sea without.

Let, then, the desire body be filled with thy desiring for thy God. May you also be filled with that desiring that I knew when, as David, I wrote down the Psalms of my communion with God, [the desiring I experienced in] my crying out [to] God that my offering might be acceptable in his sight.[10] This had been and continued to be the fervor of my heart and my reason for being for many lifetimes.

Thus, beloved, that desiring that becomes the zeal of thy house,[11] that desiring that does become the zeal of the LORD thy God shall *eat up* the substance untransmuted of [non-desire in] the astral body! And then you will know what it is to walk the earth as the one called Enoch [walked the earth].[12]

See, beloved, how that fortification [of the zeal of the LORD] does give you physical protection, spiritual protection, the protection of the soul who is one-pointed, all-infilling in her desiring to be God, God, God in the earth, to stand as that God Presence, that God-manifestation, between the multitudes of the children of light and the oncoming darkness that they must face.

Many of them shall be naked, beloved. They have not woven the deathless solar body. Pray for them, for I love them; and they are the children of my heart led astray by false pastors who have never given to them the true understanding of the sacred mysteries....

I have said, "Feed my sheep,"[13] and my so-called representatives in the world of Christendom have not fed them [the good wheat] but the husks. They have not given them my Body and my Blood as the fullness of the divine understanding [of] our Father-Mother God. They have allowed them to experience [neither] the mysteries nor [the] pain nor [the] bliss [of the path of personal Christhood].... Christianity has become a religion of the pleasure cult and of [the metaphysical] avoidance of that which must be experienced [in the psyche] as pain[—for growth and resolution require it].

Let me explain, beloved. You do not need to have a martyr complex to anticipate the experiencing of pain. Do you not experience and endure pain when you labor in travail to give birth to the child?[14] Is it pain or is it bliss, beloved? Do you not experience pain when the light enters the body—when the toxins are cleaned out and the light does enter? Is there not the sensation of pain and do you not rejoice in it, knowing that a greater light is come unto you and a [physical] rejuvenation and a [spiritual] resurrection?

Is there any creation, beloved, without birth pangs? I tell you no. To come up higher means to experience the sorrow of loss, the pain of separation as some are taken and others are left.[15] Blessed hearts, pain is not difficult to endure when you understand that in some cases it is a necessary part of the alchemy of transmutation.

Welcome adversity! Welcome the challenge! Welcome all that our God does send to you; for if it were not necessary, I would have told you.

And therefore I shall tell you what is not necessary. Your self-indulgence is not necessary. Your procrastination is not necessary. Your fatigue is not necessary. Your indolence is not necessary. The fleeting and the flirting of the mind with all kinds of things of this octave are not necessary when the mind can so easily be stayed upon God. It is not necessary to take forever to become the Son of God....

Blessed hearts, rally to the defense of the soul of light. Call to me with my Christ-vision and call to Cyclopea. Call to Mother Mary that you might know if there be a soul [in your midst] that is not of the light. And thus [realize that the] one that has no allegiance to the light will not be saved by your effort.

Do not waste precious time and energy that ought to be devoted to the saving of the children of God on such as these because you are flattered by their presence, by their attention, by their seeming intellectual brilliance [or even by their money];

and yet they are as sawdust.[16] There is nothing vital or inte-grated [in the ungodly[17]] nor are they capable of accomplishing [the] works of the Father.

For he hath sent me and I must work the works of him that sent me.[18] I work the works of Maitreya. I work the works of Gautama. I work the works of Sanat Kumara. And, my beloved, I work the works of your Holy Christ Self when you refuse to be the instrument of that Holy Christ Self yourself! And this is how much I have loved you: rather than see you lose points in the Law, I come and I perform those works. And I speak to your soul and I rebuke you and I reprimand you and I command you to allow that Christ to descend into your temple.

Blessed ones, remember that mantra, "I must work the works of him that sent me." Who has sent you? Your Holy Christ Self has sent you as the light-emanation and extension of the Holy One of God, your mighty I AM Presence.

Embody the works, beloved, and be quickened by the Word. Be not satisfied in that state of consciousness that is somewhere between the astral and the mental body, somewhere around the six o'clock line [as you chart your cosmic clock], engulfed in a sea of indecision and self-pity and all that self-justification.

Blessed hearts, I will show you how to get rid of self-justifi-cation. It is as simple as the nose upon your face. Simply get rid of the self! Then you may serve your life out justifying your Christ Self, justifying your I AM Presence, justifying their trust in you, their love in you, [you who are] that soul of light cast into the sea as a glistening pearl. Fear not, beloved. Thou shalt be made whole. Let thy God descend!

Therefore I would bring to you the vision, that you might see the filthy rags,[19] the filthy rags that you still allow your self, [i.e., your soul,] to be wrapped in. I will allow you to see the dweller that is [also] thy self; [for it is] thy *self*-creation.

I will allow you to see the ugliness [of the beast] that you might desire the beauty [of the Christ], that you might desire the Reality, that you might desire the Truth and that you might say:

"I take the sword of Christ my Lord, my Knight, my

Defender, and I take that sword and I drive it down the very middle of this personality divided, this Dr. Jekyll and Mr. Hyde![20] I take that sword and I cleave it asunder! And I will take neither the Jekyll nor the Hyde but I will take the Christ, who shall step forth, even as the mighty phoenix bird shall rise in this age from the ashes of a former self that is former and must be allowed to remain former."

I AM thy Christ. I AM thy Lord. I AM thy Saviour. Receive me in my Person, in my Sacred Heart and in your Holy Christ Self. Receive me in Maitreya and let us work the works of this age!

Beloved ones, if you make it, if you succeed, Saint Germain will be redeemed and a golden age will be possible. If you do not make it, if you do not succeed, then the possibility of a golden age becomes problematical and it may not come about. Thus, beloved, forget the self-preferences. Jump in and make it happen!

I, Jesus Christ, now give to you more than the spoken Word. I give you my love and I give you *all* of my love. I give you Communion. I give you the wine of my Spirit, the bread of my everlasting life and I call you to come Home while the door is yet open. I call you to disregard anyone's human, including your own. And love one another, for I dwell within you. Love one another, for my face is mirrored in the mirror of your soul.

I, Jesus, live in your heart. Will you not remember [this], beloved, and receive me and become who you are? This is my Thanksgiving Prayer, my Thanksgiving Call.

O my beloved, anticipate that you will need all of your strength, all of your forces, all of your integration in God. Go for it, beloved! For the more of God that is in you, the less likely you will be touched by the coming prophecies fulfilled.

Prepare for the battle. Prepare for the victory. Our eye is upon the All-Seeing Eye of God. May your eye be on it too; for in that Eye, beloved, you behold the image of God as Elohim, even as in your soul chakra you may see me face to face.

November 23, 1989
Thanksgiving Day
Royal Teton Ranch
Park County, Montana

Blessed ones, I am pivotal in this age and in the conclusion of the age, and I am the keystone in the arch of the hierarchy of Sanat Kumara that is tending the earth. And through my heart, that Sacred Heart of God that I have made my own, there is the open door whereby you may pass through into the glory of your own Christhood. JESUS[21]

We sense the urgency in Jesus' Call in this message. In his earlier dictations he has called us to be his disciples and to become that Christ. Now he says, "I speak to your soul and I rebuke you and I reprimand you and I command you to allow that Christ to descend into your temple." He comes with intense ruby-fire love and with the intent of piercing the density of our outer minds and awakening our souls to the need of the hour.

Saint Germain gave us a remarkable glimpse into the workings of heaven concerning delivering different types of dictations: "Sometimes after having had a dictation before humanity, we gather together in a little cosmic room, and we go over the dictations point by point, and we say to one another, 'Yes, I think that we would have better reached humanity by saying it this way.'

"So, I want you to understand that even at our level of thought and feeling, there is a cosmic effort on behalf of humanity, and that effort is a very real one indeed. It is not actually a haphazard gathering of concepts and then dumping them, literally, upon the consciousness of mankind. It is a manifestation of great cosmic strength and cosmic wisdom. We sometimes spend in the spiritual realm as long as what amounts to twelve years of your time producing a speech that will last thirty or forty minutes."[22]

Jesus explains here that we have a timetable to meet while the door of opportunity is open. We cannot afford to get stuck in procrastination or indecision. Jesus told his disciples: "Walk while ye have the light."[23] He is giving us the same message now. The opportunity is here, and we do not know what tomorrow will bring. He says, "I call you to come Home while the door is yet open. I call you to disregard anyone's human, including your own. And love one another, for I dwell within you. Love one another, for my face is mirrored in your soul. I, Jesus, live in your heart. Will you not remember this, beloved, and receive me and become who you are?"

The First and Second Coming of Jesus Christ

A key element in this dictation is Jesus' teaching on the Second Coming. He explains that the Second Coming of Christ is manifesting today through the Holy Christ Selves of the light-bearers on planet Earth, through those who accept his Christ light and determine to assimilate it and become it. This Second Coming "is also for the judgment of the seed of the Wicked One," those who, when they see him face-to-face (or in one of his true devotees), reject that Christ light.

In a dictation entitled "The Second Coming of the Saints," Kuthumi spoke of the Second Coming and how the saints unascended are also supporting Jesus in this alchemy. He said:

"Therefore, after much discussion and deliberation and prayer, it was the beloved Mother Mary who came and offered her suggestion that in this hour of the Second Coming of her Son Jesus, all the saints should likewise enter in to their own 'Second Coming,' to appear with him, to witness unto him and his glory and to display that portion of their own Christhood outpictured, that thereby those from every walk of life might have the conviction of their own potential Christhood and rise to acclaim the Lord and Saviour and to embrace the path of light, to shun evil, and, with supreme confidence in God, to walk away from all prior attachments to the fallen ones, however subtle, as the subtleties of fine dust begin to reduce the vibrant colors of the garments that they wear....

"Thus, the saints who gathered responded to the Blessed Mother and said, 'If we come also and show ourselves at inner levels to every lifestream upon earth to whom our Lord shall appear, perhaps by our witness to the universality of the Christ light and our closer proximity to this evolution by the nature of our lesser attainment, we might inspire those who would otherwise reject him to embrace the Lord and to accept his grace that they, too, may walk all the way back to the Sun in the Saviour's footsteps and perhaps in their own.'

"Thus, beloved, you can see that in this hour the unascended members of the Great White Brotherhood have volunteered. And they have been accepted by Lord Maitreya and Gautama and Sanat Kumara to do this very thing that they have volunteered to do, and, in so doing, to also assist Archangel Raphael and Mother Mary specifically in the rescue of souls of light who have nigh lost all the light that they once had.

"Beloved, you yourselves are a part of these bands. And I come to speak to you so that you might consciously set the sail of the mind and heart when you take your leave from your body at night and go forth in your etheric body while many sleep to contact them at the deepest levels of being that they might see the manifest perfection of the Christ in you while also noting that levels of imperfection remain.

"Thus, you have volunteered to give them heart, to give them courage, to give them the witness that though the Path be arduous, though it require a steeling of the mind and the perpetual watch that no unkind thought or unclean thing enter that mind, yet the rewards are infinite and the grace is beyond all telling. And the victory is nothing less than the statement of your soul bonded to Christ for that absolute God-victory on behalf of every other seed of Christ in all of cosmos."[24]

This is a tremendous opportunity for our souls to stand with Jesus on inner levels and witness to the universality of his Christ light within him, within us and within the souls we are seeking to rescue. Jesus has a great desire to reach his own while there is still opportunity.

The Problem of Procrastination

Jesus commands us to allow the Christ to enter into our temple. He tells us that we cannot procrastinate or get stuck in indecision—will we or won't we decide to become the Christ?

Procrastination is an avoidance technique. We know that the coming of Christ within us will cause change in our lives. We wonder if we are ready for it. And so we just keep putting off the decision. When we do this, we are continuing to live in an in-between state, not fully committed in either direction. But Jesus is telling us that we can no longer delay.

The messenger has this to say about procrastination: "There is a disease in the land.... It's called procrastination. It is the nonunderstanding of the Eternal Now. Now is the accepted time! Now is the day of salvation! Now is the time to act! Do you realize you don't own any other time but now? You don't own the past, and you don't own the future. But right now you can be God-centered. Right now you can take action. The now is very valuable. You should cherish it, not waste time. The now is sacred.... Now is the acceptable time. There is no tomorrow. We create our tomorrows today."[25]

Gautama Buddha gives his formula for overcoming the disease of procrastination: "The Path is a spiral moving to the center of the white-fire core. Many have not entered there for many incarnations. For while advancing on the track of the spiral that is the fire infolding itself, they have come to a halt, a narrow pass in rocky heights. They have turned back. They have said: 'The air is too refined. I cannot breathe the atmosphere of Spirit. The climb is too rigorous and my pack too heavy. I will tarry in this niche of consciousness and make the trek to the summit another time.'

"The delusions of time and space have ever been the weapons of deception employed by the fallen one. And his emissaries will always tell the soul moving toward the center of being: 'Another day, another year is suitable for the surrender. It is not necessary to put yourself under undue pressure. Remove yourself for a time from those fanatical ones, those devotees of the flame. Your path is not their path. There are many paths. Take it easy.

Rest yourself along the way. You have earned and you deserve a much needed repose.'

"This is the line of the fallen ones. And to it they add whatever line of reasoning appeals most to the rebellion and the perverseness of the not-self. They say: 'Take time out from the Path to indulge your family and your friends. For if you do not, they will curse you; they will leave you. And then you will be alone, and you know that you cannot make it alone.'

"What will you answer when the lies of the wicked come like smoke seeping through the cracks in the window and underneath the door? If you inhale the stench of the Liar and the lie, you will find yourself delaying the overcoming until you are overcome by the delay. For delay is the attenuation of energies that ought to be concentrated in the crucible. But he who is the flame of living truth has proclaimed, 'Behold, I come quickly.'[26] The trial by fire must be administered by angels of fire who quickly scorch the human consciousness as angels of the harvest burn the stubble of the field to set the soul free from the debris of carnality and clear the soil for a new sowing.

"The swift and sudden coming of the lightning of the mind of God is the LORD's instrument for those who would be victorious in the way of the tempter. For in the moment of victory, an intensity of soul fire must be sustained. And this sustaining of the fire is intended to remain so and not to be dispersed, for, once the fire is dispersed, the ability to summon the full measure of strength required is lost, and you must await another cycle for the concentration of energies.

"The fallen ones know that the cycles of life according to the law of the yang and the yin are alternately for the concentration of God-power in the masculine ray of the Godhead and then the release of that power throughout the Cosmic Egg in the feminine ray. Victories are won in the concentrated white-fire core of the masculine ray (the yang). Then comes the ritual of the sustainment whereby the victory spans the cosmos with the light of joy as the burst of life from the heart and the feminine realization (the yin) that I AM God here and now and everywhere."[27]

Serapis Bey speaks of the danger of indulgence in procrastination: "Remember, then, blessed ones: There was an hour when the Red Sea was parted and all of the children of the light passed through. Had some dallied and said, 'Well, the sea has parted, I will pass through on the morrow,' they would have been caught as the Egyptian persecutors were caught and swallowed up in the sea.

"Understand, then, the timing of the miracle and of the opportunity, and realize that we also respect the dates. The highway *has* been opened. Pass through while there is yet the opening, and find your place in the sun—where the keeping of the flame is, above all, the most sacred art!"[28]

El Morya states his view on the subject very succinctly: "Procrastination is a disease that is the death of the chela."[29]

The Dweller-on-the-Threshold

In this dictation, Jesus allows us to look upon our unreal self. Called the dweller-on-the-threshold, it is the *self*-creation that has become the impostor of the Christ Self. The dweller-on-the-threshold and the momentum of this human creation becomes another voice speaking to us, which the apostle Paul described in this way, "For the good that I would I do not: but the evil which I would not, that I do. Now if I do that I would not, it is no more I that do it, but sin that dwelleth in me."[30] Paul lets us know that he, too, felt a warring in his members and that this was a burden to him.

The messenger describes this carnal mind, this dweller, in the following way: "The dweller-on-the-threshold is the focal point of the consciousness behind the human creation—the mind behind the manifestation. This term has been adopted by the Brotherhood because it conveys the meaning that it sits at the threshold of self-awareness where the elements of the subconscious cross the line from the unconscious to the conscious world of the individual, and the unknown not-self becomes the known. Once surfaced, the dweller has entered the realm of the conscious will where, through the decision-making faculties of mind and heart, the soul may choose to 'ensoul' or to slay the components of this antithesis of his Real Self...

"Well, there comes a time in the life of the individual who contacts the Path, the masters or their representatives when he comes face-to-face with Christ and anti-Christ—Christ in the person of the man of God and anti-Christ in the personal dweller-on-the-threshold within himself.... This may occur at any time on the Path. People sense this, and, therefore, they avoid all contact with the Great White Brotherhood or its agents. They even take up arms against it, thinking to thwart the Law and the inevitable Day of Reckoning.

"This was so in the case of Saul on the road to Damascus. In this case it was the Master Jesus who forced the encounter and blinded Saul in the alchemical process of the light confounding the darkness. Jesus made Saul choose between his dweller, the anti-Christ or anti-Self who was persecuting the Christians, and his Real Self personified and represented in the ascended master Jesus Christ.

"When he chose his Lord, he chose the path of discipleship leading to individual Christhood. And the Master bound his dweller until he himself should slay it 'in the last day' of his karma. Endued with the power of Christ in his guru Jesus, Saul, now called Paul (having put off the old man and put on the new), went forth to witness to the Truth that had set him free from his own momentum of human creation and the human mind that created it—the dweller-on-the-threshold.[31]

"From his personal confrontation and conversion by the Lord, Paul was later able to tell the Romans with the conviction that comes only from experience: 'To be carnally minded is death; but to be spiritually minded is life and peace. Because the carnal mind is enmity against God: for it is not subject to the law of God, neither indeed can be....'[32]

"There comes a time when individuals on the Path have had the fullness of the teaching, the light, the masters and the love of the community. And that fullness is not gauged by years but by the evolution of the lifestream. It may be one year, it may be three years, it may be twenty years, it may be many embodiments.

"But there comes a point when the individual has full awareness of the Christ in the masters, in the messenger, full awareness of what the darkness is and what the carnal mind is. And he must come to the place of deciding for or against his mighty I AM Presence, the Brotherhood, for or against the false hierarchy. This is known as the Y. The Y in the Path is the point of the initiation where one actually becomes Christ or Antichrist.

"One may refuse to surrender that dweller—to bind it, slay it and send it to judgment aforehand—i.e., before the soul must give its accounting to the Karmic Board at the conclusion of this life. Jesus taught this law of karma to Paul, who wrote of it to Timothy: 'Some men's sins are open beforehand, going before to judgment; and some men they follow after.'[33]

"Instead of surrendering it at the Y, the initiate may, instead, embrace the dweller. Instead of eating the flesh and drinking the blood of the Son of God (assimilating the Light of Alpha and Omega in the Body of Christ), he literally drinks the cup of the blasphemy of the fallen angels and eats at their board the infamy of their anti-Word.

"By taking the wrong way, the initiate actually puts on, personifies, identifies with and is now become the dweller-on-the-threshold incarnate. The soul and the cancer of the carnal mind have grown together and are no longer separable. Such an individual would then be on the left-handed path. His will, not God's, is supreme."[34]

Jesus has given us a decree that we can give to call for the Lord's intercession in casting out the dweller-on-the-threshold. (See Spiritual Exercises.) Thus, day by day, as we give this decree, we can surrender a portion of that dweller and make room in our consciousness for another increment of the Christ. If we do this faithfully and daily surrender that not-self, no longer feed it our energy and light, it is gradually diminished, and, when the time for the final choice comes, the final confrontation with the dweller, it will be much reduced in stature.

SPIRITUAL EXERCISES

Read the Psalms

Jesus speaks of his life as David, the psalmist and king of Israel. He says: "May you also be filled with that desiring that I knew when, as David, I wrote down the Psalms of my communion with God." As we are filled with this true desiring, the great energy of the desire body can be harnessed to propel us forward on the Path. As you read the Psalms, ask Jesus to place his Presence over you and transfer directly to your heart this great desire to be one with God.

> *Show me thy ways, O LORD; teach me thy paths.*
> *Lead me in thy truth, and teach me: for thou art the*
> *God of my salvation; on thee do I wait all the day.*
> —PSALM 25

> *As the hart panteth after the water brooks, so*
> *panteth my soul after thee, O God.*
> *My soul thirsteth for God, for the living God: when*
> *shall I come and appear before God?*   —PSALM 42

Call to Cyclopea

In this dictation Jesus says: "Call to me with my Christ-vision, and call to Cyclopea." Cyclopea is the Elohim of the fifth ray, which corresponds to the third-eye chakra. Cyclopea focuses the All-Seeing Eye of God, the power of vision. Through calling to Cyclopea we can strengthen our own spiritual vision, which Jesus says is so important to our Path.

BELOVED CYCLOPEA, BEHOLDER OF PERFECTION

Beloved mighty victorious Presence of God, I AM in me, Holy Christ Selves of all earth's evolutions, beloved Cyclopea and Virginia, beloved Helios and Vesta, Lanello and K-17, the entire Spirit of the Great White Brotherhood and the World Mother, elemental life—fire, air, water, and earth! In the name of the beloved Presence of God which I AM and by and through the magnetic power of

the sacred fire vested in the threefold flame burning within my heart,
I decree:

1. Beloved Cyclopea,
   Thou Beholder of Perfection,
   Release to us thy divine direction,
   Clear our way from all debris,
   Hold the immaculate thought for me.

Refrain: I AM, I AM beholding All,
   Mine eye is single as I call;
   Raise me now and set me free,
   Thy holy image now to be.

2. Beloved Cyclopea,
   Thou Enfolder All Seeing,
   Mold in light my very being,
   Purify my thought and feeling,
   Hold secure God's Law appealing.

3. Beloved Cyclopea,
   Radiant eye of ancient grace,
   By God's hand his image trace
   On the fabric of my soul,
   Erase all bane and keep me Whole.

4. Beloved Cyclopea,
   Guard for aye the City Foursquare,
   Hear and implement my prayer,
   Trumpet my victory on the air,
   Hold the purity of truth so fair.

And in full faith...

Call for the Sacred Heart of Jesus to Be Superimposed Over Your Heart

Jesus tells us, "Thus, in the West my heart is spoken of as the Sacred Heart, and yet what I have realized and brought forth in my heart is something that you can do also. Your heart is the sacred heart, for God has made only sacred hearts, no other. The threefold flame of your heart is that sacredness. To be so felt and so acknowledged requires but the intensification of its dimension of that blazing sun of God-reality.

"It is only in measure of increments whereby you think of my heart as the Sacred Heart and your own in a state of becoming, but I unveil to you the threefold flame of the heart of your Holy Christ Self. I unveil to you the threefold flame in the heart of your I AM Presence. This is the sacred heart, and, in divine reality, it is your own, your very own heart."[35]

Make the following call daily:

> **In the name of my mighty I AM Presence and Holy Christ Self, I call for the Sacred Heart of Jesus to be superimposed over my heart chakra. I ask that it strengthen and protect my heart as I determine to become the Christ.**
>
> **In the Sacred Heart of Jesus I trust. (3x)**

Invoke the Ascended Masters to Cast Out the Dweller-on-the-Threshold of All that Opposes Your Christhood

The following decree by Jesus is one we can use to call for his intercession to bind and cast out the dweller-on-the-threshold, the not-self of our own human creation. Before taking on this assignment it is important to call for the protection and sealing of the soul and the consciousness in the light of God. Call for your tube of light (see "Heart, Head and Hand Decrees," page 21) and give decrees to Archangel Michael (see page 43).

"I CAST OUT THE DWELLER-ON-THE-THRESHOLD!"
by Jesus Christ

In the name I AM THAT I AM ELOHIM
Saint Germain, Portia, Guru Ma, Lanello
Padma Sambhava, Kuan Yin and the Five Dhyani Buddhas
In the name I AM THAT I AM SANAT KUMARA
Gautama Buddha, Lord Maitreya, Jesus Christ
OM VAIROCHANA • AKSHOBHYA • RATNASAMBHAVA
AMITABHA • AMOGHASIDDHI • VAJRASATTVA OM
I CAST OUT THE DWELLER-ON-THE-THRESHOLD of

_____(give personal prayers)_____.

In the name of my beloved mighty I AM Presence and Holy Christ Self, Archangel Michael and hosts of the LORD, in the name Jesus Christ, I challenge the personal and planetary dweller-on-the-threshold, and I say:

You have no power over me! *You* may not threaten or mar the face of my God within my soul. *You* may not taunt or tempt me with past or present or future, for I AM hid with Christ in God. I AM his bride. I AM accepted by the LORD.

You have no power to destroy me!

Therefore, be *bound!* by the LORD himself.

Your day is *done!* You may no longer inhabit this temple.

In the name I AM THAT I AM, be *bound!* you tempter of my soul. Be *bound!* you point of pride of the original fall of the fallen ones! You have no power, no reality, no worth. You occupy no time or space of my being.

You have no power in my temple. You may no longer steal the light of my chakras. You may not steal the light of my heart flame or my I AM Presence.

Be *bound!* then, O Serpent and his seed and all implants of the sinister force, for *I AM THAT I AM!*

I AM the Son of God this day, and I occupy this temple fully and wholly until the coming of the LORD, until the New Day, until all be fulfilled, and until this generation of the seed of Serpent pass away.

Burn through, O living Word of God!

By the power of Brahma, Vishnu and Shiva, in the name Brahman: I AM THAT I AM and I stand and I cast out the dweller.

Let him be bound by the power of the LORD's host! Let him be consigned to the flame of the sacred fire of Alpha and Omega, that that one may not go out to tempt the innocent and the babes in Christ.

Blaze the power of Elohim!

Elohim of God—Elohim of God—Elohim of God.

Descend now in answer to my call. As the mandate of the LORD—as Above, so below—occupy now.

Bind the fallen self! *Bind* the synthetic self! Be *out* then!

Bind the fallen one! For there is no more remnant or residue in my life of any, or any part of that one.

Lo, I AM, in Jesus' name, the victor over death and hell! (2x)

Lo, *I AM THAT I AM* in me—in the name of Jesus Christ—is *here and now* the victor over death and hell! Lo! It is done.

A Mantra from Jesus

"God sends us forth again and again to finish the work—his Work on earth. 'I must work the works of Him that sent me.' Isn't that a wonderful mantra of Jesus? He said it. And that's why you are here. God sent you to work his Work. And the way to do it better is to increase the light by his name, by his Word, by the use of the mantra. So you take Jesus' mantra and you say,

In the name of my mighty I AM Presence, in the name of
the Son of God and beloved Jesus Christ,
  I AM working the works of Him that sent me—
    right now today!
  I AM working the works of Him that sent me—
    in God's own way!
  I AM working the works of Him that sent me—
    by Love's consuming sacred fire!
  I AM working the works of Him that sent me—
    by Christ's own God-desire!

"The mantra is a worded formula expressing devotion to God. It is an energy matrix that sustains the qualities invoked by the science of sound and rhythm. It is a prayer, but it is also a dynamic decree. It is also an affirmation. The prayer contains the pattern of that which you desire to manifest on earth by the authority of your God-given free will, by this divine spark in your heart, and by your beloved I AM Presence."[36]

FOR YOUR JOURNAL

How Will *You* Answer Jesus' Call?

*"I command you to allow that Christ
to descend into your temple."*

What does this Call mean to me?
What will I do to answer this Call?

CHAPTER 9

"Take back unto yourself the karma I have borne for you these two thousand years."

The Way Is Cleared for the Saints to Occupy the Earth!

Take Back unto Yourself the Karma I Have Borne for You These Two Thousand Years

Now cometh the Lord with his saints! Now cometh the Lord Sanat Kumara with ten thousand of his saints this the fourth day of the Christ Mass.

I, Jesus, come to you; for I say, the way is cleared. From this day forward, one by one the saints of the etheric octave shall occupy till I come[1] in full God-manifestation, when the saints of the earth shall all have been raised to that level of the etheric manifestation that was the Garden of Eden.

One by one the saints descend to occupy. For with this clearance this day, beloved, there is a line that has been drawn and this [is the] sufficiency over the mark of the 51 percent [whereby the saints may occupy the earth]. Thus day by day there is the occupation of earth.

Blessed ones, there is room for only so many saints on the head of this pin called planet Earth. Therefore, as the saints occupy, the seats of the fallen ones are taken. And they must vacate their seats and defer to the saints. For I declare this day, "The earth is the LORD's and the fullness thereof!"

Therefore I say to you, O ye saints abiding in the physical octave, who are the mystical body of God, welcome your God, the Lord Sanat Kumara, who has tarried, who has occupied, who has not failed you but who has fulfilled his eternal Word!....

Therefore, my beloved, know this, that your heart is becoming a crystal chalice for the fire of God to burn on, to burn strong. The threefold flame is indeed the gift of the divine spark. Yet you have seen the portrayal of myself where the threefold flame does enfold my entire being. This is the sign of the Cosmic Christ, beloved.

And one day after you shall have made of your present three-fold flame a chalice for the God flame, you will know as the years, the decades and the centuries pass, even unto your ascended master activities once you have graduated from this schoolroom, that you can also experience the fullness of that God flame through and through enveloping you. Beloved ones, thus in equating with the threefold flame, know the meaning of the word of Moses unto you all: "I have said, Ye are gods and all of you are sons of the Most High."[2]

In this lily of my threefold flame, I love you, I caress you, I enfold you, I heal you, I dispel all fear and doubt. For I AM come, the Good Shepherd, and I come to feed my sheep, who are becoming head sheep and shepherds themselves....

Blessed hearts, my sheep know my voice.[3] And therefore you are my own, and any number of you are the one for whom I have gone after, leaving the ninety and nine.[4] Yes, I have gone after you and I have brought you through many lifetimes to this moment when you could see and know and understand—the inner eye somewhat opened, the inner ear hearing the inner sound, the soul knowing the vibration. I have shepherded you, beloved. I have also paid the price. For in order that your spiritual senses might be quickened I, Jesus, have taken upon myself some of the stripes of your karma.

Now I say to you, beloved, you are securely here. You have made the contact. You have tied yourself to my Sacred Heart. Thus, I am asking you this day to consider the following, that you might take back unto yourself in these remaining days of the year and throughout the New Year's conference the karma that I have borne for you. For, beloved, you yet remain under the dispensation of Hercules, who may carry your karma.[5]

But I say to you this, if you will take back that [karma] which I have borne [for you these two thousand years], for which I have paid the price, and balance it yourself and thereby grow in the stature of your Christhood, freely asking Hercules' assistance when needed, then, you see, I may leave you as the ninety and nine and I may now go after [those] other [ones], even as many as a thousand other souls who need [me to] bear their burden, that I might quicken their soul senses that they might hear my Word above the din of the press and the detractors and all those who attempt to cast shadows and aspersions upon this community, this messenger and teaching.

So you see, beloved, in the process of [doing] this so little a thing that I ask you, [for you also have the violet flame,] you are also becoming world saviours; for in a sense you are allowing me to bear another's karma. Thus you yourself do bear it, do you see?

Blessed ones, I say it is [*for you*] so little a thing. For when you have such a presence and a force united in this one place [to accomplish the labors of Hercules], you can make light work of balancing that karma [by such cosmic good deeds as these and by] encircling it [with Astrea's circle and sword of blue flame].[6] And remember this, through [your karma] you have a key and a tie to the world and the places where that karma was made. Thus you have an authority to go after the judgment [by the Lord Christ] and the binding [by Archangel Michael] of those forces that got you into that trouble and into that mess so long ago whereby the thread of contact with hierarchy became so thin that it broke.

Thus, beloved, consider this [my request to you] this day and answer me in writing out of all due thoughtfulness [whether you will take back unto yourself the karma I have borne for you] and then we shall continue our labors through New Year's Day, beginning at the beginning of this conference....

Understand, beloved, that the message of the Second Coming of Christ is a message of resurrection unto the lightbearers and of judgment unto the seed of the wicked. It is a message and a gospel—of judgment and resurrection. And those resurrected disciples of the Lord, beloved ones, are they who sit with me in glory and in the glory of this court as you assemble together. For surely the glory of the LORD is upon you! And in that glory you fulfill my words to the disciples: Know you not that you shall sit and judge the twelve tribes and that you shall judge also the fallen angels?[7]

This prophecy has come to pass and it is accomplished by the Holy Ghost. Thus, beloved, as there is the judgment of the fallen ones who have taken the light of the sacred fire, of the threefold flame of the lightbearers, you see, as their time does come and as the judgment is lawful, that light is returned to you and your resurrection does increase. For they have inverted the power of the resurrection and the power of the I AM name and the power of my own name to perform their ungodly deeds.

Therefore, this night before you shut your eyes [in sleep] read the Gospel of Jude. It is only one chapter, beloved, and you should remember it and let it be inscribed in your heart; for there [you will find what] I gave to Jude [to record as] the description of the fallen ones [two thousand years ago and] in this age. And in the coming labors of the conference I shall name those types that are described, even those apostate preachers and princes who come in this hour. Let it be done, then, beloved ones, that you deal with every category of sin and of the sinners who are of the fallen angels (and not of the children of the light) that are recounted in that gospel.

Blessed ones, I come in the name of Enoch. I come in the name of Sanat Kumara. I come in the name of the first parents and the last. I come in the name of the God and Goddess Meru.

I come in your name, beloved, for I carry your names with me in my heart and inscribed in gold in my little book. For I also have a little book and those names, as they are in that gold writing, do have the quality of registering daily the state of your consciousness and your need, the levels of your ups and downs.

This [reading] then registers upon my causal body, upon my ascended master light body, and I send needle rays from my heart that reach you with the antidote for that condition of consciousness that you may be in that may be slightly less than the fullness of your Christhood. This, beloved, happens instantaneously as the cosmic cross of white fire is the transmitter of the mind of God.

Thus understand how the Shepherd knows his sheep, even as the sheep know the Shepherd. I am tied to all upon earth who have touched the garment, even the hem of the garment of their own Christhood, through any religion, even a religion that does not acknowledge my name or victory. Unto them who truly approach their Holy Christ Self, I, with Kuthumi, am able to minister in an extraordinary way. We preach the mighty Word of the living Christ, Maitreya.

Thus as World Teachers we are continually sending needle rays of enlightenment that when there is a state [of] compromise [with the Holy Christ Self] the individual may soon learn what is the cause of that condition and what is the true way [to our heart] and may reason in his heart, as [it is written], "Come now, let us reason together, saith the LORD. Though your sins be as scarlet, I will make them white as snow."[8]

So, beloved ones, know that [in] that great truth is the understanding of the transmutation of sin as karma; and the violet flame is surely the cosmic antidote [for sin, for karma]. Transmutation comes because the mind has seen the source of the error, has acknowledged it, has taken hold of the wrong desire to be involved in that error, has banished [both the wrong desire and the error] and has willed to go forward with strength, with character, with determination and with the promise to God to put all these things, these lesser things, behind him and to embrace that Christ.

Beloved hearts, when you make that decision [to forsake sin and the sinful sense], sometimes I am no farther than ten feet before you. It would require two strides for you to be in my arms. Then do not fear to take those strides, those leaps, beloved. For I say to you, when you do make that decision to put the lesser things behind you, I strengthen you directly by the body and blood of my being, by my sacred heart, by my all-enfolding love. Your decision opens the door.

So long as you are in a state of indecision, "Shall I or shall I not put this thing behind me this day?" so, beloved, you are alone in your valley of indecision. It must be, according to the law of free will, that you have a foundation of self-determination before an ascended master can add unto you his own great God-determination and momentum of his causal body.

Therefore I say to you all, my most cherished ones, make all things right in your life! *Make all things right in your life!* Make all things right in your life. And you do know right from wrong. You know it in your heart. You know it in your Christ Self. I will strengthen you once you have firmly set your feet on your path of self-determination....

Come forward, beloved. Do not lapse back any longer into the old man or the old woman[9] of the last and the prior embodiments.

I AM Jesus. I AM the Saviour in the midst. I give my life for my sheep. I give all of my life....

There is absolutely no limit to that which you can attain to in this life. Why, beloved, some of you have attainments you know not of as you strive as humble servants and look not to your achievements but only to what else you might do to lighten the burden of community, of the messenger and of the masters.

Therefore, it is true, no man knoweth his own measure, and it is well. For the suffering servant, the humble servant and the burden-bearer, surely does awake in the glory of the garments of the Son of God. And as I have promised, to him that overcometh I will give the crown of life.[10]

May you be overcomers in all things because you can, because you know the Word with Brahman in the beginning, because you have the fiat of light, because you have all the resources and the teaching.

December 25, 1989
Christmas Day
Royal Teton Ranch
Park County, Montana

*I AM Jesus. I AM the Saviour in the midst. I give my life for
my sheep.*

The next request Jesus makes of those of us who have the
teachings of the ascended masters for the Aquarian age is
to "take back that karma which I have borne for you these two
thousand years."

It is interesting to note that this Call was given only a month
after his previous Call, "I command you to allow that Christ to
descend into your temple!" As we determine to answer his earlier Call and strive to become more integrated with our Christ
Self, we, then, have increased light and the ability to take back
portions of the karma Jesus has borne for us. Jesus is calling us
to a greater level of responsibility on the Path.

You may be feeling a little concerned about answering this
Call, and thinking, "How can I take back the karma Jesus has
borne for me when I can't even handle the karma I am presently
dealing with?" You might be asking yourself, "If I do as Jesus
requests, how will this affect me?" The messenger explains Jesus'
role and our responsibility to balance this karma in the following way:

"Jesus Christ was and is the avatar of the Piscean age. He did
bear the sin of the world, and he has borne our burdens. He has
done this for many reasons. But in each age there is an avatar
who bears the burdens of world karma. And he has many disciples who assist him in bearing some portion of that karma.

"And so we were counted among those for whom Jesus bore
karma. But he said to us that we must understand that since we
have the violet flame, since we have the ability to call to the entire
Spirit of the Great White Brotherhood and the Great Central
Sun, we have the knowledge of balancing our own karma, and
we should now bear that burden. We should take on that burden
so that he can work with others whose theology, whose traditions

in the ages of Aries and Pisces do not allow them doctrinally to accept the teachings of the ascended masters that we have accepted.

"Furthermore, Jesus desires us to become adepts, not to simply receive gifts from him but to gain self-mastery ourselves so that we will ascend, not simply because we have been good people, but because we have mastered the alchemy of our beings. We have the violet flame. We know how to call upon the numberless numbers of saints robed in white in heaven. The ascended masters have given us teachings we can apply to gain our adeptship."[11]

Jesus expresses a certain level of confidence in us, that we have the tools, the teaching and the ability to rise to a higher level of responsibility on our path and bear our own karmic burden. If you desire to answer this call, consistent use of the violet flame can help transmute this burden into light. There are also other masters who have offered to help us bear our burdens.

Jesus speaks of a particular dispensation from Hercules whereby he could bear our karmic burdens at that specific time. Although this dispensation may no longer be in effect, we can still give the decree to Hercules, Elohim of the first ray, asking him to help bear our burden and to give us strength to bear it. (See Spiritual Exercises.)

Even while Jesus asks us to bear more of our own burden, he still offers to walk with us and comfort us as we do so: "I AM Jesus. I AM the one who was and is and yet shall be in your life.[12] You have known me always, as I have known you. Therefore, come into my Sacred Heart this day, for I would take you to my heart and deliver you from the burdens of death and hell....

"I come to you as comforter. Be comforted, then! For you see, I can fill all of the vacancies and the hollowness and the hollowed-outness. I can fill the body temple with our love.

"Now you must decide if you would have me as your friend and as your comforter; for the decision involves, beloved, your commitment, your desire to let go of all other hurts, all negative encounters of this world that have become excuses not to embrace your own Holy Christ Self.

"I come as someone you know or ought to know from your readings and prayers. I come as someone who extends beyond all time and space, offering indeed my hand of friendship.

"Do you understand my point, beloved? I will make it very clear: If you can so receive me, then the very process of receiving me will involve the letting go of all other persons, considerations and experiences that have led to disappointment and sorrow and vacancy, disillusionment, cynicism, despair....

"Thus, I tell you, ere you can receive me in the offering of myself, you must desire to have the kind of friend that I am, the kind of comforter that I am. If you are ready for such a friendship and such a comfort, then, beloved, you need not go back to revolving the old records that keep you bound to the world of nothing and the not-self, that keep you from the marriage to the Bridegroom.

"And so, beloved, you will come to the place—indeed, you must if you would accept my gift—of no longer desiring this type of satisfaction but truly desiring the God-satisfaction of the true Path and the true friend and the true comforter. Your own willingness to accept me or lack of it will reveal to you just how much you are attached or unattached to all that has gone before.

"Now then, I offer you my friendship and the presence of my comfort to this end: that I may give you the gift that can be received only from friend and comforter.

"The gift, beloved, is a magnificent portion of resurrection's flame that I desire to place in your heart this day, that you may bank the fires of the heart with this sacred fire of resurrection's flame and use it to balance and expand that threefold flame and use it to increase the Christ heart flame unto the day and the hour of your testing at the two-thirds level of the pyramid, which is the point where the resurrection flame does burn.

"But the resurrection flame, beloved, is a manifestation of the threefold flame that has begun to rotate and to turn. The resurrection flame is an accelerated version of the rainbow flame of God. The resurrection flame is a mother-of-pearl radiance. And so, you see, in order to have it, in order to meet the initiation of that level, you must have balanced your threefold flame; for there cannot be rotation of the flame when the three plumes are unequal."¹³

You can say a prayer to Jesus right now and ask him for this gift of a portion of resurrection's flame to be anchored in your heart. This flame is for the balancing and expanding of your threefold flame to help you bear and transmute that portion of karma that is yours to bear.

Even as we bear our burden, Jesus can also walk beside us to strengthen us and even help us bear it. He tells us: "If you have of late become weak in your faith and lost the vision, I say, come unto me. My heart is open. I condemn you not. My burden is light. Let me carry yours for a while until you are restored by the great fountain of living waters. I yet give that water, beloved, that he who may drink of it may live forever. It is the water of my life. It is the water of life that comes from the heart and the Source.

"Do not be burdened because you go through a period of heaviness and weight and darkness. I am there. I am there, beloved. Think of yourself on a journey, journeying on the road of life. There are days that are dark, glowering. The clouds are heavy. The fog is thick. Then the thunder and the lightning and the torrential rains come, and you cannot see ahead of you. That is how it is, beloved. The patterns of the weather tell you what is going on within your soul. The sun comes out. You have direct contact with the Presence. You are joyous in that presence of Helios and Vesta. So, then, those are the days when you must internalize the sun and become the sun, for dark days will come again. So is the sine wave of your life. Get accustomed to it, beloved. Don't simply play in the summer and not prepare for winter."¹⁴

Lord Maitreya has also offered to assist us in bearing the burdens of life: "Now speak my name silently in your heart: Maitreya. In my name wrap the burden of your soul, the problem of the day. Wrap it carefully in my name, for I stand now before you in the Great Silence, ready to receive that package addressed to me...

"Come unto me all ye who are weary and heavy laden. I will give you rest. I AM the all-consuming light. The all-consuming light is my yoke. Therefore, take my yoke upon you and learn of me. I will demonstrate to you the alchemy whereby thy burden shall be light[15] and thy light shall be a flaming sword and thy sword shall be for the deliverance of the nations.

"By the flame of Saint Germain, Jesus Christ and your own dear name written in heaven, I declare unto you, the victory flame is come! In my left hand I take the package addressed to me from each one of you now. And in my right hand I make my vow. And I thrust Victory's torch and I say: 'Here, carry the torch of the fire of Victory, and I will carry the burden of your day.'

"This is my promise. May you take it and incorporate it into your morning ritual. So greet the dawn and make your little package, whether small or great. Seal it with my name. My angels will take that package and give to you the torch of Victory for your day, each and every day until your ascension in the light."[16]

The Alchemy of Judgment

Jesus explains that if we answer this Call to take back our karma, we will also have expanded opportunity for service, specifically for the judgment of forces of darkness. He says: "Through your karma you have a key and a tie to the world and the places where that karma was made. Thus, you have an authority to go after the judgment by the Lord Christ and the binding by Archangel Michael of those forces that got you into that trouble and into that mess so long ago whereby the thread of contact with hierarchy became so thin that it broke."

Jesus has given us a decree that we can use to call for his light to descend into earth in the action of the judgment. Jesus' Judgment Call, "They Shall Not Pass" (see Spiritual Exercises), invokes the light of the Cosmic Christ to separate the light from the darkness. Two thousand years ago Jesus spoke of the separation of the tares and the wheat,[17] and this cycle comes at the end of an age, after two thousand years of opportunity to serve the light. The tares are the seed of the wicked, the wheat are the children of the light and the reapers are the angels. The judgment and the separation are enacted by the angels. Our assignment is to make the call for them to enter into this octave.

SPIRITUAL EXERCISES

Write Jesus a Letter and Consign It to the Physical Fire

Jesus told us how he would like us to respond to this Call. He said, "Thus, beloved, consider this my request to you this day, and answer me in writing out of all due thoughtfulness whether you will take back unto yourself the karma I have borne for you."

If you desire to assist Jesus in his mission as World Saviour and accelerate the balancing of your karma and the putting on of your Christhood, you may wish to write him a heartfelt letter answering his request, then consecrate it and consign it to a physical fire. If you feel you are not ready to take on all of your karma at once, you can ask Jesus to return it to you in increments so that you can transmute it little by little with the violet flame. Remember to ask that your prayer be adjusted according to the will of God.

Call to Omri-Tas to Multiply Your Violet Flame Decrees

As we consider taking on the burden of our karma once again, Jesus spoke of the importance of using the violet flame to meet this challenge. The ascended master Omri-Tas asked us to give a minimum of fifteen minutes of violet-flame decrees each day, and said that if we would do this, he would multiply our offering: "If in all reverence, with inner attunement, a sense of yourself in your Christ Self as priest or priestess of the sacred fire, if with all your heart and deep within your heart you will take, then, fifteen minutes each day to give profound and loving invocations to the violet flame in my name (and please remember to use my name, for I am the one from whose causal body this dispensation comes), then we will take that offering, measure for measure, as it is devoted, as it is profound and sincere, the very weight of its power and light. Therefore, by the quality of it, quality for quality, it shall be multiplied in your life ten times!"[18] If we make use of this dispensation, our ability to deal with the karma we take on will be multiplied tremendously. You can give the following invocation to call for this dispensation after giving your fifteen minutes of violet flame:

> **In the name of my mighty I AM Presence and Holy Christ Self, I call to beloved Omri-Tas to take my offering of fifteen minutes of invocations to the violet flame and by the quality of it—as it is devoted, as it is profound and sincere, the very weight of its power and light—quality for quality, multiply it in my life ten times.**

Give the Decree to Hercules

Ask Hercules to help you bear the karma that you have taken back so that Jesus can help others.

O HERCULES, THOU ELOHIM

In the name of the beloved mighty victorious Presence of God, I AM in me, my very own beloved Holy Christ Self, Holy Christ Selves of all mankind, beloved Mighty Hercules and Amazonia, beloved Lanello, the entire Spirit of the Great White Brotherhood and the World Mother, elemental life—fire, air, water, and earth! I decree:

1. O Hercules, thou Elohim,
   I AM a child of love,
   Come and seal my being
   By might from heaven above.

Refrain: Like a bolt of lightning blue,
   Power of God flashing through,
   Take dominion o'er me now,
   To thy light and love I bow.

   Purify and guard my being
   By thine eye of grace all-seeing,
   Clothe me in thy power real,
   Fill me now with holy zeal.

I AM come to do God's will,
Give me grace now to fulfill
All the plan of heaven's Son,
With thy light I AM now one.

2. O Hercules, thy splendid shining
   Shatter failure and opining,
   Ope the way in love divining,
   Seal each one in crystal lining.

3. O Hercules, for strength I call,
   Give me victory over all;
   Let God triumph over me,
   Raise thy scepter, set me free.

4. O Hercules, beloved one,
   Crown me with thy blazing sun;
   Set thy hand upon my brow,
   Raise me to Perfection now.

And in full faith...

El Morya's Dispensation to Take Our Personal Burdens

El Morya has told us he wants to assist us with our personal karmic burdens so we can be free to do the spiritual work on world situations. He gave us a simple way to invite him to do this for us when we give our decrees:

1. List your personal needs and problems on paper. Put the paper face down on your right knee. Take a wallet-sized picture of El Morya, and put it face-down on top of your list. Then put your right hand over El Morya's picture and your list.
2. Make a quick call for the resolution of your needs and problems.
3. Then, as you give your decrees and prayers to El Morya and other masters, give your all to the work on world conditions and trust that Morya will take care of your personal needs and problems.

In order to assist us with our burdens, El Morya has also asked us to give his decree "I AM God's Will."

I AM GOD'S WILL

In the name of the beloved mighty victorious Presence of God, I AM in me, and my own beloved Holy Christ Self, I call to the heart of the will of God in the Great Central Sun, beloved Archangel Michael, beloved El Morya, beloved Mighty Hercules, all the legions of blue lightning, and the Brothers of the Diamond Heart, beloved Lanello, the entire Spirit of the Great White Brotherhood and the World Mother, elemental life—fire, air, water, and earth! to fan the flame of the will of God throughout my four lower bodies and answer this my call infinitely, presently, and forever:

1. I AM God's will manifest everywhere,
   I AM God's will perfect beyond compare,
   I AM God's will so beautiful and fair,
   I AM God's willing bounty everywhere.

Refrain: Come, come, come, O blue-flame will so true,
   Make and keep me ever radiant like you.
   Blue-flame will of living truth,
   Good will flame of eternal youth,
   Manifest, manifest, manifest in me now!

2. I AM God's will now taking full command,
   I AM God's will making all to understand,
   I AM God's will whose power is supreme,
   I AM God's will fulfilling heaven's dream.

3. I AM God's will protecting, blessing here,
   I AM God's will now casting out all fear,
   I AM God's will in action here well done,
   I AM God's will with victory for each one.

4. I AM blue-lightning flashing freedom's love,
   I AM blue-lightning power from above,
   I AM blue-lightning setting all men free,
   I AM blue-flame power flowing good through me.

And in full faith...

Give Jesus' Judgment Call

Give this call after you have put on the whole armour of God—the Tube of Light and the calls to Archangel Michael.

THE JUDGMENT CALL
"THEY SHALL NOT PASS!"
by Jesus Christ

In the Name of the I AM THAT I AM,
I invoke the Electronic Presence of Jesus Christ:
They shall not pass!
They shall not pass!
They shall not pass!
By the authority of the cosmic cross of white fire
  it shall be:
That all that is directed against the Christ
  within me, within the holy innocents,
  within our beloved messengers,
  within every son and daughter of God...
Is now turned back
  by the authority of Alpha and Omega,
  by the authority of my Lord and Saviour Jesus Christ,
  by the authority of Saint Germain!

I AM THAT I AM within the center of this temple
  and I declare in the fullness of
  the entire Spirit of the Great White Brotherhood:
That those who, then, practice the black arts
  against the children of the light...
Are now bound by the hosts of the LORD,
Do now receive the judgment of the Lord Christ
  within me, within Jesus,
  and within every ascended master,
Do now receive, then, the full return—
  multiplied by the energy of the Cosmic Christ—
  of their nefarious deeds which they have practiced
  since the very incarnation of the Word!

Lo, I AM a Son of God!
Lo, I AM a flame of God!
Lo, I stand upon the rock of the living Word
And I declare with Jesus, the living Son of God:
They shall not pass!
They shall not pass!
They shall not pass!
Elohim. Elohim. Elohim. [chant]

FOR YOUR JOURNAL

How Will *You* Answer Jesus' Call?

*"Take back unto yourself the karma
I have borne for you these two thousand years."*

What does this Call mean to me?
What will I do to answer this Call?

CHAPTER 10

"*I Call you to a life of the Holy Ghost.*"

"*I Call you to my temple of initiation.*"

"*Above and beyond all to which I have called you,… may you become all love.*"

To the Called of God
with Me in the Temple of Initiation
The Path of the Rose Cross

I speak to the called of God who are with me in the temple of initiation. And I speak to those who *would be* the called of God and who *would be* in the temple of initiation.

Let us contemplate the mysteries of self-transcendence in the holy oil, in the holy flame and in the Holy One of God.

Some have heard the Call. Some have truly come to the moment of the piercing of the heart and the piercing by the crown of thorns. Some have understood the mysteries of the secret rays and of what is required to be the chalice for the sacred heart.

I AM that chalice. I would that you might be that chalice.

Suffering and to suffer is the nature of the flesh. And in the process of the translation at the point where the Christed one stands between a Spirit cosmos and a Matter cosmos, there is that moment, beloved, when the pain of the giving up of the light itself [from the four lower bodies that can no longer contain it] unto a higher vessel is experienced unto the being of the bliss of God all one.

Some linger, for my sake, at that point of the cross for centuries. They count not the time, for I have called them. They have heard. And therefore daily and hourly they must deal with the world momentum of the force of Antichrist that will not stop, that will not let go the blessed one becoming the all of me until they [the legions of Antichrist] may no longer touch that one, for that one is not only resurrected but ascended in the light and wholly free.

Thus, it is the tarrying [with me upon the cross of life] in which the saints have engaged. And they have allowed themselves to be the targets of the fallen ones, who think that by assailing the saints they do despite to the Godhead. But on the contrary, it is this affliction that brings about a distillation whereby the soul of the individual and the spirit become one as an Alpha-and-Omega in this octave.

I speak of the spirit here below and not of the [Spirit of the LORD, who is the] I AM Presence. Therefore listen well. It [the ritual] is for androgynous being, whereby thy spirit fiery [the masculine, or yang, aspect of self] and thy soul [the feminine, or yin, aspect of self], as the essence and heart of the evolving one, do merge. And thus there is a wholeness, there is a beingness and there is the profound desire to extend into this octave even portion by portion of the Infinite One. For in this process, beloved, many are healed, much is consumed by sacred fire.

Thus, know and understand that this is the inner temple initiation, yet it is walked in the outer world in these days.

Let it be known, therefore, that when you are the called for this blessedness, when you are called to be the blessed who receive fire for fire for the devouring of the onslaughts that seem perpetual, so it is well to answer and to say:

> O LORD my God, I am not able but thou art able in me.
> Because thou hast called, I will answer,
> Trusting that thou knowest surely what is the capacity
> Of my soul and my spirit to take my turn, to play my part
> And thus to increase the opportunity for the little ones of
>   God
> To be drawn up by the very draft of the Holy Spirit
> That will surround me as I come into consonance
> With this point of initiation of the rose of the heart.

The symbol of the rose is the sign of this path, beloved—the symbol of the rose. Thus, the rose of the heart must increase her petals and Rose of Light has offered you her assistance. And so you have been given, too, the initiations of the heart, the meditations of the heart by my blessed father, Saint Germain.[1]

Coming in, then, to the understanding of this calling, you may begin to examine and to discern all events of your lifetime leading to it, understanding that all other initiations and the balancing of karma and the increase of the cosmic honor flame [have been that you may] come to that place where surely the momentum of the bliss of the rose of the heart itself does displace the transmutation that may be experienced, [albeit momentarily,] as pain or sorrow or burden. And yet in the moment, in the twinkling of the eye of God, once again, *once again* you have passed through another round for world transmutation, for world conflagration, for sacred fire.

Bless God. Bless the enemy. Bless the adversity and the adversary, as you have heard the Beloved One speak and say.[2] But feel the blessedness of the love of the Holy Spirit that passes through you, even an all-consuming fire whereby the burning of the heart does, according to the sine wave, carry you up into the ecstasy of the Holy Spirit.

O blessed ones, truly it is blessed to have the opportunity and the certain freedom that comes with this path to exult in the glory of the LORD and to know that on the etheric plane one carries the stigmata.[3] And thus, the flowing light, as the flowing blood of Christ, and the superimposing of my body upon your [body] enables you to be in the earth, in heaven at once but most especially at the point of the nexus where [the] one becomes the other.

Thus, you remain visible in the world, but all who see you will begin to see through you into the portals of heaven and gain an understanding of what is the life universal and the life triumphant and that earth provides stepping stones. And those who may be the exalted and those who may fulfill a certain way of the Path of the Rose Cross may appear in the earth as Saint Thérèse of Lisieux, being in the earth a powerful presence, ascended and unascended all at once.

There are goals that you can aspire to, goals that you can set. Their attainment does correspond to the yearning of the heart, to the willingness to groan in travail that the Holy Spirit might take up his abode within your temple. And to the love—O the love and the desiring to fill and fill again the empty, the incomplete, to provide the I AM Presence to those who know not who they are or who I AM, truly to be the instrument for the engrafting of the Word!⁴

Therefore, there are sacred labors of the heart that the saints have won. And if there were but one among you who were ready for this initiation, I would speak to that one this day, for I have spoken to [the] many on prior occasions. Yet I tell you that there is more than one. And those who receive the increasing of the fire by the increasing of the desiring for God, as it has been said, "My soul panteth after the living God,"⁵ so they shall receive my answer when they shall call in answer to my Call.

Many are called but few are chosen.⁶ Therefore I call all of you, but I choose those who bring the prerequisites. And I take you [to my heart] as [I did take the disciples and the holy women] in the inner circle of old where I did give much.

Blessed hearts, understand that there are among you [those] who, thanks to Saint Germain and two thousand years of your increase of light [in your temple] and [the] dispensations of God [upon you], have gone beyond the attainment even of the twelve, who, beloved, in the hour of my departure from that part of the world yet did indulge in their unbelief, their human questioning and their doubt. And thus, to some of them my final and parting words were the upbraiding of them for their hardness of heart.⁷ You can understand, beloved, that those who have now had for decades the violet flame and the Call should be past this place of being in my presence and yet doubting that I am the representative of the Cosmic Christ.

Fear and doubt are as [a] desert of desolation. They render the soul desolate, for the soul cannot grip Reality when in the grips of fear and self-doubt. Thus, I do come as the Piscean Master and Initiator always, counseling you that that God-mastery will come only to those who abandon their doubts, abandon their fears and cast them into the fire.

O the mastery of the flame of love!
O the presence of the flame of love!
O the power of the flame of love!
O the wisdom of the flame of love!

I, Jesus, speak to you of the heart and essence of love as being the fulfillment of the whole law.[8] And I speak to you of all these things of the world as paltry before the treasures of the Spirit and the gifts of the Spirit that we would bestow.

It is time for self-emptying and for the infilling. It is time to reduce oneself, to be the spirit of the living God juxtaposed against the backdrop of the Cosmic Spirit of the living God. It is time to despise all else. It is time to know the true meaning of the heart of Saint Francis.

Blessed ones, those of the orders of Francis and Clare saw outer poverty as the vacuum whereby the inner riches of the Spirit could be attained. They left "all these things"[9] and thus nothing, nothing stood between them and my presence.

I call you to a life of the Holy Ghost. Some of you have been here since the days of Mark,* yet you have not yet received the Holy Spirit! And you walk among us as hollowed-out ones. And why? Because you have preferred your independent/dependent ego stature. You have stood apart. You have not let me embrace you. You have not allowed me to draw you to myself, to breathe upon you the breath of the Holy Spirit, but instead [you] stand as the accuser of the brethren[10] and in judgment of one or another or another....

Let none attempt to measure his place but rather to know that life is a perpetuality of seeking and finding, self-emptying and increasing of the Holy Ghost. Do not attempt to fix your position on the Path, but do ask for guidance of me through my messenger or through your Holy Christ Self. Do not seek definitive answers or promises or commitments from God, but seek them in your own heart, of your own soul.

Fear not to stand in your Christ Self to command your soul

---

*Mark Prophet, founder of The Summit Lighthouse, who ascended in 1973.

to come out of the doldrums of negativity and to rise to new planes of being. Fear not in the spirit to be fierce with the lesser manifestation of self and to compel the [soul's] ascent to God, just as you would speak firmly to the child or one entrusted to your care.

Many saints have walked the earth, and among many saints only a single saint has been called apart to become the rose of the heart. What is the difference, beloved? What makes one devotee be received into the courts of the kingdom of heaven and another working side by side with that one to return into embodiment?[11]

It is the quality of the heart. It is the quality of grace. It is the quality of forgiveness and forbearance. It is the quality of love discovered in all of the millions of facets of its potential expression. It is care and carefulness and the rough places of the human will planed[12] by the diamond of the inner Christ.

Commend your spirit unto the Father, saying, "O my Father, into thine arms I commend my spirit!"[13] But the key is, except you become [as] a little child, you will not enter in to the Holy of holies of the temple initiations with me;[14] [you will not enter in except you have the] childlike quality of trust and innocence and purity, knowing only the love of God and trusting that love.

Now come my legions of angels, for I would not leave you to wonder or despair this day. Therefore they come with swords to cut you free from worldliness, intellectual pride, the entrapments of the carnal mind and all those things that have taken you from the sweet innocence of your childhood and the simple faith you knew.

I, Jesus, have walked up and down the earth, placing my Electronic Presence [before the people] that all might see the Christ. And you, the saints, have revealed your path at inner levels to millions.[15]

All know it is the time of the coming of the Son of man. Yet they will not know how or where or when unless some of you enter into the bliss of God, knowing that the portal to bliss is pain. But it is a peculiar pain, beloved, and it is one that surely, I tell you, can be endured.

In the great mystery of love I call you, for you have loved and cherished the lives of the saints. You have loved each of my footprints in which you have placed your own feet. You have supped on the words. You have been drenched in the glory of my light released, as again and again you have received my testimony.[16]

The testimony is not in the mere worded dictation. It is in the light that flows and flows again and flows, beloved, that touches you and leaves a radiance in your temple that cannot be scrubbed away. It is there as the shining aura of one who has touched my garment and, yea, more, one who has touched my heart.

I send ruby fire this day for healing, for disassociation of atoms that are not in harmony, for the regrouping of atoms forming the foundations of the whole man that is to be made whole in this life.

O Great Central Sun Magnet of the Ruby Ray, draw the fragments of self scattered to the four corners of the universes back, back to the magnet of the heart!

Blessed one, if you would be all of yourself, you must develop the heart as a magnet so that all that has your imprint upon it, and even fragments of the soul lost here and there, will come back to you as though spiraling to the center of a great sun. Without the quality of the ruby-ray magnet of the heart that is the very expression of the rose, you cannot become here below that "fire infolding itself,"[17] which draws to you all of the components of selfhood that divine wholeness might appear here below, as Above.

One glimpse of the face of a saint, a Christed one, a light-bearer by those who are open and listening and yearning and calling for their God, and they know. They know it is possible.

Some of you have had this effect on those who have watched and seen you as you walked through a crowd thinking you were unnoticed. You yourselves may remember how once or twice in this lifetime you may have seen someone whose eyes told you that God dwelt in his temple. And you have been spurred on, understanding that purity of heart has enabled that one to be a shining one in the earth. And you have said, "There by the grace of God I will go, for I see it is possible by his Spirit."

"Holiness unto the LORD!"[18] is a most powerful fiat for establishing and reestablishing the fire and the magnet of the heart, for it is [your] declaring that here below all holiness is the LORD's. And this holiness becomes the dazzling sun [within your heart] to increase and increase and increase....

There are many ways to ascend to God. But if I had to do it again, I would still prefer the way of overcoming in the earth [wherein and whereby] every public statement, example and act might be recorded in akasha that others might know, "If I take the same steps [and] make the same stand, I, too, will arrive at the fount of truth in the etheric temple of Pallas Athena. I will arrive at the point of the Logos and the Solar Logoi."

All that is accomplished here below, beloved, does increase your [self-] mastery [that enables you] to help others, and it does accelerate the entire world momentum of entering in. All things that are truly permanent happen at inner levels and you do not see the signs of them until the victory is almost complete in the physical.

Much inner preparation is going on amongst the saints in the earth who have become saints only by the crumbs from the Master's table.[19] But because of the fire of their hearts and their love, they have seen that one crumb *is* the whole loaf. And though they have been given the whole loaf by me, they could not receive it in their outer consciousness, for the whole loaf of the divine doctrine is unacceptable to their programming in this life, their belief systems.

Yet, on the inner, beloved, they know the truth and therefore progress does continue. And finally, when it comes time to enter the temple of the Christ where I initiate my own, it does not take too much to deliver them by the magnet of my heart's love from the mental set, the mind patterns of an outworn theology.

Remember this, beloved, how one crumb has given to so many the love to live as I would have them live. And therefore by merit, by determination and by faith they have arrived at the place where finally they could balance the threefold flame by [the fullness of Christ] illumination.

Thus, there is much wisdom teaching given in my temple. And I call you to my temple of initiation. May you ask to be taken there at night, for when you see what is the wisdom teaching and put it all together, you, too, will find the balance of the threefold flame.

Some have a karma for not entering in, for they have not seriously studied the teachings already given in the physical through this mouthpiece. Let it be understood that these teachings and dictations are preparatory to your inner temple work. To whom much is given, much is indeed expected.[20]

May you become world teachers, as I have said before. But above and beyond all to which I have called you, I say, may you become all love, all love and all love.

I, Jesus, would share with you now my Body and my Blood, for by this wise I truly give you my life and my heart as the engrafted Word. Receive, therefore, Holy Communion, which I serve to you personally by my angels' hands.

I seal you on the path of initiation according to your will, which I trust will be God's will this day and forever.

I seal you, beloved, into that which you desire, for I can give you only that which you desire of God. I say, cast out lesser desires that all of your energies might flow into the one, great all-consuming desire for *God, God, God.*

April 15, 1990
Easter Sunday
Royal Teton Ranch
Park County, Montana

Let none attempt to measure his place but rather to know
that life is a perpetuality of seeking and finding, self-emptying
and increasing in the Holy Ghost.   *JESUS*

In this address Jesus is speaking to those who have heard his previous calls, have understood and have responded. They are therefore referred to as "the called of God." Because they have answered the Master's calls, now God has called them, and they are with Jesus in the temple of initiation.

The Rose of the Heart

Jesus is calling us to expand the heart and the flame of the heart. The rose is the symbol of the heart chakra, and the heart chakra with its twelve petals must be expanded as we walk this path with Jesus. He speaks of the ascended lady master Rose of Light, who has offered to help us in the expansion of the heart chakra.

Rose of Light says: "Thus, I come again, and my mission is to come and to stay with you, for Saint Germain has called me to be your special mentor of the heart. Therefore, I bring my angels of the rose of light, and we place upon your heart chakra the thoughtform and the manifestation of the rose of light unfolding petals that are multiplying the twelve of the heart chakra. You may have a thousand-petaled rose of the heart chakra, beloved, for the petals increase by mercy's flame and compassion and wisdom....

"I, therefore, have come forth on this day, as scheduled by the Great Law, to begin the process of the tutoring of the heart and the opening of the rose of the heart—not that you have not already been God-taught by many of the ascended hosts. And Saint Germain himself has given to you his heart meditations.[21] These ought to be pursued.

"Yet we understand the preoccupations, the dharma of the

day and the requirements of the hour. Therefore, it is necessary to develop thoughtforms, beloved, which you can then visualize by second nature and which you can anchor by mantra. Let the mantras of Maitreya and Manjushri[22] give to you the balance of the heart, and may you visualize the most beautiful golden pink rose of light assisting you to unfold the petals of the heart chakra.

"Let each unfolding of the petal of the heart be a strengthening of the petal and of its release of light.* Let there be the Godmastery of the petals, signifying a greater and greater release of light, which does require, as has been explained to you at length, a greater protection and likewise a mounting spiral of attainment in the flame of God-mastery."[23]

Rose of Light gives meditations and visualizations that can assist us in expanding the heart. "Thus, I begin by counseling you to breathe out the fragrances of love and wisdom through the heart. And sense when you breathe out, beloved, that you are sending this light around the world to circle it and to return to you multiplied in kind. [deep inhalation]

"Now exhale, but visualize the sacred breath passing out through the heart and see it as a mist that is truly a sacred fire tinged with golden pink, sending a missile of hope throughout the planet....

"Then, beloved, know that the breath of life itself as well as the sacred fire breath you invoke to charge the breath of life and the atoms, cells and electrons is able to kindle and rekindle and to expand and intensify the threefold flame. Therefore, let the breath of life be instrumental in the balancing of the threefold flame. Therefore, let Djwal Kul's breathing exercise[24] be that which expands the power of the light in the chakras, in the lungs, in the heart, and in the rose of light that you visualize.

"Now draw a circle of light around the rose that you visualize in the center of your chest at the level of the heart filling the entire upper portion of your body. And this circle of light around the rose is pure gold. It extends to a wider circumference than the

---

*The light-emanation of the heart chakra is the Christ consciousness that radiates the balance of power, wisdom and love of the threefold flame.

rose itself, and it is a ring-pass-not whereby the rose cannot be touched.

"Therefore, you have heard the admonishment: 'Guard the heart.[25] Guard the secret place of the heart. Guard the beating of the heart. Guard the bird of the heart.'

"Heart, therefore, is the seat of sacred fire and of agni yoga.[26] Heart must be protected, beloved. Let not the heart be jolted or jostled or overcome by anything beneath or above. Practice, therefore, stillness in the heart, peace in the heart, strength in the heart and God-centeredness in the heart....

"Feel yourself to be as that fire infolding itself seen by Ezekiel.[27] Feel yourself spiraling inward to the center of your Sun Presence, following the spiral formed by the rose petals back to the center, there to commune in the threefold flame, there to sense the balance of Alpha and Omega, once again to be renewed and restored, physically and mentally strengthened and above all focused in the heart of hearts of your Holy Christ Self as you visualize your Holy Christ Self not separate from you but super-imposed over you, your hearts as one.

"This, beloved, is a simple exercise, but many who are too spread out in their consciousness and thinking faculties, often because they are too 'yin' in their four lower bodies, and have no God Self-mastery over that attenuation from the center, scarcely know how to spiral backward into the heart in a counterclockwise direction that is seemingly backward. Therefore, spiraling to the center is a necessary exercise if the soul would establish her Christ Self-mastery sealed in the twelve-petaled chakra of the heart.

"And therefore, 'I AM Alpha and Omega in the white-fire core of Being' is the mantra you recite in addition to the Maitreya/Manjushri mantras. It is wondrous to be silent when you engage in this exercise as a holy ritual of going within. And as you come to the center of the thoughtform of the rose of light through the spiraling inward, you pass beyond it through the heart chakra to the eighth-ray, secret chamber of the heart.* And

---

*the eight-petaled chakra

here you have a few moments to bow before Lord Gautama and his bodhisattvas who have become Buddhas, who tutor your souls as they keep the flame of life for you here in the Holy of holies of your temple.

"Therefore, a mighty trinity have you, beloved, of power, wisdom and love in the Lords Gautama, Maitreya and Manjushri. See, then, how they come in the tradition of the Trinity and how the great power of the Lord of the World is ensconced by those who flank him with the adoration of love and wisdom. Thus, visualize your threefold flame as ensouled and embodied and personified by these three beings, even as you often visualize in those three plumes the Father, the Son and the Holy Spirit, or Brahma, Vishnu and Shiva."[28]

As we enter into these exercises and ask these great beings to abide with us and assist us, we can see our hearts and our lives transformed as we are remade, day by day, in the image of the divine.

The Path of the Rose Cross

The Path of the Rose Cross is the path of the Sacred Heart of Jesus—the path of the ruby ray. The ruby ray is an intense action of the pink ray, the third ray of divine love. It is the path of perfecting our souls through the initiations of love. The tests and initiations we must face on this path are not unlike those the saints of East and West have encountered throughout the ages. The ruby ray with its intense fiery love separates the Real from the unreal within us and prepares us to receive further testing on the secret rays.

The ascended masters in the lineage of the ruby ray include Sanat Kumara, Gautama Buddha, Lord Maitreya and Jesus Christ. These and other ascended masters initiate us on the path of the ruby ray—the path of sacrifice, surrender, selflessness and service.

As we walk the path to our ascension in the light, we will pass through the initiations of the ruby ray. And as we walk this path and assimilate this ruby ray, our souls are perfected through the initiations of love. This leads us to the alchemical marriage, which is the fusion of our soul with our Holy Christ Self.

The Path of Francis and Clare

Jesus' first Call to us in this dictation is "to a life of the Holy Ghost." He tells us that to be filled with the Holy Spirit, we must first self-empty, and he gives us the example of Francis and Clare, who "saw outer poverty as the vacuum whereby the inner riches of the Spirit could be attained."

In answering this Call, we can consider what we could do to simplify our lives, to have less of ourselves invested in material things. Francis and Clare demonstrated an uncompromising path of physical poverty, almost Eastern in its austerity. This can be one way of liberation from materialism. But the messengers have also taught that it is the attachment to material objects rather than the things themselves that fills our consciousness to the exclusion of the Spirit.

The path of desirelessness and nonattachment that Gautama taught can also be walked by the disciple who is given steward-ship of the things of this world. The key to walking this path is to see the things given into our keeping as God's possessions rather than our own. Seeing ourselves as stewards rather than owners, we can make wise decisions as to what God would like to have done with his abundance without becoming personally preoccupied with material things and missing the greater gifts of the Spirit.

The Call to a Life of the Holy Ghost

Jesus points out another element of consciousness that would block the Holy Ghost from entering in. It is wanting to maintain a certain independence, or separateness, from God. This may come from fear or from experiences where we have opened our-selves to others in love, only to receive rejection or hurt in return. Somehow, we never quite trust in the same way again. Thus, we see the need for healing our soul and our psychology.

Having overcome our desire for separateness and made room

in our life, what might a life lived in the Holy Ghost look like? We know that ultimately it would mean a path of walking and talking with the Holy Spirit and seeking the initiations of the Holy Spirit.

The Maha Chohan is the Representative of the Holy Spirit. He teaches us of the nine gifts of the Holy Spirit[29] and the path of initiation that we can pursue to receive these gifts: "I am the Maha Chohan, so named the Great Lord, and I do preside over the seven chohans of the rays. Each of these rays comes forth from the heart of the dove of the Holy Spirit. And that ray in manifestation to the planet is first and foremost the individualization of the God flame by each of the seven lords.

"Thus, when you desire to receive the Holy Spirit of the first ray, you apply to El Morya. And when you desire to receive the Holy Spirit and the gifts thereof of the second ray, you apply to Lord Lanto. And when you desire to receive the gifts of the Holy Spirit on the third ray and the flame thereof, you apply to the Lord Paul the Venetian. When you desire to receive the Holy Spirit of the fourth ray, you go to the heart of Serapis Bey for those fiery gifts.

"When you desire to receive the Holy Spirit of the fifth ray, you make application to Lord Hilarion that you might also qualify to receive the gifts thereof. When you desire the Holy Spirit of the sixth ray, then you appeal to the heart of Nada to receive the gifts thereof. When you desire the Holy Spirit of the seventh ray, you go to Lord Saint Germain and to his heart.

"Thus, it is well to desire the Holy Spirit in each of the seven rays and to chart the chohans and their rays on your cosmic clock, beginning at the twelve o'clock line and ending at the six.

"Thus, in increments of sacred fire, you do receive this light. That which you receive, you must keep and guard as treasure. If you lay up treasure in the earth, thieves will come and steal, moth and rust will corrupt.[30] But, beloved, while you are in the earth, you are expected to guard the things of the earth and to be a just and wise steward[31] of all energy forms. So it is true of that which you may receive of the Holy Spirit. For the Holy Spirit, even in one-seventh of its measure, may not be misqualified, may not be violated.

"Therefore, it is well to establish the discipline of calling forth that which one can keep and of keeping that which one calls forth. To keep the sacred gems, beloved, this is the mark of balance, of self-mastery, of objectivity. For when one becomes too subjective, one's views of life become warped, and then one may lose the treasured gift while defending the trinkets of life.

"When you desire to receive the power of the three-times-three and the all-power in heaven and earth that was given unto Jesus Christ at the conclusion of his Galilean mission,[32] you appeal to my heart, beloved. In my heart is the synthesis of the seven rays and the nine that precipitate these gifts.

"I would come to you, then, with a path of initiation that you might see as real, as doable, and that you might see your heart and your soul and your mind focused at the point of light where the three flames of the threefold flame are one. I step forth from your threefold flame embodying all of love. And all of love is the recitation of the gifts and of the callings of the members of the body, the mystical body of God.

"Be content to master one of the offices, one of the levels of service—even one of the rays. For when you do, beloved, the rest will come. Be at a state of discontent when you have the self-knowledge that you have not the mastery of one of these. For it is then that you are vulnerable, and it is then that I may not enter and approach as close as you would have me.

"Yes, I may teach you, beloved. Yes, I may comfort you. Yes, I may hear your prayers and be with you. But the giving of fire, beloved, is always and only according to the deepest desiring of the soul, which exceeds and must exceed all other desiring. For you see, beloved, if your cup of desiring for the flame that I bear—O look at it now!—be not the cup that is fullest, then you may take this cup when there is not another to be taken. But as soon as the cup of your greatest desire is offered, you will let go the one that I bear and take the one that you desire most.

"Thus, the beginning of the path of the Christ and the Buddha must be the soul's inner co-measurement based on self-examination: 'What do I desire most?' And if the answer be the Holy Spirit and the nine gifts, then understand, beloved, that you *will* hold that desire against all other offerings of all other worlds and all other levels, even in the face of the karmas that come due. When all of thy desiring and all of thy getting is to get the Holy Spirit, beloved, then I assure you, you will attain this goal.

"Such was the desire in the heart of the child Mark Prophet. Having lost his earthly father, he sought with all his heart his heavenly Father and his Lord and Saviour and, unbeknownst to him, myself. This little boy, beloved, knelt by the hour on the hard floor at his attic altar in the heat of summer and the cold of winter imploring God to come unto him, to give him those gifts of the Holy Spirit. This was his great and only desire. Surrounded by poverty and left fatherless, he and his mother made their way during the Depression, and there was nothing to intrude itself between him and his greatest desire.

"These gifts I gave to him, anointing him as a young man. These gifts he kept unto the hour of his ascension."[33]

Each of the lords of the seven rays has a path of initiation that they open to us so that we might receive the gifts of the Holy Spirit on that ray. The book *Lords of the Seven Rays* is a good place to begin your relationship with these servants of the Lord. You will find that, as you read about a particular master you feel close to and study his dictations, the master will place his attention upon you, and you will develop an ongoing relationship. As in any relationship, ours with the masters is nurtured and sustained through love.

Wisdom Teaching at Jesus' Temple of Initiation

Jesus' second Call to us in this dictation is, "I Call you to my temple of initiation." He is extending again the invitation to journey to his retreat and receive his teaching and initiation. You only have to accept his invitation and make the call for your soul to be taken to his retreat. There he will initiate you personally in the mysteries of his Sacred Heart and give you keys to pass your tests on the physical plane.

Jesus tells us, "There is much wisdom teaching given in my temple…and when you see what is the wisdom teaching and put it all together, you, too, will find the balance of the threefold flame."

Become all Love

The third request that Jesus makes is, "Above and beyond all to which I have called you…may you become all love."

Jesus speaks to us of "the heart and essence of love as being the fulfillment of the whole law" and directs us to the lives of saints who have been willing to walk the path of the Rose Cross and become the embodiment of love.

He speaks of Saint Thérèse of Lisieux as one who was in the earth, who was ascended and unascended all at once because she fulfilled the path of the Rose Cross. She was all love.

We also think of Saint John of the Cross and Saint Francis as those who knew the piercing of the heart in the initiations of divine love. We can read the lives of these saints and thus gain a sense of co-measurement for our own walk with God. In this day and age the world does not promote a path of holiness, but as we read of those who have walked this path, we find that we are following in the footsteps of many who have gone before us.

SPIRITUAL EXERCISES

Self-Emptying

As you think about the example of Francis and Clare, consider what can you do to simplify your life, to be less concerned with the things of the world, to create the vacuum that can be filled by the Holy Spirit.

Ask to Be Taken to Jesus' Retreat

Before going to sleep, ask the angels to take you to Jesus' temple of initiation. (Chapter 4 has an example of a prayer you could use.)

Remember to keep pen and paper beside your bed to write down anything you may remember from your inner experience upon awakening. You may not have a specific memory of a retreat experience (although many people have had such a remembrance on more than one occasion), but sometimes the insights we have upon awakening—about life, the path or challenges we face—represent that portion of our experience in the retreats that is given to us to bring back to our outer awareness.

It is important to commit these things to writing. At the time they are so vivid and alive that you think you will never forget them. But we often find that memory fades, and during the dark night of dealing with karma or challenges in life, it can sometimes be hard to remember ever having had a spiritual experience. These are the times that your journal and your personal testimony of the reality of the path can be of great assistance.

Saint Germain's Heart Meditation

Jesus and Rose of Light ask us to take up Saint Germain's heart meditations. These are services of prayers, meditations, decrees and songs directed by Saint Germain for the opening and expansion of the flame of the heart. They are available on audiotape and CD, and, as you listen to the recording, you can give them with the messenger and many other disciples.

Saint Germain tells us: "Neglect not my Heart Meditations; for as you increase the fire of the heart, so, beloved, I increase my presence in your heart. The increase of the threefold flame is your key to the all-power in heaven and in earth[34] that may be given unto you as a part of the initiations of the Holy Spirit, even the power of the three-times-three."[35]

Djwal Kul's Breathing Exercise

As we seek to expand the rose of the heart, Rose of Light directs us to a breathing exercise to expand the light in our chakras: "Therefore, let Djwal Kul's breathing exercise be that which expands the power of the light in the chakras, in the lungs, in the heart and in the rose of light that you visualize."

The Maha Chohan also asks us to give this exercise as a means to internalize the light of the Holy Spirit: "Blessed ones, in the reality of thy walk with the Holy Spirit, I AM at thy side, the Maha Chohan, for the victory of life in you. O keep the flame of life and know that the breath that is breathed upon you in the hour of your soul's descent into form is truly the breath of the Holy Spirit!

"As the years go by, through absence of mantra or prayer, the sacred fire breath is no longer native to the body but must be reinvoked by you. To this end the ascended master Djwal Kul dictated the *Intermediate Studies of the Human Aura* that you might have a simple exercise for the breathing in again of the breath of the Holy Spirit."[36]

This exercise can be found in *The Human Aura*, by Kuthumi and Djwal Kul, Book 2, chapter 8. It takes only a few minutes to complete and can be done daily for the strengthening and integration of the aura and the chakras.

Give the Mantras of Maitreya and Manjushri

In Tibetan iconography, Maitreya, the bodhisattva of love/action, and Manjushri, the bodhisattva of wisdom, are often depicted to the right and left of Gautama.[37] Rose of Light explains that these three form a trinity of the flames of power, wisdom and love comprising our own threefold flame. She asks us to give the mantras to Maitreya and Manjushri for the expansion of our own heart flame.

Mantras to Manjushri:
Om Ah Ra Pa Tsa Na Dhih
(Manjushri's mantra for developing wisdom.)

Om Wagi Shori Mum
("Hail to the Lord of Speech! Mum!")

Mantras to Maitreya:
Namo Maitreya
("Homage to the sacred name of Maitreya.")

Maitri Maitri Maha Maitri Svaha
("Loving-kindness and great loving-kindness,
please grant me that, Maitreya,")
or
("Maitreya, Maitreya, I will worship him.")

Rose of Light asks us to give this mantra also:

I AM Alpha and Omega in the white-fire core of Being.

Give the Mantras of Jesus

Jesus gives two mantras in this dictation. These are short prayers you can give at any hour of the day or night. While you are waiting for the light to change or for the web page to download or during any spare moment, you can make the call and reconnect to the heart of Jesus.

Holiness unto the Lord!

Jesus tells us this mantra is "a most powerful fiat for establishing and reestablishing the fire and the magnet of the heart, for it is your declaring that there below all holiness is the LORD's."

"O my Father, into thine arms I commend my spirit."

"Except you become as a little child, you will not enter into the Holy of holies of the temple initiations with me. You will not enter in except you have the childlike quality of trust and innocence and purity, knowing only the love of God and trusting that love."

A Prayer from the Maha Chohan

The Maha Chohan has dictated a prayer that we may use to invoke his Presence for the magnification of love within the heart. Give this prayer as you meditate on the flame within.

Beloved Maha Chohan, I want to be a comfort flame to every part of life. I want the flame of my heart to flow out daily toward the rising Sun—to sweep the world around with your wonderful comfort flame, to enter into the consciousness of the tired and the poor and the ignorant and to infuse them with a sense of the divine goodness of God.

I recognize that as a manifestation of God, I play a very

important part in awakening the consciousness of mankind. For as I think, so I send out the arrows of my love in all directions.

I will be an eternal cupid for God. I will fill my quiver with the arrows of God's love. I will shoot them into every heart that I meet until the world is so infused with comfort and love that the perfect example of the healing of Christ is extended through me toward all upon earth.

I will not look upon men to see imperfections, mortality and grossness and all of the stain and doubt and fear and negative possibilities. I will not dwell in a consciousness of *if,* but I will dwell in a consciousness of: *Now God is! Now God lives!*

And as the LORD liveth, so live I. And as I live, so I live for him. And as I live for him, I AM determined to be an ascended being. I AM determined to be an ascended master!

I have had embodiment upon embodiment upon this planet. I have been surfeited in human wandering and misery. I have accepted the dust of the road from mankind, the offscouring and the filth of the world.

I call now to the angels of purity to cleanse my consciousness of all that is not of the light. Wash me and make me white as snow![38]

FOR YOUR JOURNAL

How Will *You* Answer Jesus' Calls?

"I Call you to a life of the Holy Ghost."

"I Call you to my temple of initiation."

*"Above and beyond all to which I have called you,...
may you become all love."*

What do these Calls mean to me?
What will I do to answer these Calls?

CHAPTER 11

*"Become agents of the Cosmic Christ…
that the children of the light might
enter into this sheepfold."*

*"I Call you to… the perfecting of
the soul as my apostle."*

*"I have come to Call you to
be my shepherds."*

Become Agents of the Cosmic Christ!
I, Jesus, Have Called You
The Perfecting of the Soul as My Apostle
Please Feed My Sheep!

Now from the heart of a cosmos I greet you, beloved, in this hour that you keep the vigil for the servants of God upon earth. I am come to you even as I ensoul the planet in my garments this day.

I come, then, holding the balance in the earth for all conditions untoward you observe and some you do not. I come that I might extend to you even the thread of contact with my heart whereby you should also become agents of the Cosmic Christ to hold this balance to that end and for that purpose that the children of the light might enter in to this sheepfold.

These are the "other sheep"[1] and therefore these souls are gathered. I place my seal upon them but you must be myself as shepherd to go out and gather them.

Therefore all [of you] on this staff and beyond who have no better occupation shall now be God-taught that you might become spokesmen for the Great White Brotherhood, for myself [and] even for Magda.

Blessed ones, the Law has decreed that the hour may no longer advance that you are not equipped to speak the Word, to comfort, to counsel, to admonish, to raise up and to carry that child-man across the rapids and ultimately across the sea of samsara.

I am with you in this hour by the magnet of love of the Great Central Sun. I demagnetize from you all those things of which you desire to be delivered,[2] those things that you are through with, throughly* so.

Yes, beloved, if you can say to this or that state of consciousness, "Have done with it! I want it no longer!" and mean it with the fire of your heart, I will take it this day. Surely I shall. For the night is o'er, the day is come and it is the day of gladness of the Christ's descent into your temple.

I am that Christ! You are that Christ-potential emerging now into the fullness of your mission. The signs in the heavens and the earth all point to this day as the day of the Son of God appearing in you. Therefore let your mouths be unstopped! Let your ears be unplugged! Let your tongues receive the fire of seraphim[3] to consume all misuses of the spoken Word!

I, Jesus, have called you. And in this hour you shall be my manifestation where'er you go. This opportunity comes to you, beloved. Therefore I bid you to ride the crest of the wave; for when the wave of this dispensation moves on, it shall no longer be a choice. And therefore, fit into the cosmic scheme else jeopardize your mission and enter the possibility of becoming misfits insofar as the divine scheme is concerned.

There is a great panorama of life. This panorama unfolding is a giant mural that is in the grand hall of a magnificent building upon Sirius. Before you left that God Star aeons ago, you did study that mural and all of its portents for your life and the future. It does present on succeeding walls in other halls options and turning points, [showing] what shall be the outcome for those who choose a lesser path and what shall be the glory of the LORD upon those who continue to mount, to exert themselves, to move up on the high road, first through the foothills and the mountains and then on to the high places of solitude where only God and man are known.

Therefore, the consequences of all actions and turnings have been made known to all sons and daughters of God and even to the children of the light in their time and season. Each one in his own heart and time is a prophet of his destiny, for he does read the same record written in his inward parts. And therefore, the

---

*throughly; archaic: in a thorough manner

consequences of choices are always known and people know what they should have done even at the time they did not do it.

Therefore, beloved, there is indeed a tide in the affairs of men and angels. I come on that tide of light. I do even ensoul it.

May you contemplate how you can best deliver the message that has been brought to you. May you begin to write the story of your own conviction, your own conversion, your own inner knowing of your I AM Presence, your own confirmation of this path by your own telling and intelling of that Word that you have heard resounding from the altar, yet which also originates with your own Spirit of the I AM.

May you come to understand how you came to know the truth of the mysteries of God. Contemplate step-by-step what was required for you, and then you will understand what many souls need as points of transition and understanding and then a lessening of the intensity—a going within, a retreat perhaps, a coming to the ranch.

Yes, beloved, souls have need of the necessary food and light and contact with the stars and a great sense of love and belonging to the mystical body of God, which is in truth in heaven and on earth. By compassion and the flame of love, by identifying with individuals who are at a certain place on the Path, you may personally assemble those teachings that you know are pivotal as turning points in the way.

This is surely the hour for the perfecting of the soul as my apostle. I call you to this, beloved, because it is the hour. It is a cosmic moment when this opportunity is come.

I tell you, my beloved, that I would bring to you the understanding of the first resurrection.[4] The power of that resurrection, beloved, is given to you by the Spirit of the Resurrection when you use the mantra of the resurrection written down by your beloved Mark.

Take that mantra, together with my mantra—"I AM the resurrection and the life!"—and know that resurrection's flame must first burn in your heart congruent with the threefold flame and then [it must] ignite the cells and atoms that have become chalices for that wavelength, [thereby] igniting the chakras. Thus prepare this body temple [by resurrection's flame], by violet flame and by the pure water and the pure diet that you need.

Thus, beloved, understand that you may walk the earth in the Spirit of the Resurrection, but the true initiation of the resurrection will come to you only after you have sought and achieved that fusion [of your soul] with your Holy Christ Self and that fusion with myself. For when you contain the fires of the resurrection, beloved, you possess the power (given unto you as an endowment) whereby you may endow other parts of life with a semipermanent immortality, [albeit] that full immortality is not defined until the ascension is attained.

But, beloved, if you desire the ascension, you must seek the resurrection. And if you desire the resurrection and to walk the earth as a resurrected one, then, beloved, you must seek that fusion [of your heart with my heart].

I will tell you about [the soul] who achieves the fusion and another who does not. The one who achieves it has a sense of her own sinfulness, her own uncleanness and her own worthlessness in that lowly estate of the flesh yet, confident in noble purpose and design from Elohim, [she] does embrace the true identity of self and does break the shackles and the barriers and the confinements and the prison house of the psychology of the lower self.

[She] does seek to enter in, does weave the wedding garment, does perfect that seamless garment day by day, does remember that the manifestation, though it may be in the lowly estate of the flesh, yet contains that pearl, yet contains the fire; and therefore [she] does amplify that fire, makes no pretense at being perfect but understands that I AM the All and that [I AM the] perfection in her—that the lesser vessel is the nothing while I AM the All.

I have given this teaching to Catherine[5] and other saints. Those who have truly understood it have not felt debased when they acknowledged that they were the nothing and that I, the Christ in them, was the All. For they understood the process of displacement, the process of transmutation; and therefore [they] could come into the dignity and the integrity of the son, the daughter of God.

These are they who have received the washing of the feet and the cleansing of the blood. These are they who enter into that fusion by adoration, by love, by tears and by washing my feet with those tears and with the hair.[6]

Beloved ones, I tell you, the one who does not enter in is the one who trots about with the self-image that the definition of chela is perfection. But [in that one's mind] the quality of perfection is not the perfecting of the heart but the perfecting of performance, the perfecting of movement, the perfecting of speech.

Now, if this [perfecting of modes] were done to the glory of God and [according] to the true inner and deep understanding of the indwelling light, it would be a worthy goal. But those of whom I speak are those who come and go like martinets, even marionettes; and therefore stiff, stiff-jointed, stiffed in their mentality, they march about with a sense of spiritual pride, which they ignore that they have at all. They have no sense that they have missed the point and they cannot get through the eye of the needle any more than the camel can pass through....[7]

Let those chelas who are imitating the fantasy of the fallen ones and the ways of mechanization man cease to do so! Let those who admire the world and its levels of a material perfection remember that [the worldly] have not entered in, lo, in aeons! Yet they may perform well. They may be thought well of. They may appear to have genius. But where genius leaves off, beloved, *there* is the mind of Christ and many do not have it.

May you understand that noncommunication is a sign of the suppression of the Word itself and [of] the denial of that Word. Noncommunication of the truth, of the details necessary to move on in life and to make an organization run. Noncommunication with the heart of the ascended masters, with loved ones, with friend or stranger or with the messenger.

This noncommunication, beloved, indicates that there is no tie, there is a cutoff. And in that state of consciousness individuals think that salvation may be won by moving about in a robotic

manner; and [then] they become angry when, though they may
be robotically perfect, they have failed to please their God. Such
was the consciousness of Cain, and his offering was rejected.[8]

I find it necessary to speak this message to all who will come
to this place on the Path where they must make the effort in the
full fervor of the fire of the heart to transcend that former state
of the condition of *Homo sapiens* and enter in to the *true* walk,
the *inner* walk with God—moving from the known quantity of
the mechanics of a mechanical creation to the unknown realms
of the free form and the absolute God-freedom of the electron
itself that is the sign of the son of God who is never out of alignment with God's will or geometry and yet is ever new, ever creative, ever approaching the same equation with new input and
new energy and moving on with the cycles [of God's perfection,
not man's]!

For that one knows that nothing can ever be the same as [it
was] yesterday. Yesterday is not good enough, for the earth and
the entire galaxy have moved on at tremendous speeds into new
dimensions, wavelengths, timetables, options.

Thus, beloved, know the signs! Follow your beloved Melchior[9] and understand that in many instances astrology does tell
you the limits to as well as the unlimited potential for freedom of
creative action. See to it that you are in attunement [with the ebb
and flow of cycles] and that you ride the crest of this wave!

**I am Jesus, your Lord. I have come to call you to be my shep-
herds. I have come to compel you![10] I have come to warn you
that you who have not studied my Calls as they have been
released in cycles of dictations may come to this place [of my
present Call] where you consider yourself not ready.**

**Beloved, that is not an acceptable state of consciousness. If
you are not ready, you must get ready in the next five minutes!
Do you understand?**

You must make that five minutes five hundred or five thousand years but you must decide that there is a coiled spring in
your causal body that can be unleashed as soon as you will
declare:

> *There is no more night here!*
> For I AM the manifestation of that Holy City where
>   I AM!
> And I do not procrastinate my union with my God
> Or with that City [Foursquare]
> Or with my Christ or with my Divine Mother.
> I enter the Spirit of the Resurrection now!
> And if in my tardiness and in my dalliance
> My entering in may cause me some pain,
> Then I welcome it!
> For I understand that if I would be ready,
> Then the spirit that is anti the living Christ in me
> Must be broken!

Blessed ones, the times and the cycles come again and again but they are never the same. We have spoken and spoken again. The reward for our speaking must be with us and in hand. And if you would tie yourself to that moving star of destiny above you, then you must do it quickly. For the stars of destiny move on. They are bright in the heavens in this moment, but there may come a period in the earth when the earth itself should go through the dark night of the Spirit when you will not see the star. You will see it only in the memory of God.

Understand this principle and understand that there is indeed an urgency. There *is* a warning and things are brewing in the earth. And all that I can tell you of prophecy in this hour is that when things happen in the earth, from this day forward they will happen swiftly and suddenly. And all of your preparation will have had to have preceded those events, for there will be no time to prepare or to react but only to be.[11]

Be, then, in the heart of the Buddha, in the stupa of the Buddha. Make your own causal body of light and your aura that haven, that resting place, that place of samadhi and [that place of] the invocation of the Word, its intonation in the sound of the Om. May you contain in your space the house of the Buddha.

What do I say? I say, let the aura be expanded! Let it be increased by the fire of the Kundalini, by the fire of the chakras!

Use the fire you have while you have that light! Expand the dimensions of your auric field so that you do contain the whole house of the Buddha where you are and so that in that canopy and forcefield of light there may enter lesser souls from various planes who may be shielded in the day of the LORD's appearing.[12]

For in the day of the LORD there is a tremendous light and cosmic burst of energy, and it is for the annihilation of the [mechanization-man] misusers of the light. And it is for the clearing of the entire material cosmos for the descent of the Buddhas and bodhisattvas of Maitreya, of Gautama, of Sanat Kumara and of myself.

Yes, beloved, I come to you now as you see me in the posture of my Buddhahood[13]—that you might see about me and in me those rings of light and that presence that you think of when you think of Lord Gautama. I reveal myself to you, then, in the Buddhic presence that you might hold that image of me, for those of the Christian world will not. And therefore there must be some who understand the meaning of my Buddhahood. There must be some who aspire to be bodhisattvas that they might be linked to the layers of my causal body that are my Buddha manifestation.

Therefore know the path of the bodhisattva. Know the sweetness and the compassion, the peace, the fierceness, the strength, the *virya!*[14] Know the wisdom. Know the ability to rule the city because you rule yourself.[15] Know the geometry of God and expand [your soul-awareness] into it as a Michelangelo.

Understand that you can know many things beyond what happens to be in your outer [conscious] mind. Yes, you can contact the level of genius. And if you do not have [that level of genius developed in your four lower bodies], then let the violet flame consume all records of anger and hatred and fear [that prevent its development]! For these [vibrations], beloved, do surely consume the fineness [and the refinement] of the mind of God within you—that piercing quality, that manifestation [of needlelike rays] that is able to probe a cosmos and bring back discovery and new dimensions of thought.

You have been limited by fallen ones and by yourselves. No longer accept the limited condition! You need not. For when you step forth from this body you wear, when the day comes that you are called to enter into the octaves of light and in the twinkling of an eye you have all knowledge of all things in God, your I AM Presence, you will say to yourself:

"I should have made more fervent fiats to break this sound and mental barrier that existed around me as iron bands! I could have walked the earth in a greater fullness of my Christhood had I only recognized that the laws were there to be applied and the call was there to be given. And therefore I could have been more [the manifestation] of God if I had only transcended the density of the lesser self."

You will wish that you had embodied more of God when there is no longer opportunity, for you shall have been called to the resurrection and the ascension.

Thus, beloved, I bid you this greeting and this message in this hour that you might understand once and for all that heaven is ready to bestow upon you truly bowers of loveliness in an eternal springtime. If you can think of the most beautiful day of spring [you can imagine] and the songs of the birds and the blossoms and the sun in the heavens and all of the joy of nature, think, then, of the etheric octave.

Think, then, of that opportunity that you do have in this hour. Think, then, of walking and talking with me. Think of what we must do to gather these souls of light. Think of it, beloved, for they are called and they are touched.

Now I say, *please* gather them! *Please* feed my sheep! For it is the law of the cosmos that those in this octave must do the gathering. I can do all things and many things for you and through you but you and only you can feed my sheep.[16]

Let us take stock, then, each one, in this hour. Let there be the rejection of negatives as limitations instead of in the sense of the condemnation of sin. Simply look at that which limits you and see how it is a creation of the mind or other minds and of programming. I, Jesus, say to you, you are with God and in God the Limitless One. May you discover this and become an avatar. [17]

Yes, I said "become." For the process of becoming is the realization in outer manifestation of that which is, was and ever shall be your true [inner] God-manifestation. Therefore I have unveiled many levels of my Christhood and [my] Buddhahood and my Godhood along life's way, and this is the nature of the grand evolutionary spiral of life throughout a cosmos.

Let the mechanization-man concept of religion tell you that Christ simply is and I will say that even the I AM THAT I AM is not simply that which is. For the I AM THAT I AM is ever moving, and even as I speak the Word, the I AM THAT I AM has transformed itself a million times and released all manner of light rays [and spirals of the mind of God]. There is nothing but progressive revelation and [progressive] realization of God where you are.

Do not impede the process, beloved, and do not let yourself calcify in a certain mold from now until the hour of your victory.[18] For if you do, beloved, you may not have the victory over death and hell; for calcification is the signal and the sign that you have sealed yourself at a certain level. All who do this enter the spiral of mortality—of disintegration, disease and death.

Therefore know this, that your challenge as a son of God, *which you are,* is to move on in the creative spirals of being every single day and to not accept the defeats of yesterday or its limitations as having any power over the sun at dawn, the sun of your Christ Self, which rises every day from dawn to the zenith of the heavens, whereupon you cry out:

> O LORD, I AM THAT I AM
> The fullness of thy resurrection and thy life
>   within me this day!
> And I AM alive forevermore in thee
> And in the Central Sun and in the earth!
> Behold, I AM with Lanello:
> Everywhere in the consciousness of God!

I bid you a joyous Christ Mass, ever unfolding unto the fullness of the Christ in you, Amen. 🌸

December 25, 1990
Christmas Day
Royal Teton Ranch
Park County, Montana

I am that Christ! You are that Christ-potential emerging now into the fullness of your mission. JESUS

Jesus' first Call to us in this dictation is to "become agents of the Cosmic Christ." As the ascended master who holds the office of Cosmic Christ, Lord Maitreya teaches us the same path of individual Christhood that he taught Jesus more than two thousand years ago.

Jesus is one with the heart of his guru, Maitreya, and he calls us to also enter into that oneness. Maitreya, as Jesus' guru, provides a thread of contact to Jesus' heart. We, as disciples of the master Jesus, receive in turn that thread from Jesus' heart, and, thus, we may also become representatives of Maitreya.

Jesus calls us to hold the balance for all untoward conditions in the earth so that the lightbearers might have the opportunity to enter in. What does "holding the balance" mean?

It means holding a light in the earth. As we intensify and expand our threefold flame and embody more of the Christ light, this light can sustain a world. As Jesus declared, "I am the light of the World,"[19] so he calls us to be that light today. This is the real meaning of being a Keeper of the Flame.

It also means bearing a certain weight of world karma. Jesus has asked us to take back to ourselves the karma he has borne for us for two thousand years. He bore this karma so we would have an opportunity to walk the spiritual path and come to the place where we would be able to balance that karma and not fall under its weight. We also have the opportunity to take on a portion of karma that is not our own so that others might have renewed opportunity to enter in. In order to do this, we must have a momentum of light that is great enough to bear this weight.

"The Perfecting of the Soul as My Apostle"

In a previous dictation, Jesus called us to be his disciples—to study his teachings and to enter into a direct relationship with him. Now he is calling us to apostleship—to take what we have internalized of his path and teaching and go out into the world as his representative to share that teaching with others.

He tells us that we need to prepare for this mission, and the mission is not only to deliver the teachings, but also "to comfort, to counsel, to admonish, to raise up and to carry that child-man." An intellectual knowing or impartation of the teachings clearly will not suffice for such a mission. It is the teaching that we can apply and make real in our lives that can make the difference for others.

Jesus asks us to write the story of our own conviction, our conversion and our own confirmation of the Path. If we speak from the power of our own experience, then what we have to say will reach our audience. This is why it was said of Jesus that he spoke "as one having authority,"[20] and not as the scribes, who knew the words of scripture but had not internalized the Word.

The Mantle of Apostle

Jesus Calls us all to be his apostles, but it is up to each of us to answer the call and claim that office. And as we take up the office, we also receive the mantle associated with it. A *mantle* is a cloak of light, a grid or a forcefield of light that is given to an individual who is sponsored by the Great White Brotherhood or by an ascended master. Worn at inner levels, the mantle contains specific keys that are a formula of light, hieroglyphs of the Spirit—a quality of light necessary to fulfill the office.

The apostle Paul, who was a great preacher of the Word of Christ and who is now the ascended master Hilarion, explains that God will place the mantle of apostle upon us if we do our part: "The instrument of hierarchy is a very tender instrument. And if you do not neglect the requirements of the service, you will find that God will come into you and live through you, and you will feel the broad shoulders and the robe of the apostle upon you. You will feel the mantle of Elijah or Elisha drop upon your shoulders.[21] You will hold your head high because you stand where the Lord stands."[22]

The life of Saint Paul is a tremendous example of the path of apostleship. We see how a single individual, one with the Lord and empowered by the Holy Spirit, can indeed change the world. Hilarion asks us to study the example of Paul and the apostles as part of our own preparation to be apostles of Jesus Christ. "Now then, beloved, you ought to know by heart the Book of Acts, chapter by chapter, for then you will know and believe that the acts of the apostles may be repeated by you today."[23]

Hilarion offers us his assistance and his mantle of apostle if we will take the first steps: "I bring that empowerment, beloved, for my heart has been kissed by my Saviour. And I am bonded to him, and I would assist you in the bonding of your souls to your Holy Christ Self through Jesus Christ.

"And I offer you my heart. I offer you my mantle. I offer you the staff of the Lord this day if you will but place yourself on that path of being tutored and God-taught, that you may indeed know the scriptures and impart them by the Holy Spirit.... My beloved, it is this gospel of salvation that must be preached in every nation before the end shall come[24]—the end of opportunity for souls of light to be bonded to their Lord. Therefore, understand that many have thought that it is the orthodox Christian message that had to be preached in every nation, but I tell you: it is the true mysteries of Jesus Christ that must be preached."[25]

The Resurrection Flame

Jesus then asks us to invoke the resurrection flame so that we can walk the earth bearing the power of that flame. Gautama Buddha speaks of the tremendous effect the resurrection flame can have on the planet and why it is so essential that we strive to prepare ourselves vibrationally to be at the level of this flame as it descends:

"I come in the hour when resurrection's fires can no longer be withheld: the power of the resurrection flame can no longer be withheld from the planetary body, beloved. And the effect of this flame upon the environment where it descends may be comparable to the energy released in the splitting of the atom.

"By resurrection's flame not only was the stone rolled away, but, beloved, boulders were cleaved asunder, the mountains moved, the thunder and the lightning descended; and that which was mortal was set aside as Jesus walked the earth to complete his life span and service, fully the embodiment of the Spirit of the Resurrection. The blessed one, as the Son of man, did demonstrate what must be demonstrated by the evolutions of the planet in this hour.

"Thus, beloved, know that such unpreparedness as you see on the part of the vast majority of the people of earth for the resurrection experience may itself be the cause of cataclysm or war or turmoil or disease outcropping when resurrection's fires are released. Understand that the nonpreparedness of humanity at the conclusion of 25,800 years of cycles of the coming of the Buddhas and the bodhisattvas must now be dealt with.

"It is not that calamity may not be postponed. *It is that the resurrection may not be postponed!* And the Second Coming of Maitreya and of Jesus Christ will be in the hearts of all.

"Blessed ones, the resurrection cannot save that which does not present itself vibrationally as the equivalency of the resurrection. You must provide the negative polarity, the Omega, for the positive polarity, the Alpha, of the resurrection flame. And, thus, you will be fused to Christ when that resurrection fire does descend."[26]

Jesus explains that while the fullness of the resurrection experience comes as a definite initiation on the Path, we are called to walk the earth now with a portion of that flame, and we can experience that flame as we use the mantras that invoke it. (See Spiritual Exercises.)

The Call to "Be My Shepherds"

Jesus' third Call in this dictation is to be his shepherds. He understands the human condition, and he knows that we might consider that we are not ready for this calling. But he will not allow us to use this as an excuse. He says that we must be ready "in the next five minutes," and that in those five minutes we can accomplish the preparation that would have taken five hundred or five thousand years. (How many lifetimes have we delayed answering the call of the Master?)

Jesus says this miracle can be accomplished if we have the determination and make the fiat for the light to descend from our causal body. This light can instantly transform us. He says that there is an urgency, and it is important that we catch this cycle as there may be a time in the earth when "there will be no time to prepare or to react but only to be."

Then the Master goes on to plead: "Now I say, please gather them! Please feed my sheep! For it is the law of the cosmos that those in this octave must do the gathering. I can do all things and many things for you and through you, but you and only you can feed my sheep."

Here is one key from Jesus on being a shepherd: "Know, then, beloved, that to be a good shepherd is to give the word of kindness and compassion again and again. Whether you journey to lower levels of the astral plane with Archangel Michael or to the highest levels of the etheric plane, remember to give kindness to all. For you never know when those who have strayed far from the center of Being, under the influence of black magicians and fallen angels, will melt by the tenderness of your heart that says, 'No matter how filthy or dark this one has become or how great his wrongs have been, I will give the word of kindness.' "[27]

Each of us needs a personal strategy on how we will fulfill Jesus' Calls. You can be a shepherd if you are willing to embody a morsel of the Master's teaching and give it heart-to-heart to someone. Watch as they receive this Truth, and see how the light of the Master can transform a life.

SPIRITUAL EXERCISES

Hold the Balance in the Earth

Take some time to consider the following questions:
- What does it mean to you to hold the balance in the earth "for all conditions untoward you observe and some you do not"?
- How can you hold this balance more effectively?

A Dispensation from the Master

As a grace and a blessing, Jesus gives us the following dispensation in this dictation: "I am with you in this hour by the magnet of love of the Great Central Sun. I demagnetize from you all those things of which you desire to be delivered, those things that you are through with, thoroughly so.

"Yes, beloved, if you can say to this or that state of consciousness, 'Have done with it! I want it no longer!' and mean it with the fire of your heart, I will take it this day. Surely I shall. For the night is o'er, the day is come and it is the day of gladness of the Christ's descent into your temple."

Even if you were not present when this dictation was originally delivered, you can ask Jesus for this dispensation today. If it is God's will, he will grant your request.

Write Your Personal Story

Respond to Jesus' request and write the story of your personal conviction, your conversion and your confirmation of the Path:

"May you contemplate how you can best deliver the message that has been brought to you. May you begin to write the story of your own conviction, your own conversion, your own inner knowing of your I AM Presence, your own confirmation of this path by your own telling and intelling of that Word that you have heard resounding from the altar, yet which also originates with your own Spirit of the I AM.

"May you come to understand how you came to know the

truth of the mysteries of God. Contemplate step-by-step what was required for you, and then you will understand what many souls need as points of transition and understanding."

Give the Mantras to the Resurrection Flame

Jesus asks us to invoke the resurrection flame by using the resurrection mantras. You can give these mantras individually at any time during the day, or you can give the complete ritual outlined here. The messenger suggests giving this ritual for fifteen or thirty-three days for the resolution of personal and planetary problems.

RITUAL OF THE RESURRECTION FLAME

**The Disciple's Prayer
by Jesus the Christ**

There is no more night here!
For I AM the manifestation of that Holy City
    where I AM!
And I do not procrastinate my union with my God
Or with that City Foursquare
Or with my Christ or with my Divine Mother.
I enter the Spirit of the Resurrection now!
And if in my tardiness and in my dalliance
My entering in may cause me some pain,
Then I welcome it!
For I understand that if I would be ready,
Then the spirit that is anti the living Christ in me
    Must be broken!

**Beloved Flame of Resurrection
(written down by Mark L. Prophet)**

Beloved mighty victorious Presence of God, I AM in me, my very own beloved Holy Christ Self, and Holy Christ Selves of all mankind, by and through the magnetic power of the immortal victorious three-fold flame of love, wisdom, and power anchored within my heart, I AM invoking the flame of resurrection from the heart of God in the Great Central Sun, from beloved Alpha and Omega, beloved Jesus the Christ, beloved Mother Mary, beloved Archangel Gabriel and Uriel, the angels of the Resurrection Temple, beloved Lanello, the entire

Spirit of the Great White Brotherhood and the World Mother,
elemental life—fire, air, water and earth!

> Beloved flame of resurrection,
>   Blaze through me thy light always;
> Beloved flame, resuscitation,
>   Make my heart to sing thy praise.
>
> O blazing white Christ radiance
> Of God's own I AM fire,
> Expand thy blessed purity
> And free me from all wrong desire.
>
> Beloved flame of resurrection,
>   Rise and rise to love's great height;
> Blessed flame, regeneration,
>   Guide all men by thy great light.
>
> I AM, I AM, I AM thy chalice free
>   Through whose crystal substance clear
> All can see the Christ flame lily
>   Of eternity appear
>
> Blazing, blazing, blazing!
> Blazing, blazing, blazing!
> Blazing, blazing, blazing!

Transfiguring Affirmations
of Jesus the Christ

I AM THAT I AM
I AM the open door which no man can shut
I AM the light which lighteth every man that
  cometh into the world
I AM the way
I AM the truth
I AM the life
I AM the resurrection
I AM the ascension in the light
I AM the fulfillment of all my needs and
  requirements of the hour
I AM abundant supply poured out upon all life
I AM perfect sight and hearing
I AM the manifest perfection of being
I AM the illimitable light of God
  made manifest everywhere

I AM the light of the Holy of holies
I AM a son of God
I AM the light in the holy mountain of God

Resurrection

I AM the flame of resurrection
Blazing God's pure light through me.
Now I AM raising every atom,
From every shadow I AM free.

I AM the light of God's full Presence,
I AM living ever free.
Now the flame of life eternal
Rises up to victory.

Resurrection Mantra

I AM the resurrection and the life!

The Disciple's Affirmation
by Jesus the Christ

O LORD, I AM THAT I AM
The fullness of thy resurrection and thy life
    within me this day!
And I AM alive forevermore in thee
And in the Central Sun and in the earth!
Behold, I AM with Lanello:
Everywhere in the consciousness of God!

And in full faith I consciously accept this manifest, manifest, manifest! (3x) right here and now with full power, eternally sustained, all-powerfully active, ever expanding, and world enfolding until all are wholly ascended in the light and free! Beloved I AM! Beloved I AM! Beloved I AM!

FOR YOUR JOURNAL

How Will *You* Answer Jesus' Calls?

"Become agents of the Cosmic Christ... that the children of the light might enter into this sheepfold."

"I Call you to... the perfecting of the soul as my apostle."

"I have come to Call you to be my shepherds."

What do these Calls mean to me?

What will I do to answer these Calls?

CHAPTER 12

"Drink this cup of my Christhood!…
Be the instruments of my light… to the
youth of the entire world, to children
bruised and battered."

"See the great calling… to embody that
light, that I AM THAT I AM, that portion
of Christos that is yours to claim."

"Save the homeless and the street people
from that sense of abject self-negation.…
Be converted to serve those who sense
they are the poor in spirit."

Drink This Cup of My Christhood
Let Us Get On with the Science of Being!
The Quickening of the Heart

My Own and My Beloved,

I call you holy ones of God, for this is the nature—the true nature—of your soul. I descend into this city, consecrated to my Mother, to tear from you the veil,[1] that you might see face-to-face[2] and know your God.

I am Jesus, your brother, and truly I am Saviour, but I cannot save that which does not consider itself worthy to be saved. I speak to the soul, then, who may discover her worthiness in the mirror of that Christhood, which I bear:

Ye are all made in the image and likeness of God from the beginning. You may have sinned, beloved, but you are not forever "sinners."[3] You are ascending the cycles of being. You are destined for immortality. You are destined to shuffle off this mortal coil and enter the coils of ascension's flame!

Yes, my Magda* is with me and we are in the glory of the white-fire body. And we bring to this city and all servants of God within it truly the comprehension of the new heaven and the new earth.[4] You shall not all weep but you shall be transformed, and that transformation by the Holy Ghost can come upon you whenever you are truly ready to receive it.

Let the walls of doctrine come tumbling down! Enter ye into the gates of my heart, for it is my heart that is the open door whereby you enter in to the Holy of holies. Wash thy garments, O my beloved! Receive the Refiner's fire and be taken up now in that sense of the rapture of my Presence!

---

*Magda, now ascended, is the twin flame of Jesus. She was embodied as Mary Magdalene, and most recently as Aimee Semple McPherson.

My Presence is upon you all, each and every one. Yet each of you will appropriate my light as you are able to establish a sense of coequality with me from the beginning.

Are we not all born out of the same white-fire body of God? Is not the Logos, the living Word, the fount of creation?

I say to you, either you are sons and daughters of God or you are not. And if you are, and I say that you are, then dispense with the shrouds of death and hell put upon you for centuries of incarnations!

Rise in the mystery and the spiral of the resurrection flame! Rise in vibration and in consciousness and in oneness and claim your sonship! And then go forth to prove it, to set the example. Be willing to retrace your footsteps, karmic footsteps, one by one, putting off the skeins of a lesser self and internalizing that Word.

To this end was I born and for this cause came I into the world: to give you the great mystery of the Christos. Yet they have taken away that mighty presence.

O beloved, receive Communion as my Body and my Blood in this hour. This is the Alpha-to-Omega, for I have said it:

"I AM Alpha and Omega, the beginning and the ending."[5] Therefore I am one in you in the beginning and the ending of the cycles of the Father and the Mother. I am there for the re-creation of your worlds. I am there for the inner resolution. I am come to make you whole.

Resist not your wholeness! Were there not a point of light in you from the beginning, there would be no point from which that wholeness could be expanded. Thus, as the seed of God in man does grow and does mature and bring forth the newborn babe, so the seed of light does contain the whole cosmos of thy becoming.

Is not Nature thy teacher, O beloved ones, in this regard? Therefore every tree does come forth from its seed after its own kind[6] in its own time.

Thus your soul is ready, beloved, but the overlay of the intellectual mind, the doubting mind, the fearful mind does place that wall between you and me. And I, beloved, must leave to your free will the taking down of that wall. But I establish a quickening in your heart whereby faith might be born in you to know that God has also endowed you with eternal life.

Let us get on with the science of being! Let us get on with our reason for being and let us know that in a state of sin and the sense of sin, struggle and the sense of struggle, there is not the vessel that we need upon earth to carry the light to neutralize the momentums of darkness moving in the earth.

Truly the Divine Mother does weep for her own on the battle-ground of life. Truly, beloved, let the light descend! Let it be directed into the Middle East for the consuming of ages-old conflict!

Were the war to end tomorrow, the war would continue, beloved, as Arabs and Jews continue to dispute land occupation, matters of religion, matters of supply and economics.

Blessed hearts, these things ought not to be! Yet the entrenched divisions between these peoples have come down for centuries and millennia as they have reincarnated again and again, only to not let go of the causes of their original division.

Now I come. I come knocking upon the door of each and every one. I come again with my flame, the all-consuming flame of divine love. I come to heal the hurt and the sense of vengeance.

Yet, beloved, understand that the response of free will is needed. It is a requirement. As God has endowed all of his creatures with free will, so they must exercise that free will to receive the transfer of light that can indeed in the twinkling of an eye[7] bring about the healing of ancient records.

Thus, beloved, some cry out in anger against God, "Why does God allow it?" God [allows it because he has first] allowed free will. And the rest is the responsibility of man. To understand this is to begin the true path of a cosmic accountability for all of your foot-steps day by day.

I come to tell you that my teachings were indeed lost and that they are being restored today. It is almost too late, beloved, for so much has been lost over the centuries and so much karma has been made by the sins [of omission], as has been discussed this evening.

Thus, beloved hearts, may you become shining ones! May you embody the light and may your light so shine[8] that they will know that this inner light is truly the transfer from my heart, is truly the sign that you are disciples indeed[9] and that all can so become and none, not even the hardened sinner, is left aside. All can enter in [if they repent of their deeds].

But, beloved, if you cannot see and accept my Christhood, how can you see and accept your own? Even those who can see my Presence cannot accept that this Presence is also the Presence of God with them and that this is the heart and reason of my coming. This, then, is the lie of division[—that the Christ can be and is in Jesus, but that the Christ cannot be and is not in you].*

The quickening [of the heart], beloved ones, [were it to take place] in the millions of planet earth who are already servants of God, already of the faith, could bring about a tremendous turning of worlds, even the healing of the economy, even a mitigation of those things projected upon this decade of which you have been taught.

A change in consciousness upon earth by the simple application of the teachings I have brought would bring about the healing of the nations and a liberation of all the churches.

Truly I come, even burdened in this hour to see how the children of light on every continent and in every faith have been deprived of my offering of the cup of Selfhood.

Drink this cup of my Christhood! Drink ye all of it [10] and fear not to enter in to the mystical union with your God.

Ye are of the Father-Mother, who love you with a profound love, who do not condemn you, who do not call you "sinners" but call you Home. "Come Home, our children!" they say. And I bring their message.

O cherished ones, ye who are loved, be not dismayed by the condemnation of the world! For I, Jesus, have overcome the world[11] and you shall also. May you receive the mantras of the violet flame and know the supreme worth of giving unto God the joy of your

---

*This lie sets up a division between you and Jesus and you and God. The Holy Christ Self as Mediator, as point of Reality in you, is the very key to your oneness with God and Jesus and the Holy Spirit. Likewise, Jesus the Christ is the key to your fusion with your Holy Christ Self and to your soul's union with God.

heart and voice in invocation and prayer. This weaves the connection between God and man and man and God. And the soul is weaving her wedding garment through prayer, through the Hail "Ma-Ray."

Blessed hearts, drink of this cup of my Selfhood and recognize the God-potential in yourself and everyone whom you meet and see how the world takes on the sense of the rapture of God's holiness.

O beloved, let us turn around an age! Let us see the darkness be consumed by the sacred fire of our love! Truly we are one in the living flame of love.

I direct my heart's light to the youth of the entire world, to children bruised and battered. I direct light to them. Will you be the instruments of my light to them, God's hands and feet and hearts extended to save the children? to save them from reaching that point where they become a part of the many who partake of drugs and marijuana and of unwholesome substances?

Be my hands and feet, O beloved! Go for me and awaken them, quicken them, speak to them! As I spoke with a loud voice, "Lazarus, come forth![12] so I speak to the souls of the youth:

"I have a path and I would take you on that path to reunion with God. I am not removed from you. I, too, knew childhood and youth midst adversity and challenges untold. My love is with you, each and every one."

O parents and teachers and wise ones among you—all of you, I say—go after the youth who have been betrayed! They are the ones who are crucified upon the cross this day and the Christ in them is crucified. And they are not fed the bread of life, they are not fed therefore that body and blood of my teaching whereby in the assimilation process they may come to understand themselves, too, as extensions of the Most High.

Do you not see how the forces of death and hell concentrate on the destruction of the youth and how the people are hypnotized to neglect them, to not give to them the true teaching and a reason for living instead of dying?

There is a psychological suicide and a spiritual suicide that precedes the destruction of the body day by day and drop by drop by drugs intaken. Pray for them! Dedicate prayer vigils in their behalf. Go after and save that which is lost![13]

Truly I did declare, "I AM the light of the world!"[14] But I also said, "Ye are the light of the world. A city that is set on an hill cannot be hid."[15] So long as I AM in the world, I AM the light of the world, beloved, but I am no longer of this world and therefore you, my disciples, [who are in this world,] must embody that light, that I AM THAT I AM, that portion of Christos that is yours to claim.

See the great calling and see how the doctrines of sin and the sense of sin have denied most of the people of this planet the sense of self-worth [they need] to go forth in my name. Let all of this, as with the sound of the seven archangels and the hosts of the LORD, be stripped from those who deep within their hearts know that God is real and is real in them.

Save the homeless and the street people from that sense of abject self-negation. No one has told them that they are worthy to follow me in the resurrection. Their tenure upon earth wanes. What will happen to those souls as they depart this life?—a life that has been ended in the uselessness, the non-will, the non-sense of being of those who vegetate in the streets of the cities of the world.

Reach out, beloved, and my hand shall reach out through you! Be converted this night to serve those who sense they are the poor in spirit and are ready to become the rich in spirit.

I claim you as apostles of Christ, as revolutionaries who shall go forth to establish my revolution for woman—archetypal Woman who does bring forth the Manchild, the Woman in each of you that does give birth to the Christ of the heart.

Ye are all feminine in nature and all masculine. Weigh, then, the issues of life and death and the hereafter and go forth in my name and service. I will be with you, and where two or more gather[16] you will see the multiplication of your forces by my Presence.

I am anchoring a light in this city for the reversing of the spirals of violence, of crime, of teenagers lost in street battles when they could be walking the path of the high Himalayas and could know the Great Lights of all centuries of East and West.

Where are the role models for them? Who will teach them that

I have established the Way? Who will go and do likewise in the imitation of my heart's love and therefore stand in the cities and in the country and everywhere in the highways of life as my representative, my disciple?

I pray you will say, "We will!" my beloved.

["We will!"]

In this hour, then, I seal you in the power of the Trinity, in the power of the Mother. And as Above, so below, I bring the higher and the lower self into greater proximity by my intercession and my mediatorship.

In the eternal love of our Father-Mother God, I, Jesus, bow to their light within you. 🍇

February 15, 1991
Pasadena Convention Center
Los Angeles, California

O cherished ones, ye who are loved, be not dismayed by the condemnation of the world! For I, Jesus, have overcome the world and you shall also.

One of the most important messages in this dictation is how "the doctrines of sin and the sense of sin have denied most people of this planet the sense of self-worth" to be able to receive the true message of Jesus Christ—that the Christ in Jesus is the same Christ that lives in all of us. A sense of unworthiness can prevent us from receiving Jesus or our own Christ Self.

As we seek to walk the path with Jesus, it is very important to know the difference between unworthiness and humility. In humility we surrender the lesser self and allow God to enter in. In unworthiness we identify with the lesser self and keep God out. Mother Mary speaks about the consequences of accepting the limitation of unworthiness:

"Your assessment of yourself defines and limits your self-expression. If you think you are of no more worth than a certain level, then you will not perform above that level; for, should you do so, all of the theories of the carnal mind should crumble, and you should find yourself as the living Christ. Do you see, beloved? When you entertain any sense of worthlessness whatsoever, or unworthiness, then that is the highest level of expression you reach. And you determine this each day.

"Because you have said to yourself, 'I am not worthy to be that Christ, I am not worthy to be one with Mother Mary,' you act the part, and you have placed that ceiling above you. Well, beloved ones, that ceiling does not stay put. Once it was twelve feet high, then it was nine, then it was seven. And pretty soon, if you are going to stay in that box of worthlessness, you will find that the room will shrink, and you will know the shrinking-man, the shrinking-woman syndrome.[17]

"Do you understand what I am saying, beloved? That which

ceases to grow will cease to be. And, therefore, if you allow these conditions and matrices of negativity to remain much longer, you will find that they will become the law of your life, and you will have a tremendous struggle getting out of them. If you should ever be cut off, by a path of initiation or karma or whatever, from the direct contact with our Brotherhood through the messenger or through your own God Presence, then you will know just what an opportunity you have lost."[18]

Mother Mary desires us to realize that it is God in us who is worthy, not the dweller-on-the-threshold or our ego self. If we have feelings of unworthiness, they are of our human self, not our Real Self. If you feel stuck with these limiting thoughts and feelings, the first step is to recognize them for what they are. Ask the masters for help and seek therapy to get to the cause and core of the problem and find out why you identify with your low self-esteem.

In *Messages from Heaven*, a soul who has newly made the transition to the etheric retreats of the Brotherhood gives his perspective on the problem of unworthiness:

"Unworthiness that will not go away has usually been present for more than one lifetime. We have all performed acts that were not worthy of God or we would not still be in embodiment. Some people fear being whole. If they truly let go of their sense of unworthiness, they would have to acknowledge their wholeness in Christ.

"Unworthiness creates a tremendous block between the individual and the fulfillment of his divine plan. When you hold on to the unworthiness, it is as if you are saying, 'I believe my dweller (the synthetic self or carnal mind) more than my Holy Christ Self.' It is also a denial of divine justice. Trust that you will be given opportunities to work out any violation of God's laws. You do not need to impose a life sentence on yourself. Ask yourself: Why am I unwilling to forgive myself and trust in divine justice?"[19]

Feelings of guilt, shame and a sense of unworthiness because we have sinned and made negative karma can lead to low self-esteem. It is very important to work on this, because if we hold this image of ourselves (consciously or subconsciously), it can keep us locked in negative habit patterns and continually revolving our past mistakes. Even when we ask God for forgiveness, negative thoughts and feelings about ourselves may not allow us to receive his forgiveness and the healing that comes with it. We can get stuck in a rut that can prevent us from internalizing the Word and experiencing the divine love that Jesus so desires to give us.

Save the Children and Youth

Jesus' first Call is: "Drink this cup of my Christhood.... Be the instruments of my heart's light... to the youth of the entire world, to children bruised and battered." Even as Jesus Calls us, he reassures us: "Drink ye all of it and fear not to enter into the mystical union with your God."

We realize that in order to be effective instruments of Jesus' light to the children and youth, we must rid ourselves of our fears that we are unequal to this task. Negative states of consciousness prevent us from taking action and being the masters' hands and feet for the rescue of souls. We must recognize our God-potential and the divine potential in everyone we meet if we are to help them realize that potential.

The plight of the youth of the world is something we see in the news almost every day. Whether it is drug addiction, abuse, teen pregnancies or children being abandoned in Africa due to a high percentage of parents dying of AIDS, our children and youth are sounding an alarm and crying out for help.

Jesus asks us, "Don't you see that the forces of death and hell concentrate on the destruction of the youth and how the people are hypnotized to neglect them, to not give them the true teaching and a reason for living instead of dying?"

The Elohim Astrea speaks of the peril of the youth and the necessity of our extending ourselves to help them: "I tell you again as you have heard it before, *none* are so crucified upon earth in this day as the little children! Little children in every nation—*they* are bereft of the true love of the living Christ and the Divine Mother.

"Feed them! Console them! Teach them! Teach them how to read and write. Teach them the inner sensitivities of the heart. Teach them to know angels and elementals—gnomes, salamanders, undines, sylphs—all those who service the garden of God upon earth. Teach children to be sensitive to Mother Earth, to balance their bodies, to tie into their intuitive faculties in order that they might be the full expression of the Mother.

"Guard them, beloved. Their inner sight is assaulted through television. Their bodies are destroyed by a high content of sugar and caffeine in the drinks that they drink.

"O blessed ones, without the strength of a balanced physical body strengthening the mind, where shall the chalice of that child appear when he comes to his teenage years and later on? If the body has not the strength and the balance, the soul's option for Christhood may be lost for an entire lifetime.

"Take care of these little ones. They are your leaders and your fathers and mothers of tomorrow. O feed my sheep, these souls who come trustingly. Yet parents and teachers often know not what they do in not dealing with them as they should."[20]

The dark force concentrates on destroying our children and youth because they have the pure light of God and are destined to take their rightful places and lead us into the golden age of Aquarius. Another more insidious reason is that fallen angels need their light to sustain themselves. These fallen ones have no light of their own because they rebelled against God and chose to cut themselves off from him. Now, they take God's light from our children by involving them in drugs, rock music, alcohol and early sexual encounters.

As well as taking practical steps to help our children and youth, Jesus begs us to pray for our young people and dedicate prayer vigils on their behalf. They need to have a vision of who they are in God and to be inspired to become all God intends them to be.

Embody That Light

The second Call from the heart of beloved Jesus is "to embody that light, that I AM THAT I AM, that portion of Chris-

tos that is yours to claim." Again, in order to receive this great
calling, we must feel worthy enough to claim it. If we could just
remember to keep firmly fixed in our minds and hearts that it is
"God in me" who is worthy and keep our eyes focused on our
Real Self and our mighty I AM Presence, we would make accelerated progress. This process is simple, but we know that in
practice it is difficult to stay focused and live in the higher consciousness. In order to achieve a sustained contact with our
Higher Self, we must be willing to set aside time daily and build
a momentum in doing it.

The masters have told us that they can do nothing in the
physical octave without our prayers and invocations and our
willingness to go forth and fulfill their direction according to
God's will. We are indispensable to the heavenly hosts in their
efforts to accomplish God's work in the earth.

Save the Homeless and the Street People

The last Call in this message is: "Save the homeless and the
street people from that sense of abject self-negation.... Be converted to serve those who sense they are the poor in spirit."

Jesus is asking us not only to deal with our own sense of
unworthiness, but also to rescue others who are even more burdened than we are with this state of consciousness. He calls us
not just to provide physical help, but to offer the spiritual solution. Jesus desires that we go tell the homeless and the street people that they are worthy to follow him in the resurrection. By our
very service to those who are less fortunate, we may even be
healed of our own sense of unworthiness.

The ascended masters have always encouraged us to minister to life wherever we find ourselves. The messenger gives the
following advice to those who would answer this Call of Jesus:

"Maybe take a day out of your month or a day out of every
two months and go and work with people who are working with
the homeless and the street people. Experience life at all levels,
and learn how to reach life at all levels. And recognize when
you're dealing with street people, you're dealing with people

with enormous depression and an absence of will to live in the mainstream.

"To really help them, once you have physically gone to comfort them personally, you have to go home and go into your closet, and you have to pray and give the decree to Astrea for them, to cut them free from these entities of depression and the burdens that are on their souls. You can't save people with physical, human kindness alone. It requires efficacious, fervent prayer."[21]

Jesus, through us, wishes to embrace the homeless and the street people all over the world. In a dictation delivered in South America, Saint Germain spoke of our responsibility to care for the homeless in those nations, especially the children. He said: "I tell you that among these children you will come across advanced souls in the guise of beggars. Truly, you never know when you may be turning away a Christ Child. But if you care for all children without discrimination, you shall not miss a single soul who has the potential to contribute mightily to the flourishing of this civilization.

"Watered with love and nourished with wisdom, these precious flowers of God's heart will know that you have empowered them with God's grace—so much so that they will carry their communities and their countries to new levels of opportunity for all. No, you must not neglect the children! For they are your most priceless heritage. And you must acknowledge that they are the hope of the future."[22]

Astrea and Her Circle and Sword of Blue Flame

Purity and Astrea are the Elohim of the fourth ray of purity. Astrea explains that Jesus called upon her in his healing work: "I am reminded now... of the episode that occurred at the time of Jesus when the young man lay on the ground frothing at the mouth. The disciples had attempted, again and again, to cast out the demon from that boy, and I tell you they exerted themselves to the fullest. But they lacked the faith, and they lacked the knowledge of our octave of light.

"If my cosmic circle and sword of blue flame had been invoked around that boy by any one of those disciples, they would have found that that demon would have left on the instant and would not have remained for a second. This was the power of light that Jesus himself invoked. He invoked that energy of the blue flame, and it immediately fulfilled the destiny that God intended it to do. And, thus, the boy was effectively cut free and healed of that condition."[23]

When invoked, Purity and Astrea come with their circle and sword of blue flame to cut free souls who are caught in the astral plane and to bind the demons and discarnates that prey upon them. Just by living on planet Earth, especially in the large cities, we all pick up a certain vibration and energy of the world. Astrea can also assist us in this by helping us keep ourselves clear of this substance, which can accumulate as a kind of astral soot in the aura.

Astrea explains the importance of giving her decree: "I need your help! I enlist your help! I say, try me. See what will take place when you use the circle and sword of blue flame! See how a hundred entities can be bound by our legions in answer to your call as you give that decree to Astrea. I am the Starry Mother. You will see how that loved one can be cut free and kept free and how that one will return to the dignity of a child of light and find his mission before it is too late....

"Thus, my beloved, if you would keep the vigil for a loved one or a number of loved ones, know that the power of the circle and sword of blue flame will work as you pray for them each day and for every other child of God on this planet who is similarly enslaved!

"I, Astrea, make you this offer: Pray for your loved ones; put as many photographs as you like upon your altar. And when you pray for them, pray also for all others upon this planet who can be delivered by Astrea. I will place my Electronic Presence over all of them, a billion times over if needed and more. This is the capacity of a cosmic being who is one with God, hence, fully God in manifestation. I need only the call of single hearts on earth."[24]

The decree to Astrea is a key tool we can use in answering Jesus' Calls to help the children and youth, the homeless and the street people. El Morya has told us that this decree to Astrea (see Spiritual Exercises) is the most powerful mantra to the Divine Mother that we have been given.[25]

The Power of the Rosary

In this dictation, Jesus speaks of the prayer of the Hail "Ma-ray," the Hail Mary. This is another devotion to the Divine Mother, and to Mary as one representative of that universal presence of the Mother, who has always sought to save all her children.

The Hail Mary has been given for centuries by devotees of the Mother in the West. Mother Mary has now given us a new form of the Hail Mary for a new age. She has explained that we should not affirm our sinful nature, but, rather, our rightful inheritance as sons and daughters of God. Neither should we dwell upon the hour of death, but, rather, upon the hour of victory. Thus, she asks us to pray:

Hail, Mary, full of grace. The Lord is with thee. Blessed art thou among women and blessed is the fruit of thy womb, Jesus.

Holy Mary, Mother of God, pray for us, sons and daughters of God, now and at the hour of our victory over sin, disease, and death.

Mother Mary has also given us a number of scriptural rosaries, which braid the Hail Mary and other prayers with readings from the scriptures.

She has told us that through giving the rosary we gain access to the power of light in her causal body:

"I extend to you access by the rosary to my causal body, to the attainment on those fourteen stations gained throughout my long spiritual history.... This I transmit to you that it might become close to the physical world and physical problems through your own physical body and heart...."

"I have added the forces of my angels and those of Raphael's bands to the armies of the Faithful and True and of Maitreya and Sanat Kumara and Archangel Michael to wage war at inner levels with these unseen forces, principalities and powers, and spiritual wickedness in high places...."[26]

"I turn your attention, then, to the rosary as never before. For it is the single prayer that does draw down the universal power of *Omega*—Omega fire, Omega light. The power of the Mother moving with the forces of the Trinity is the missing dimension in the victory of Armageddon."[27]

Saint Germain tells us: "When you give the Hail Mary, even then the violet flame is released. For Mother Mary has determined in counsel with us, with the Darjeeling Council, that in response to the Hail Mary said by those of the New Age, there shall be accordingly a release from her heart of her own full-gathered momentum of the violet flame from her own causal body of light."[28]

When we say "Hail Mary," we are saying "Hail Ma-ray," or "Hail Mother ray." The Hail Mary is thus given to Mary, as a representative of the Mother, and to the Divine Mother in all her representatives. It is also a devotion to the light of the Mother within each of us, known in the East as the *Kundalini*, the energy that rises from the base-of-the-spine chakra to the crown. This prayer is the safe and natural way for western devotees to purify their chakras and raise the light of the Kundalini.

SPIRITUAL EXERCISES

Heal the Condition of Unworthiness

These are practical steps you can take to heal the condition of unworthiness:

1. Try repeating the following affirmation for several weeks: "Christ in me is worthy," or "Lord, I AM worthy, make me worthier still."

2. Take some time to meditate on the concepts of humility and unworthiness. What do you see as the difference between the two? When do you find yourself engaged in one or the other? Write your thoughts in your journal.
3. Give decree 20.09, "I Cast Out the Dweller-on-the-Threshold." (See chapter 8.) Call for the binding of all sense of unworthiness from within and without.
4. Use the violet-flame decrees for the transmutation of all feelings of unworthiness and any contributing causes or karmic conditions stemming from lives, all the way back to your first incarnation on earth. "See yourself standing before Saint Germain and Portia (Saint Germain's twin flame) in a room with amethyst walls. Hand them your burden—your bundle of unworthiness—and watch them cast it into the violet flame once and for all. Then go forward free to serve the light."[29]
5. Ask the masters to show you anything in your psychology that is blocking your freedom from this negative momentum.
6. If you find that a sense of unworthiness is limiting your path and that you are unable to deal with it effectively by yourself, seek spiritual guidance or counseling.

Sometimes we resist tackling certain states of consciousness that burden us. We resist talking to a counselor about our burdens and our psychology because it is painful to do the inner work. And yet, if we trust what the masters have told us, we know that on the other side of any pain we may go through there is the bliss of our union with our Holy Christ Self.

Help Save the Children

Consider what you can do to answer Jesus' Call to help save the children. Do you have children of your own? Do you have friends who have children? If so, you have ready-made opportunities. There are also many organizations that provide organized programs with children where you can assist as a volunteer—including schools; churches and Sunday schools; youth organizations, such as Boy Scouts and Big Brothers and Sisters; museums and libraries.

And, of course, there is always the great necessity of prayer for the protection of children. You can name children and youth and their special problems following the preamble to any decree. You can also give the following decree by El Morya.

PROTECT OUR YOUTH

Beloved heavenly Father! Beloved heavenly Father!
  Beloved heavenly Father!
Take command of our youth today
Blaze through them opportunity's ray
Release perfection's mighty power
Amplify cosmic intelligence each hour
Protect, defend their God-design
Intensify intent divine
I AM, I AM, I AM
The power of infinite light
Blazing through our youth
Releasing cosmic proof
Acceptable and right
The full power of cosmic light
To every child and child-man
In America and the world!
Beloved I AM, beloved I AM, beloved I AM!

Give the Rosary to Mother Mary to Rescue the Lost Sheep

The Blessed Mother has given us her Hail Mary and the New Age rosary to give on behalf of all lightbearers and for the raising up of the feminine ray in this age. You can give this prayer many times daily.

Hail Mary

Hail, Mary, full of grace, the Lord is with thee. Blessed art thou among women and blessed is the fruit of thy womb, Jesus.

Holy Mary, Mother of God, pray for us, sons and daughters of God, now and at the hour of our victory over sin, disease and death.

Take Action for the Homeless and the Street People

1. Find out what organizations in your area provide assistance to the homeless. Volunteer your time a day or two a month at a soup kitchen or some other place where you will be working

with the homeless. See what it will do to change your life and how your love and caring impacts their lives.

2. Give your daily prayers to Astrea and Archangel Michael to cut these people free from entities and depression and a sense of unworthiness to receive the light of Jesus and their Holy Christ Self.

As you give the decree to Astrea, visualize the circle and sword of blue flame around the situation or circumstance for which you are giving this decree. See the circle of blue flame—a sapphire blue burning with a white diamond-like brilliance—around the individual at the waist, around the group of individuals, around entire cities, states or nations, or around the whole earth. See this as a ring of fire, spinning like a buzz saw, cutting away layers and layers of density and discord.

See the sword of blue flame perpendicular to the circle of blue flame, breaking up matrices of darkness, and magnetizing elements of being to return to their original divine blueprint.

As you give this decree for yourself or for an individual, you can visualize Astrea holding the blue-flame sword parallel to and two inches from the spine, demagnetizing the being and consciousness from all that is not of God, all that is not of God-design.

DECREE TO BELOVED MIGHTY ASTREA— "THE STARRY MOTHER"

In the name of the beloved mighty victorious Presence of God, I AM in me, mighty I AM Presence and Holy Christ Self of _____ [names of people for whom you are decreeing] _____, by and through the magnetic power of the sacred fire vested in the threefold flame burning within my heart, I call to beloved Mighty Astrea, beloved Lanello, the entire Spirit of the Great White Brotherhood and the World Mother, elemental life—fire, air, water and earth! to lock your cosmic circles and swords of blue flame in, through, and around:

Insert 1: my four lower bodies, my electronic belt, my heart chakra and all of my chakras, my entire consciousness, being and world.

[Give your own insert for individuals or situations for which you are decreeing.]

Cut me loose and set me free (3x) from all that is less than God's perfection and my own divine plan fulfilled.

1. O beloved Astrea, may God-purity
   Manifest here for all to see,
   God's divine will shining through
   Circle and sword of brightest blue.

First chorus:* Come now answer this my call
   Lock thy circle round us all.
   Circle and sword of brightest blue,
   Blaze now, raise now, shine right through!

2. Cutting life free from patterns unwise,
   Burdens fall off while souls arise
   Into thine arms of infinite love,
   Merciful shining from heaven above.

3. Circle and sword of Astrea now shine,
   Blazing blue-white my being refine,
   Stripping away all doubt and fear,
   Faith and goodwill patterns appear.

Second chorus: Come now answer this my call,
   Lock thy circle round us all.
   Circle and sword of brightest blue,
   Raise our youth now, blaze right through!

Third chorus: Come now answer this my call,
   Lock thy circle round us all.
   Circle and sword of brightest blue,
   Raise mankind now, shine right through!

*Give the entire decree once through, using the first chorus after each verse. Then give the verses again, using the second chorus after each one. Conclude by using the third chorus after each verse.

And in full faith...

FOR YOUR JOURNAL

How Will *You* Answer Jesus' Calls?

*"Drink this cup of my Christhood!... Be the instruments
of my light... to the youth of the entire world,
to children bruised and battered."*

*"See the great calling... to embody that light, that I AM THAT
I AM, that portion of Christos that is yours to claim."*

*"Save the homeless and the street people from that sense
of abject self-negation.... Be converted to serve those
who sense they are the poor in spirit."*

What do these Calls mean to me?
What will I do to answer these Calls?

CHAPTER 13

The Call to "espouse the higher calling in God" and "to stand in defense of life."

Rise to the Higher Calling in God!

Salvation through My Sacred Heart
The Fire of Pentecost for the Judgment of Abortion and the Abortionist

It *is* I. I AM come this day to show thee my body of light—no longer the nail prints, no longer the marks of the crucifixion, for I AM in the light and the glory of the living Christ, whom God has placed where you are as I AM.

I AM that living Christ come to you and I come to my own who have the temple of the heart and would bid me enter.

I AM the Faithful and True.[1] My armies with me, I descend this day for the resurrection and the life of all souls seeking entrance [to the physical octave] through the portals of birth. We come to support woman and her mission in bringing forth the Divine Manchild in every child whom God has made.

I AM Jesus, your Master, and you may call me Rabboni[2] if you will. I come, beloved, in answer to the Call, the heartfelt calls of millions who desire to undo the curse of death upon woman that has now these eighteen years[3] been extended to the child in her womb, that portion of herself more precious even than her own soul: the soul who should become even the living, breathing awareness of Almighty God.

I come to bind the Death Rider through you, beloved. May you be the voice of the ones who have been silenced, who wait and who weep and who mourn a lost opportunity to be at your side, to be as children in your arms, to be in my churches throughout the world this day and in those of religions other than Christianity.

They long to be cradled by mothers and fathers. May it be so. May it come to pass, as you have prayed, that all souls who have been aborted may now be received because the people are awakened, because there is enlightenment by the Holy Spirit!

And I promise you that on the day of Pentecost 1991 you shall know the descent of the Holy Ghost with the full fire of the judgment upon the seed of the wicked who have descended from Herod to snuff out the Christ flame in those who come to rescue a world and are denied entrance by their hand.

I promise you that on the day of Pentecost, if you will prepare yourselves, you shall receive some glory of my causal body of light and you shall keep it if you are ready to keep it. And you will know the empowerment of the Holy Spirit[4] as the disciples knew it, as the apostles knew it, as the inner circle knew it.

Empowered by that Spirit, you shall do what others have not done, and that is to turn around the consciousness of the nation and the nations.

I, Jesus, call you. Feed these my lambs and deliver them to their earthly habitation! Let the abode that is the temple of man and woman be sanctified! Let it be purified and let the uses of the sacred fire be purified. And let there be the knowledge of the LORD within this temple, which is my temple.

For my house has become a den of thieves![5] And I cast the moneychangers (who run their abortion mills) out of the temple of the living God! For they have committed the sin against the Holy Ghost that is not forgiven until it be forsaken and forsaken ten thousand times ten thousand. They have much to do ere they shall be received as one of these my little ones.

Blessed hearts of light, I enlist you in the army of Christed ones to go forth and claim life on behalf of those who are helpless. I ask you and I implore you with the same fervor with which I implored Peter: Will you feed my lambs?[6] ["Yes!"]

My beloved, it is a higher calling and I tell you of this higher calling. For to stand in defense of life and not be moved and not descend into fanaticism or anger or hate and hate creation but to manifest the fullness of the living Christ that is the fire of the Divine Mother and even the "wrath" of the Great Kali—this is to have the center of God-free being! And it does come, beloved, because you pray on your knees to me for my Sacred Heart to be your own heart.

This is the day of salvation through that heart. If you desire to win this victory, and win it fully, that a nation and many nations might be spared the karma of the murder of their own children, then I say to you, you must have the engrafted Word![7] You must have my sacred heart. You must desire this burning heart within you and visualize it within your own breast and know that that fire burning will be a sign unto all those who are of Antichrist. And the line of division will be drawn, even more than you have seen it drawn before.

Beloved ones, to succeed in the defense of life demands that you espouse the higher calling in God and in Christ and that you be willing to sacrifice "all these things" for that calling!

I tell you, those who have mouthed the right words have not been willing to sacrifice the human consciousness to win the victory. And therefore the forces who speak in my name do not have the fervor of my flame and they have not succeeded in preventing 25 million abortions* in the United States of America in these eighteen years!

Blessed ones, know it, and know it well: we come upon a threshold [in the abortion of human life such] that should this continue and continue and continue, God will not spare the karma of a mighty people. For as you have been taught, the LORD God prefers that the chastisement be upon those whom he loves that they not be allowed to advance their [unjust] cause any longer, lest in so advancing it they might believe that their cause is just. Therefore the Law, the Law itself, must [chasten the children of God and] stop the evildoer.

And those who would marshal themselves in defense of life must also know that they have not done enough or given enough or risen to the true heart of my beloved Saint Joseph—my true and noble father. They have not risen to claim his violet flame and to use it.

They have not called upon Saint Michael the Archangel with the necessary fervor that his legions might be empowered by those in embodiment to go forth to slay this dragon of Antichrist that

---

*By the year 2001 over 40 million abortions had been performed in the United States.

does devour the holy innocents and beings of great light who have endeavored to enter into the community of nations but who have been forbidden—forbidden by the fallen ones and that ignorance that is still all-pervading through the nations [concerning the crime of abortion].

And those who are the blind are they who will not see my own life in every newborn child. Lo, it is I! And I smile at you through the eyes of the newborn babe. And therefore those who would deny me have done so [by aborting that babe], yet they are they which testify of me.[8]

Let those liberal clergy in all nations and in all world religions who have denied the life of God in the offspring of his sons and daughters know that they shall face the judgment of the false teachers and the false pastors and the false prophets, *and they shall not escape their karma!*

Suffer, then, the little children to come unto me and unto you. Let there be the "Life Begets Life" family counseling centers. And if you will, take counsel together to form adoption agencies that you might offer to receive children of those who are not able to keep their babes [and give them to those who will love and care for them].

Blessed ones, there need to be offices, there need to be adjuncts to our teaching centers and study groups where the information of the ascended masters [on "Life Begets Life"], of Saint Germain concerning the soul, and such teachings as the messenger has given to you [on abortion][9] are taught to those who come. You need to put a sign on your door and let it be known that you are there to counsel others [concerning the sanctity of life from conception].

There are many mental health practitioners and psychologists in this community. There are those of the professions who can serve and give of their free time on a part-time basis to counsel young women and families and to assist them in [family] planning[10] and show them the reality of the continuity of the soul. [They can teach them] that the soul needs and desires and is ordained by God to come into embodiment at that moment, that cosmic moment in eternity that is ordained for that one by my Father and by my Mother, [who are] also your Father and your Mother.

For we are of one seed and that seed is the eternal Christ; and to deny it in yourself is to deny it in me, and to deny it in me is to prevent it from manifesting in yourself, beloved.

And therefore let the false doctrines come tumbling down! And let the false doctrine that the soul is created at the moment of conception be stripped of its "reality"! And let us go back to first principles. Let us go back to Origen.[11] Let us go back to my words written in akasha, which come to you by the Holy Spirit.

Every one of you may receive by the Holy Spirit—if you will sacrifice [in order] to receive that Holy Spirit—my words originally spoken and written in the sand, written in akasha. Your Holy Christ Self is one with my Christ. There is but one universal body of Christ, in which we all share, and therefore my words are already written in your heart. So the Holy Spirit may deliver them. So your messenger may interpret them.

But the LORD God is speaking to his people this day and I AM speaking to their hearts! And they must be shown the folly of their ways in the squandering of the light that is in their chakras. They must *hear* the Word of the LORD! They must *see* the LORD himself! And they must live because they both hear and see and have the witness![12] And you do have the witness as the testimony of myself.

Therefore, you who know the Everlasting Gospel that I deliver in this age for all time, you who know what doctrines must be stripped from those individuals who are devout and yet know not their limitation and the limitation that has been put upon them by orthodoxy, *you,* beloved, must rise to the higher calling this day!

I have called you for many a month and many a year. Understand that there is a ceiling upon those [serving under the yoke of orthodoxy] who would serve me and love me and who would save my own. It is the prejudice of the mind. It is the fear to believe those things that I speak to them in their hearts, fear that they will be found in disfavor with the Church.

Blessed hearts, let us love this day! Let us enter the love feast! And let us release such a powerful love that it does cast out fear[13] in those who are desiring to seek me and know me and to walk on the road to Emmaus with me[14] and who would walk out of their churches and follow me down the highways of life to bring in those souls who can yet save an age and can yet put to an end the very possibility of nuclear war and earth changes and all of those karmic predictions that will surely come, I tell you, if this nation does not stop the practice of abortion, legalized and government-sponsored and [tax-]supported abortion.

Blessed hearts, it is the karma of a people. It is becoming heavy and heavier until no power will be able to stop it from descending.

Therefore if you have love for those in embodiment who have been led astray [by the Supreme Court's decision to legalize abortion] and love for those young women who are bringing forth babes, even at an early age, as Mary did bring me forth from her womb, [you must see to it that] these young ones know the truth, for the truth is in their hearts. They need be told only once. For these young maidens, beloved, are surely of my heart and surely desire to truly know me.

I present myself to them, beloved, and I present myself to them through you. They must have a teaching they can understand. They must have a spiritual path instead of a path that is of a dead ritual. Religion is not necessarily spirituality. Therefore let the spiritual path be opened unto them! Let their spiritual eyes be opened!

So many of them have the courage to carry their young ones in the face of all adversity and obligations. Blessed hearts, I praise the angels who tend them and their pure hearts who are bringing forth souls. And they are bringing forth souls of light and many of them are being reared in homes where there is light and where there is opportunity.

This is the hour indeed to be on your knees daily in prayer unto my Mother that you might have from her again the empowerment of the immaculate heart. It is the day and the hour to do penance on behalf of the sin of a nation, to atone for that sin by speaking the Word and preaching it.

Do not fear the reaction of the world! Do not fear to become unpopular! Do not fear to be put down! Only call upon me and upon Archangel Michael and the hosts of the LORD for your protection and the protection of the ears and the hearts who must know this truth!

For they are thirsting for it, they are hungering after this truth and they *must know* that that soul is integral to that body, to that mind, to that memory, to that sheath of desire, all coming together in that embryo, in that fetus in the womb, beloved.

Now I say to you, if this entire momentum of death and hell be turned around, *nothing* shall be impossible to the Church of God upon earth, to his people! For this [abortion of unborn children] is the most deadly of all plots against humanity and the children of light. It is greater than nuclear war itself, for the destruction of the nucleus of life that is God is the most horrendous crime that is (or can be) practiced, that is (or can be) committed against the backdrop of eternity.

Before it is too late, beloved, I say to you, take my staff this day, take my hand. I shall walk with you.

I AM he! I AM Jesus and I will keep my promise. I will be at your side in the defense of life—all life, any part of life. Wherever you defend the right of life to be the full expression of God in embodiment in a healthy body, a harmonious home and on a path of light, wherever you defend the right of the individual to know the truth of my message of all ages that is the path of the resurrection and the ascension in the light, *I will be with you!* This is my promise. May you not lose it by departing into old patterns.

Therefore I commune with you as you pray now on your knees to be delivered of the ancient patterns of going astray from the Christ into the human consciousness. [Congregation kneels.]

My angels come and attend you and the angels of Magda come. And now, beloved, know the presence of my legions. For they themselves are masterful beings and they serve your soul, they guard your soul.

In this hour surrender your burdens, your cares, your anxieties, your fears of the future, beloved—your fears of your yesterdays coming again and your resistance to taking the next step on the Path, which will require new levels of commitment of your own self-mastery, your expanding heart and less and less regard unto the selfish self.

O soul of mine, O soul of mine, I speak to you, each one. You are my brides. You are my beloved. I would hold you in the Master-disciple relationship. I say, let there be permanent change wrought this day! I, Jesus, declare it unto you.

It is by the power of my resurrection flame released this day from the Great Central Sun that you *are healed!* And I, Jesus, say to you, you are *healed* in this hour if you will accept it.

Accept it, beloved. Call unto me! Call unto God now! And do not be ashamed, for you are in the Temple Beautiful in the etheric octave in this moment and you may receive blessings without limit. [The congregation offers individual calls unto Jesus and unto God for blessings without limit.]

I now command you in the name of my God and your God: Rise in the newness of your Christhood! Rise in the wonder and the glory of the Christ Presence above you! See how your souls are clothed with garments of light, dressed by angels.

May you know the meaning of the higher walk with God. May you hold that footstep and hold that word and that thought and that feeling. Release it into the violet flame; but do not take a backward step, do not fall into the old patterns.

Struggle if you must, strive if you will to overcome the patterns of the past. Self-correct! Call to me! Call to your Holy Christ Self! For I have said to you, "Occupy till I come."[15]

Therefore you may call to me and say, "O Jesus, my Lord and my Master, occupy my mind! Occupy my memory body! Occupy my heart! Occupy my soul! Occupy my temple, my physical body that is prepared for thee!"

And you may call to your Holy Christ Self to enter into these tabernacles of being, to enter and prepare the way for me, even as you serve as my assistant, as the handmaid of the Lord, that you might receive that Christ in your heart.

I pray that you will know that dispensations from God are limited according to your own self-limitation when you do not receive our Word and rise to it and understand that a dictation itself is the pinnacle: it is the crown upon the recitation of prayer and dynamic decrees and mantras and the imploring of God....

Blessed ones, now is truly the time. It is the time indeed for you to cast forth the net of the consciousness that you have carefully woven by your prayers and to know that the power of God is able to tear down the erroneous teaching [of orthodoxy] that has been held too long, that is the teaching of man and not of God.

Therefore, bring in the nets! Bring in the fishes! Feed my sheep, beloved! They are there. They are waiting. They are suffering. They are dying in every nation. May you not forget to offer the prayer whereby they might be taken to octaves of light to make progress on the Path before they must descend again, once again to enter the battle of Armageddon.

For so many upon earth life and death are just a line apart. May you know how many suffer in this hour and now give of your hearts in the greatest love the world has ever known. And that love is the love of Christ and my disciples—Christ and my disciples.

"O drink of the fount from which I have drunk and be like me!"—the words recorded by Thomas that I spake.[16] Let them become your words. When one does acknowledge your light, say to that one: "I have drunk from the fount of the mighty I AM Presence, truly the I AM THAT I AM. I have drunk from the fount of my Holy Christ Self. I have drunk from the heart of my Lord and Saviour Jesus Christ. I am filled! Wilt thou be filled, O friend? Come and drink with me, and now come and dine."

Thus offer the friend in the way my cup, my bread, my heart. But above all, do not leave him without the teaching, beloved, for without it he will be led astray again and again....

The hour is late, beloved. It is too late to be a halfhearted disciple. It is the hour when the King of kings and the Lord of lords, it is the hour when Sanat Kumara, the Ancient of Days, does approach and there is the sifting of hearts and souls.

Go all out for the mission and behold my Presence with you! This Communion is for your sending to the farthest corners of the earth and to your own backyard.

I AM Jesus, always with you, and I say, "Onward, Christian soldiers!"

Receive ye now Holy Communion and tarry for the receiving

of the Holy Ghost as never before on this Pentecost 1991.
[Holy Communion is served.]

March 31, 1991
Easter Sunday
Royal Teton Ranch
Park County, Montana

*I AM he! I AM Jesus and I will keep my promise. I will be
at your side in the defense of life—all life, any part of life.*

As we read this dictation we are brought face-to-face with
the awareness of the very serious karma of the abortion of
incoming souls. By the year 2001, over 40 million souls had
been aborted in the United States alone.

Jesus tells us that the key to the whole issue of abortion is the
spiritual understanding of the soul and its destiny. The messenger explains: "What is abortion? It is not only the abortion of a
body, it is the abortion of the divine plan of a soul whose body
temple is being nurtured in the womb. It is the abortion of an
individual calling; for God chooses the special moment in history
for each soul to return to earth to take part in the divine plan of
the decades and the centuries."[17]

Jesus Calls us to "espouse the higher calling in God" and "to
stand in defense of life." In order to take on the responsibility to
defend life, we need to understand the masters' teaching on abortion so we can share it with others. We also need to do the spiritual work that Jesus says is central to turning the situation
around, and we need to have an awareness of events and issues
so our prayer work can be intelligently directed.

Fundamental to an understanding of the abortion issue is the
idea of the continuity of the soul—the concept that the soul has
lived before and comes again to fulfill a special calling and mission. Saint Germain tells us that "the first and greatest contribution of God to man is *the gift of life as a continuum*—identity
preserved through the divine spark, the threefold flame of life.
And the second, which is like unto it, is *the gift of free will* in the
exercise of power, wisdom and love—choosing step-by-step eternal life."[18]

The soul also comes with debts to pay from previous lifetimes, and in order to graduate from earth's schoolroom and

return to God, the soul must fulfill her special mission and balance this karma. Many in the early Christian church understood the concept of karma that they had learned from Jesus.* The law of karma can be summed up in the words of the apostle Paul in his letter to the Galatians, "For whatsoever a man soweth, that shall he also reap."[19]

If an opportunity to live on earth is denied, then the soul is not able to balance this karmic debt until another opportunity for life is available. The evolution of the soul is delayed, and when so many souls are denied entrance to earth, the spiritual evolution of the planet as a whole is also delayed, since those individuals and mandalas of souls that are meant to be pioneers in many fields are incomplete or absent altogether.

Thus, we see that abortion is something that affects us all. When we consider how many millions of people were meant to be in embodiment but have not made it, we realize that some of those in our own soul mandala, who should be working alongside us—even a soul mate or a twin flame—may not be here.

The Karma of Abortion

Jesus gives us some guidelines as we take our stand in defense of life. He tells us that we must not be fanatical, get angry or send out hatred toward those who are perpetuating the practice of abortion. Our role is to embody the Sacred Heart of Jesus, be his hands and feet and bring to people the enlightenment of the Holy Spirit. We must also be willing to do sacrificial prayer work to protect the incoming souls. And if, for one moment, you doubt that prayer can make a difference, listen to the words of the ascended master Saint Germain:

"Well have I observed over the centuries how important is the service of ordered prayer. The daily offering of petitions has saved the lives of millions, expanded the lives of other millions and blessed all life without limit.

---

*If you would like to learn more about Jesus' teachings on karma and reincarnation, see *Reincarnation: The Missing Link in Christianity,* by Elizabeth Clare Prophet with Erin L. Prophet (Summit University Press).

"Prayer opens the door of God's intervention in human affairs. It provides an avenue whereby the ascended masters and cosmic beings who desire to serve the planet Earth and its evolutions can walk within the folds of universal justice and render special assistance because they have been called upon to do so. For the Law decrees that the heavenly hosts must be petitioned by some among mankind, must be invited to intervene, before they are permitted to intercede on behalf of humanity."[20]

Mother Mary speaks of the gravity of the abortion issue and the judgment (return of karma) that it brings upon the individual and upon the nations:

"I am your Mother and the Mother of all who will receive me. Untold numbers of angels and servants of God are with me as we care for the diseased, the dying, the homeless children and the unborn who will never reach incarnation because parents and others who have committed to bring them into this world have gone back on their promises. And because of those broken promises, so many souls who could one day right the wrongs, even of Western civilization, are not in embodiment.

"On this subject I am intense! I am intense because many of the great ones who must take embodiment are being denied entry into the twenty-first century. In the past I have spoken softly. Today I deliver a stern warning. Let it be clear that souls are destined to incarnate *when God ordains it* and not at the convenience of others or even not at all. Blessed ones, if the coming decades bring cataclysm and upheaval in the earth, it will be because the wrath of God* has descended.

"Up until now God, Elohim, has withheld his wrath that you might right the wrongs of this civilization. For through your invocation of the violet flame, there is yet time wherein you might atone for the sins of this world. But the open door of opportunity is soon coming to an end. And those who selfishly indulge their lusts, those who have no time to love a child or to

---

*wrath of God: The term used in the Bible to denote mankind's karma when God allows it to return according to the cycles of the Law rather than holding it back in an action of mercy.

bring children into this world (though they themselves have come through mothers and fathers) will be judged when that day and that hour finally descends. And I tell you, it shall be a planetary judgment upon those who have either refused to bring forth children* or who have aborted them.

"Abortion is truly the most profound crime of the century, for it is the murder of souls as well as bodies. The children who are finally born, often having tried a number of times to enter this world in order to fulfill their mission, may become angry children. For, believe it or not, they *remember* their abortions. They remember them, beloved! And these aborted souls are outraged before this injustice, and they cry out in anguish, pleading for mercy from the wombs of their mothers. Know this and teach this, that all may come into alignment with God's plan for every soul on earth."[21]

Saint Germain has also spoken of the seriousness of abortion and the karma that results: "Out of the mouth of the messenger I spoke this day, before a television camera, the pronouncement of God's judgment upon any nation that enacts a law authorizing murder through abortion. The nation that allows these laws to rest upon the books, and therefore govern life itself, is judged. And unless it be overturned, cataclysm has always been the judgment upon those who have defended death, through their own selfishness and self-intent, rather than life in the sacrificial sense."[22]

Jesus tells us, "God will not spare the karma of a mighty people. For as you have been taught, the LORD God prefers that the chastisement be upon those whom he loves that they not be allowed to advance their unjust cause any longer, lest in so advancing it, they might believe that their cause is just. Therefore, the Law, the Law itself, must chasten the children of God and stop the evildoer."

There are many ways in which this karma may return. Some that the masters have spoken of in relation to abortion are extreme weather conditions, pestilence and diseases, war and

---

*when this was the mandate of their karma and their mission in life

problems in the economy, and a general insensitivity to life lead-ing to an increase in murder and crime in general.

What Can I Do If I Have Had an Abortion?

Jesus speaks of souls of light who need to hear his message on the defense of life. He also speaks of those who have been led astray and have had abortions, not understanding the real issues. Great pressure from circumstances and from other people also may result in a mother making a decision for abortion even when her heart would lead her to bear life. These are the com-forting words from the heart of Mother Mary to those who may have had an abortion:

"If abortion has entered your life, I say, call upon the violet flame for the healing of the soul in pain for its mission cut off. Call on the law of forgiveness for yourself. Do not condemn yourself, for I, Mary, do not condemn you, but I urge you to seek early the opportunity of serving life and caring for children that you might learn to love your own inner child and balance the karma of abortion.

"And pray that in due course you might have a family and bring in the soul or souls whom you aborted through ignorance in an hour when you were perhaps distraught, misled, faced with choices without being given the facts about the life that was aborning in your womb—or perhaps you knew and denied what you knew."[23]

If you are a woman who has had an abortion or a man who has encouraged a woman to have an abortion, the messenger assures you that whether or not you knew about the sin of abor-tion at the time, it is not going to prevent your ascension in this lifetime if you give yourself to God in a service that can balance that karma. Such service would include helping children in some way, working with children, praying and decreeing for the youth or bearing a child if it is God's will.

SPIRITUAL EXERCISES

Take a Stand for the Defense of Life

Jesus outlines the practical steps we can take to answer this Call. The essence of the mission is to "turn around the consciousness" of the people. It begins with education—teaching people the continuity of the soul and the unique mission of each incoming soul. It is not only giving people the teachings, but also extending care and assistance, one-on-one, to those who feel pressured into making a decision for abortion, whether ignorantly or because they feel they have no other alternative.

Here are some steps you can take to answer Jesus' call. First, there is the spiritual work:

1. Jesus asks us to pray on our knees for his Sacred Heart to be our own.
2. Invoke the violet flame to transmute the cause and core of abortion and the pain suffered by the aborted souls.
3. Call upon Archangel Michael and empower his legions "to go forth and slay this dragon of Antichrist that does devour the holy innocents and beings of great light who have endeavored to enter into the community of nations but have been forbidden." (Use the decree to Archangel Michael, page 43.)
4. "Be on your knees daily in prayer unto my Mother that you might have from her again the empowerment of the Immaculate Heart." Give the Hail Mary and the Rosary.
5. Give Jesus' Judgment Call for the judgment of forces of darkness and fallen angels promoting the practice of abortion. (See page 182.)
6. "It is the day and hour to do penance on behalf of the sin of a nation, to atone for that sin by speaking the Word and preaching it." Consider how you can answer this and previous Calls of Jesus to give people his true teachings on karma, reincarnation, the violet flame and the spiritual path.

Jesus is also calling us to take the very physical steps to help those who may be considering abortion. He asks us to form "Life Begets Life" family counseling centers and adoption agencies. Are there Keepers of the Flame or other individuals in your area who could work with you to establish these agencies? If you want to answer this Call, ask Jesus to put you in direct contact with all those you are supposed to work with to make it happen. When Jesus issues the Call, we understand that he does have a plan. Also along with the Call, Jesus gives an impetus of light that can be the means of implementing that plan if we can "catch" it and use it.

If you are not able to set up your own organization, there are probably existing agencies and organizations in your area that do provide these services, and where you could offer your services in answer to Jesus' Call.

Call to the Great Divine Director for the Arresting of Spirals

In 1973, the Supreme Court of the United States initiated the spiral of legal abortion in America. This spiral can be arrested and turned back, and the Great Divine Director gives us a key to doing this:

"Ask, then, the Almighty to arrest those cycles not of the light that are continuing in the world, in your consciousness and in the planetary body. The mighty I AM Presence has the authority and the power to instantaneously arrest and reverse any cycle and to cause a complete erasing, a disintegration of it, right back to the twelve o'clock line.

"It is as though you would see a moving picture in reverse. All of a sudden, the figures go back into their little holes from which they came, and they reverse the order of their activities. This is the process of transmutation. This is how energy is freed of an imperfect cycle.

"I say to you, you must demand and command it in the name of the Christ—that every single cycle of every single cell and atom within your form that is not outpicturing the perfect cycles of the Christ consciousness is now dissolved, is now arrested and turned back by the authority of your God Presence!

"If you will but make that invocation each morning, you will find in a very short time that only the cycles of immortal life and your divine plan fulfilled and your ascension will prevail."[24]

Here is a prayer by Lanello for the arresting of spirals:

> In the name of my mighty I AM Presence and the Great Divine Director, in the name Jesus Christ, I demand and command the arresting of the spirals of negative karma throughout my entire consciousness, being and world! [including the following conditions:
>
> _____]
>
> I demand and command that every single cycle of every single cell and atom within my form that is not outpicturing the perfect cycles of the Christ consciousness be now dissolved, be now arrested and turned back by the authority of my God Presence! And in the name Jesus Christ, I demand and command that the cycles of immortal life and my divine plan be fulfilled and that my ascension prevail![25]

Meditation on Jesus' Sacred Heart

Jesus said, "You must have my Sacred Heart. You must desire this burning heart within you and visualize it within your own breast and know that that fire burning will be a sign unto all those who are of Antichrist."

Take a period of time to visualize the Sacred Heart of Jesus superimposed over your own heart. See and feel his heart burning intensely within your own breast. Hold this visualization and then softly repeat the following words several times: "In the Sacred Heart of Jesus, I trust."

You may wish to include this as part of your daily devotions or use this visualization while you give decrees each day.

Give a Rosary to Mother Mary Daily

Consecrate your rosary for the protection of families and of souls aborning in the womb. Ask Mother Mary to intercede in the minds and hearts of those who can be converted to the understanding of their calling to bring forth life.

Forgiveness for Abortion

If you have had an abortion or encouraged someone else to do so, take the opportunity to seek forgiveness and the means to balance this karma. The following steps may be useful for you:

1. Write a letter to God asking forgiveness. Tell him your thoughts and feelings about the situation, and let him know what you would do to seek forgiveness and balance the karma involved. Consecrate the letter and burn it so the angels can deliver it.
2. Give the prayer, "Forgiveness for Those Who Have Had an Abortion."
3. Take a stand for the defense of life as outlined above.
4. If you are married, consider whether you can sponsor another child in your family, either through birth or adoption.
5. Find ways to help and serve children. There are many organizations in need of volunteer assistance for their programs that help children and families.

Finally, accept your forgiveness from the heart of God, and be willing to forgive yourself and others. Sometimes we feel that we cannot forgive ourselves. Should you find yourself so burdened, consider the words of Kuan Yin:

"And now that you have made Him the centerpiece of your being, now that you have understood that the word *Christ* is truly the identification of your soul, one with Jesus, not only can you become a repository of Christ's mercy and a giver of Christ's mercy, but you can become humble before God, you can forgive yourself—yes, forgive yourself even as you can now be accepting of God's forgiveness. This is the key to the foundation of the path of the bodhisattva, the path of the Buddha."[76]

Prayer for Forgiveness for Those Who Have Had an Abortion

In the name of the I AM THAT I AM, I call upon the law of forgiveness for myself and every child of light who has ever unwittingly undergone an abortion or consented to an abortion or encouraged an abortion. I call for the encirclement now of that entire cause, effect, record and memory!

I call for the cutting free of the soul aborted! I call for the cutting free of the mother and the father! I call for the raising and the elevation of their consciousness into new service to life, into renewed opportunity to serve to set life free!

I call for divine opportunity for that soul to incarnate, if she has not already done so. I call for the path of peace, enlightenment and ministration and service to be the way of atonement unto the children of God who have been drawn into the culture of death and now desire to espouse the culture of the Divine Mother in life.

Therefore, Lord Christ, we ask for the pronouncement of thy Word unto these whose hearts are troubled by the events of abortion in their own lives. Pronounce the Word, O Lord, as we speak it: Thy sin be forgiven thee. Go and sin no more! Go and serve to set life free! Go and be a mother of the world, a father of life aborning. And, therefore, nourish and encourage life to be free—all life everywhere manifest.[27]

FOR YOUR JOURNAL

How Will *You* Answer Jesus' Call?

*The Call to "espouse the higher calling in God"
and "to stand in defense of life."*

What does this Call mean to me?
What will I do to answer this Call?

CHAPTER 14

"I Call you to repentance."

"The Hour of the Choice"

It is an hour of opportunity. It is the moment of the descent also of Lord Gautama Buddha. Therefore receive me, as I am also the Buddha, and know that I have called you from ancient times to this hour that you might finish that which you have begun.

May you know, then, preeminently the cycles turning and that there is an hour of the Call. There is an hour to set aside the defiance against the LORD God and his Son, [who yet lives] within you and within me. It is the hour, then, to accept full responsibility for thy word and thy work, to have humility to receive and know true forgiveness and the true undoing, line upon line, of that which was wrought in pain and in sorrow.

I have come for the restoration and to redeem every erg of light that you have squandered. I have come as a magnet of the Sun to draw all elements of your being that you have carelessly scattered to the winds back to the vortex of the whirling Sun of Being and the sun of the soul in the seat-of-the-soul chakra.

I am your Jesus. I belong to you, if you will have me, and you belong to me, beloved. And if I have anything to say about it, I say, indeed I would have you! I would have you unto the rose of Sharon of my heart. I would have you unto the light of my causal body. I would wrap you in the swaddling garment of my Mother. I would renew you in the fire of the aura of the Sun, which you have allowed to be stripped from you in the folly of following false teachers.

Yes, my beloved, there is an hour for reconciliation with your God. I come to announce it to you this day. For the meeting of the signs of the heavens and the signs in the earth does therefore open a door that has not been open to you individually and others of that ancient golden-age civilization, 33,000 B.C. It has not been open [to you] since the hour of its decline.

Thus the cycles turn in a wide, wide orb. Begin, then, to imagine and to understand that the wide circling of the cycles of karma, of initiation, of light and light descending all come full circle in this hour of the turning of ages.

Be not deceived by those who deny the law of cycles! For I have written the law of cycles in your inward parts[1] and I have written the comings and the goings of your soul into and out of the house of the Father-Mother God. And each time you have gone farther from the center, you have created another wide orb that must be retraced for the return. Even so is the law of the universe and the planets in their courses. So even is the homecoming of the sons and daughters of God.

Now then, make no mistake: I call you to repentance. It is repentance from the violation of the Law of the One, the crossing of the line of the law of love. Where you have sown anything contradictory to love, may you reap quickly and cast it into the fire as the tares you have sown among the good wheat of your own field of consciousness and the fields of many others.

Watch the thought! Watch the thought! Watch the thought as it does depart from you! Therefore let arrows of the violet flame trace the thoughts that you have sent that have not measured to the level of your own dignity in Christ.

Yes, beloved, watch the feeling! Watch the feeling! Watch the feeling! Let the full momentum of the water of life flow freely as violet flame to go after and consume all besmirching of the pristine purity of the white snows of the fire of cosmos.

Let all these things return, and may you bank the fire of the heart that when they return the fire shall *consume* and you will not be consumed by earlier sowings. Unless you bank the fire of the resurrection in this day and in this hour, what shall you say when you must face the dark night of the soul and the dark night of the Spirit, the eclipse of the sun of the Presence?

Where shall you be found, beloved?

Where *shall* you be found if you have not the fire to greet the fire of darkness that long ago you did invert from light itself?

You have sown. This day face the sun and retrace your footsteps back to the center of Being and know that you must harvest as you go. It is a joy and a cause for rejoicing to cast into the sacred fire all that is not worthy of permanence in God. "This, not that." Thus sort the memories. Thus sort the records and the past, and therefore retain that which is worthy to be made a permanent atom in your being and in the kingdom of God's consciousness.

I am Jesus the Christ. I have been with you far longer than I shall tell this day; for I desire a shortening of the days of the elect[2] and surely not to heap upon you that condemnation that comes only from the fallen angels. And I would not have you condemn yourselves for your going out of the way of the path of life and of truth and of love.

Yet, behold, you are weary in your wanderings in the wilderness of Zin![3] Let it be understood, then, that the soul has suffered enough outside of the circle of the Father and the Mother, of the Son and the Holy Spirit. I bid you enter, painful though the process may be—and more painful yet for those souls who desire to accelerate the process of the return.

Yet, as I have taught my messenger, pain is the other side of bliss. Be willing to push through the pain to transcend the lesser self and to enter in to the bliss of union with my heart.

Thus is the way made plain. May you know surcease from all that would hinder you and may you not shirk responsibility to challenge the arrogance of the former self, to challenge the adversary, to challenge that which would thwart your new beginnings unto the fulfillment of certain endings that are come.

I desire to find you, ere this year has concluded, surely in the fire—in the fire infolding itself of the resurrection flame. I desire to see you walking the earth in the sense of the dignity of your Christhood. I desire to see you washed clean by the light, purified by the Refiner's fire.

For who shall stand in the day of the coming of my messenger?[4]

Therefore let it be fulfilled and let the ancient prophets come full circle also, to know their redemption and to know that their prophecies are nigh. All things do come full circle and coil into the center.

May you know when you see the light and the wave of the
Central Sun approaching that this is your wave and this is the ship
Maitreya that you enter to cross the sea of samsara and to enter
new portals of light unto the Holy City.

I am your Jesus. Will you have me? ["Yes!"]

Yea, Lord Gautama Buddha! Yea, Lord Sanat Kumara! Let us
harvest the pearls and the pearls of souls who now may come to the
feet of their Holy Christ Self to be wholly washed, to be set on
course and to begin a course where there is no turning back, no
looking back but building increment by increment up the spinal
altar until light, all light, does infill this temple!

May you go forth with a sense of zeal to find those who are of
my house of the God-reality! May you go forth with a quickening,
with the good news of the Everlasting Gospel that I have preached,
that I have demonstrated, that has been outplayed in numerous
golden ages past. And you who seek, know you have been a part of
[this preaching, this demonstration of the law of Christhood, this
outplaying of the Everlasting Gospel] and you will not be satisfied
until you awake in the likeness of your Holy Christ Self.

Wield, then, the sword of the Spirit! Bind each and every foe
that would separate you from your God! May this be your walk.
May you shut out the din and the noise of this world and all of the
attention-getting devices of an electronic age that take your heart
and your inner ear and your mind from listening to the Great
Silence, from entering in to the Great Silence.

Cherish every breath you breathe, the inbreath and the outbreath, even a lifetime in one of these cycles. Cherish the moments
for the reconsecration of self, for the atonement; for atonement is
a necessary process. By atoning for karma, or sin, you enter that
oneness, that "at-one-ment" with your God, and no man shall
take thy crown.[5] No woman shall take thy crown. No force of evil
shall take thy crown.

Be sealed, then, in the wholeness of your causal body. Be one in
the Spirit with your twin flame and know that my heart is the open
door whereby you shall be protected and preserved for the day and
the hour when you are called—called to fulfill your mission, called

to make your statement, in your finest hour of the declaration of the Word, when you may stand before the world and witness unto the glory of God that truly has come for your salvation in this age....

These are days of accounting and accountability. And the false pastors preach from their pulpits *no* accountability, when I have not preached it! No, never have I said there is not accountability for the misuses of the kingdom of God, which is his vast consciousness!

No, beloved. Let the true Gospel that is everlasting be preached! May you open your mouths! May you receive the fire of the Holy Spirit for the cleansing of the throat chakra as the ancient prophets received it, that you might speak and [speak] only by the Holy Spirit and not by foul spirits.

I say, be cleansed this day! Let them come out! And know that it is time to walk a straight line that others might know the way to go and the way ye know, and it is surely unto the center of your God.

Look neither to the right nor to the left. Know that you can indeed skip steps on that spiral staircase by the acceleration of the mantra, by the Mother within you, by absolute mercy of heart that does forgive and forgive and forgive. And "Let vengeance be mine," saith the LORD.[6]

So therefore give love and know that you can indeed beat the Fates and your karma! You can transcend! You can go on! You can move and you can defy prophecy and make it fail and collapse before you as the legions of light go marching in.

Yes, "saints of God" I call you, for you have been labeled "sinners" too long. Now fit into the garment of saint and know that it is neither a martyrdom nor a boring experience but the most joyous experience in all eternity to feel the fire of God blazing through you and to know it as the power that can challenge corruption until corruption is consumed by the sacred fire itself....

I have Called you. And may you know that it is your turn to call, to call and to call again to me, crying out:

O Jesus, come into my temple!

O Jesus, my Lord, receive me as thine own.

I will answer you! I will tutor you! I will chasten you! I will take you firmly and show you the way [in which ye ought] to walk, the way in which ye have not walked in this life.

Yes, I speak to all! Let none feel so smug that they cannot become a child again and learn of me and take those sure and certain footsteps whereby, [having so taken them,] they might later leap and arrive at the gate.

Yes, beloved, this is the hour of the choice. It is the hour! May you choose this day and live forevermore.

April 28, 1991
Sir Francis Drake Hotel
San Francisco

COMMENTARY

These are days of accounting and accountability.

JESUS

In this dictation Jesus speaks of an ancient golden-age civilization. The time was 33,000 B.C. The place was Atlantis. Jesus, because of his great spiritual attainment, was ruler.

He speaks of the law of cycles and wide cycles of karma and initiation converging in this point in time and space as opportunity. After a very long cycle, the story of this golden age, lost to recorded history, can be revealed.

Before this dictation the messenger delivered the lecture, "The Golden Age of Jesus Christ on Atlantis." It is important to briefly review this lecture to understand more fully the teaching Jesus gives during this dictation.

In this story of Atlantis, we see many who turn away from God, and even from Jesus personally. Jesus says it is an hour for reconciliation with God, and he calls us to repentance. And so we understand that reconciliation and repentance may require us to go deep within and revisit ancient scenes where we perhaps first turned away from the Path.

The messenger tells us of this great people and this great land at the pinnacle of their civilization, with Jesus in their midst:

The Golden Age of Jesus Christ on Atlantis

"Jesus was the emperor of that golden age on Atlantis, 33,000 B.C. His consort was his twin flame, who we know today as the ascended lady master Magda. They ruled because they were the highest representatives of God in embodiment in that civilization.

"In this golden age, more than 50 percent of the people had risen to the bonding with the Holy Christ Self and walked the earth as Christed ones. All of the people of this civilization knew and accepted God's will. Jesus and Magda did not have to impose any rules on the people because they were all in attunement with their Divine Source.

"The people were not dependent on others for their food.
Every citizen of this civilization was capable of precipitating his
own food and also of levitating. They also were able to levitate
objects. Even those who were not yet fully clothed in their Christhood had these abilities, since they knew and practiced the laws
whereby they could accomplish these things. They maintained
the soul's tie to their God-source and applied the power-wisdom-
love of their I AM Presence to every aspect of their lives with joy
and gratitude.

"There were ten million inhabitants in this civilization, a
group of souls destined to be embodied under Jesus Christ and
who had embodied many times before. Some of them had come
from the Mystery School of Maitreya, having failed their tests,
and they had risen to the point of the bonding to their Christ Self
once again and now had the opportunity to make their ascension
if they would fulfill all things.

"The top twenty percent of the people dedicated themselves
to meditation and worship and also to teaching others. The lower
eighty percent pursued various occupations. The capital city was
made of white marble and gold. Gardens and monuments could
be approached from the air as well as from the ground.

"In a square paved with white marble in the center of the capital city burned the resurrection flame. It had a translucent
mother-of-pearl radiance and was 150 feet in diameter. The citi-
zens could walk into and through the flame without being burned.
In this way their bodies were recharged, their cells were invigor-
ated and they could be healed of any burdens in their bodies. Others less evolved could stand in arms of flame that spiraled from the
center as less concentrated extensions of the resurrection flame.

"In the great temple of the capital city, there burned another
flame. It was 180 feet tall and 60 feet wide. The flame, like the
latter, had no source of fuel. It was an 'unfed' flame, sustained by
the devotion of the people.

"After Jesus had reigned for 450 years, the people began to
be corrupt. The seeds of corruption were sown by one called
Xenos, who was chief counselor to the emperor. By and by,

Xenos wearied of giving glory to God for the civilization's achievements. Xenos reasoned in his heart that if he could gradually draw the people into outpicturing their lower animal natures, he would be able to control them, because, once they should consent to the lowering of the sacred fire, the descent of the Kundalini, they would lose the ability to provide for themselves.

"So he began by showing the people how to adorn and glorify their bodies. Jesus did nothing to stop the obvious ploys of Xenos. He stood back to allow the people to deal with this test that must come. They should have seen through the machinations of Xenos, especially those who were enlightened.

"One day, Jesus saw that the lower fifty percent of the people were no longer capable of providing food for themselves. They had followed the false guru, the false priest Xenos. Now Xenos, together with a band of fallen angels that he had gathered around him, was producing food for them.

"By the time fifty years had passed, only 20 percent of the people embodied the Christ. The other 30 percent had lost their tie to their Holy Christ Self. This is a shocking record, but we must hear it because one of the greatest problems that we all face today is to understand the nature, the logic, the modus of embodied evil. We cannot believe that embodied evil exists. Yet, Xenos had chosen consciously to now embody, not the light but the darkness. He had chosen to use his occult powers, his adeptship to make the people his slaves instead of to liberate them as true disciples of Jesus.

"The people had achieved the perfection of their physical bodies and had mastered elements of the physical octave. Now, under the influence of a false guru, they would become engrossed in those bodies. They would use them to control other people. They became addicted to sex and the spending of the sacred fire in pleasure.

"Over the fifty-year period the people's anger waxed strong against the emperor, and their hearts were not right with God or his Son who had faithfully served them for centuries. The people were also angry at the top 20 percent of the people who still embodied their Christhood.

"Finally, after they no longer had the power of destiny in their hands, Xenos convinced them to revolt against the government (personified in Jesus) because the government (in the person of Jesus) was supposedly not supporting them. Xenos raised an army of these 'disenfranchised' ones.

"Jesus and Magda left Atlantis with the two million of their subjects who retained the bonding to their Holy Christ Self. They went to the land of Suern, which includes modern-day India and Arabia. Xenos sat in the seat of the Christ, Jesus, and took his place. The once golden-age civilization gradually descended into barbarism as the people, imperceptibly to themselves, grew dense and insensitive to life. Looting and anarchy prevailed to the point where even Xenos lost control. Over time the cities disappeared and crumbled.

"You might be asking yourself, 'How could Jesus have allowed such a thing to happen?' Why does God allow anything bad to happen? The answer is, as simple as it may seem: *free will.* There is a law of hierarchy—and hierarchy means the entire range of unascended masters, masters, cosmic beings, archangels and the entire hierarchy of the servants of God, of light. And that law is that God sends his Servant Sons to earth— great avatars, Buddhas and Christs—and they reign over the people as long as the people will accept them and be obedient to the Law of the One.

"The Law of the One is the law of your I AM Presence—one God, one Christ, one Son and one chalice. And that one is multiplied billions of times over for every lifestream upon earth. That doesn't make millions of gods or millions of Christs. It is the individualization of the God flame where each one of us is. Those flames come together, and there is still only one flame and one God. Time and space enable us to behold a separateness that really does not exist in God consciousness.

"The people were influenced by false teachers. But they are still accountable for their actions. In any age, the people have free will to pass or to fail their tests. Their tests involve defending their right to be disciples of the Son of God and joint heirs with

Jesus Christ and of his Sonship.

"Do you daily defend your right to be a disciple of the living God, of Jesus Christ or Gautama Buddha or an ascended master, or of your own Holy Christ Self? Anything that you allow to come between you and your God is a breach in that sacred trust. Your reason for being is to be attached to one whom you can call teacher, one who will lead you in that path of the ascension.

"God has promised us that we can be heirs with Jesus of that Christ that he bore. But we ourselves must do it. We must do his works and follow in his footsteps. The Law says that if we fail our test, we must learn our lessons from the toiler. If we turn our backs on the true and living God, then we must be faced with a false teacher, a black magician who will have all the powers of Christ and yet use them to subjugate us instead of to elevate us and make us independent.

"We then come under the toilers and the spoilers and the fallen angels until that karma of the failed test is spent and we cry out for the living God and his true heir. If we do not challenge the false teachers and take our stand for the Son whom God has sent to us, even our Holy Christ Self, then that Son must withdraw. And that is how we get detached from the Holy Christ Self—by denying the inner voice of conscience that speaks so clearly to us with such clear, divine direction.

"So the Christ recedes because our vibration and consciousness is so opposed to that very light. And so there is a separation, and that separation increases until the bond is broken because our attention has been placed elsewhere.

"The Atlanteans rejected the living guru and replaced him with the false guru. Jesus was with them in the flesh. Yet they cast their vote for Xenos, the thief who took from them their life and their light and cut their tie to God. [We see the pattern repeated in a later embodiment when the people voted for Barabbas to be freed and for Jesus to be crucified.[7]] And, as has happened so many times in history, when the people lost their light, the light descended on the spinal altar. When this happens, they are no longer able to hear their God. They no longer hear the voice of

their I AM Presence, even when his emissaries stand before them
face-to-face.

"Of the two million who went with Jesus to Suern, half
made their ascension in that life. The other half of the two million have continued to evolve on earth until today. Most are in
embodiment right now, ancient Atlanteans come again to fulfill
their destiny in the present hour. These are the most highly
evolved lifestreams on earth, yet most of them have lost their tie
to their Holy Christ Self.

"Jesus said that some of these will be saved by him because
they will accept him and understand that he is necessary to save
their soul once again for the bonding to the Christ. He comes to
reestablish the tie."[8]

Meeting the Tests on the Path

We see in this history that the loss of the tie to the Holy
Christ Self, the fall in consciousness, did not happen overnight. It
happened little by little, almost imperceptibly. This is how we may
also fall away from the Path. Not all at once but very subtly we
move from our Christ centeredness and lose the perspective we
once had. We are pulled by the outer senses, and the ego begins to
hold sway. We gather around us others who support our position
and state of consciousness, and so we feel justified. Finding others to agree with us, however, does not mean we are on the right
path. As Proverbs says, "There is a way which seemeth right unto
a man, but the end thereof are the ways of death."[9]

The ancient Atlanteans faced their test. They met their
returning karma from ages even further back in history where
they had turned away from the Christ. They also faced the test,
as in the Garden of Eden, of the tempter, who would provide an
alternative to the path of the true Guru.

We will also face these tests. Perhaps one reason Jesus brings
the record of this golden age to our awareness is so we can
understand the past karma that will come due, understand the
mistakes we have made and learn from them. With an understanding of the teachings and the Path, we can make a conscious

decision to make a different choice this time around.

Jesus seeks to prepare us for these tests. He exhorts us to "bank the fires of the heart" so we will have the spiritual fire necessary to consume the karma that is returning to us personally. Each of us must pass through the dark night of the soul and the dark night of the Spirit, and we must be ready.

As we saw in chapter 7, in the ascent to perfection, the soul passes through what Saint John of the Cross describes as the "dark night." The first dark night is experienced as an individual encounters the return of his own personal karma—the human creation that almost completely obliterates for a time the light of the Christ Self and the I AM Presence. This dark night of the soul is in preparation for the dark night of the Spirit, which involves the supreme test of Christhood faced by Jesus on the cross when he cried out, "My God, my God, why hast thou forsaken me?" In this initiation, the soul is completely cut off from the I AM Presence and the heavenly hierarchy and must pass through the crucifixion and the resurrection, sustained solely by the light garnered in her own sacred heart, while holding the balance for planetary karma.

Beloved El Morya shows us how we can approach these initiations victoriously and pass through them as a whirling sacred fire of diamond light—thereby avoiding much suffering:

"Yes, beloved, loving the will of God and his Law, which is truly the law of profound love and wisdom, you shall then take heart—take courage to take on the path of the dark night of the soul and the dark night of the Spirit. And you will become such a whirling sacred fire of diamond light as my diamond heart is superimposed upon you that you will literally *charge* through that dark night of the soul and charge through the initiations of the dark night of the Spirit!

"You will not languish. You will not attenuate this suffering through your karma. Nor will you suffer, for you will have that mighty sword in hand and you will slay every foe and you will beam such a concentrated, God-controlled ray of the seventh ray of the violet flame through that third-eye chakra that you will see

the parting of the Red Sea of your own returning karma, the parting of the Red Sea of the fallen ones! And you will march through
triumphant! And you will be riding your steed, and it will not be
riding you. And I say it is true, and you must do it! You must
accelerate, for *acceleration is the key!*

"Go through it. Get it over with. Become the master of your
life. Come to that place where I may speak through you, where I
may dwell in you, where I may deliver the momentums of the
highest levels of the etheric octaves through you. And, therefore,
we together, guru and chela one together, may pass through this
earth and leave the foundations for our children and our children's
children that they might build that golden-age civilization."[10]

Jesus, the One Sent

Jesus has not left us since that ancient golden age of Atlantis.
He came again to Atlantis many times to establish the law, to
teach the people, to seek to reconnect them to their Christ selves
once again. He came two thousand years ago, in his final embodiment, to open the path of Christhood to all. And he is here today
on a rescue mission. He is looking specifically for the one million
souls who were once tied to his heart, and he also calls all other
souls who will open their hearts, hear his voice and be converted
in this hour of supreme opportunity.

The messenger explains the significance of Jesus' mission to us
throughout the ages: "One of the reasons I am giving this lecture
today is that I believe many lightbearers are in the New Age movement, and many of you have gone out of your churches of orthodoxy because you could not accept orthodox doctrine. You could
not accept what the preachers are telling you about Jesus, the
only Son of God, and you a miserable sinner, et cetera, et cetera.

"And so you have gone forth to seek a true teaching and a true
understanding, and, in the process, you have rejected a man-made
Jesus that has been created by Roman Catholicism and carried
through Protestantism to this hour. This is not the full and living
Great Guru Jesus Christ that I know. The fullness of the stature of
this Son of God and his greatness and the power he has had

throughout the ages to deliver us comes home through this vast understanding of the continuity of his presence on the earth with us.

"God appointed this Son of God to reunite us to that Christ Presence. And God has said to us, 'This is the particular ascended master, this is the specific Son of God that I have appointed to this task. If you will not bend the knee and recognize the light in him as the salvation of your soul, then you will not be able to raise up the light in yourself. You must first acknowledge him and the light in him, and then he will assist you to raise up the light in you.' This is the real message and the understanding of why... we must receive it from him and why he is the Saviour and the Lord of all people upon earth who wish to reattain, or to attain for the first time, that bonding.

"I believe that a false doctrine of orthodoxy that has been handed down to us has been the cause of the separation of Jew and Gentile, of Christian and Muslim, because they have made a god of a flesh-and-blood Jesus and denied that individuality of the God flame to all others.

"I believe that if these true teachings of Jesus Christ were known...that the whole world would understand the necessity of going through the open door of this one who has been holding this door open for us for so long....

"Why do we need him? Because we've squandered our light. We've let go of the hand of our Christ Self. And we cannot pick ourselves up by our own bootstraps any longer. Through the heart of Jesus you get to the heart of any ascended master of your preference, whether Gautama Buddha or Maitreya or Sanat Kumara or any other saint.

"But Jesus says, 'I am the open door which no man can shut. I am the open door to this union of your soul. And no man will enter by any other door....'[11] And that is his message."[12]

I Call You to Repentance

Jesus' Call in this dictation is expressed very simply as the Call to repentance. At first, the answer to this Call might seem easy—certainly when compared with previous calls to save the children and youth or to end abortion. And yet the Call to repentance really takes us to the very core of our being. It is no less challenging than the outer work in the world.

As we ponder our response to this Call, we must consider the real meaning of repentance. What is it that requires our repentance?

Jesus says, "I have called you from ancient times to this hour that you might finish that which you have begun." He tells us that cycles have turned and that "there is an hour of the Call. There is an hour to set aside the defiance against the LORD God and his Son who yet lives within you and within me."

Seeing some of the ancient history of our souls, we perhaps have a clearer idea of why we need to repent. It is not just the day-to-day mistakes and wrong decisions. In the ancient past we may have made a wrong choice that set the course of our evolution since that time. Unless we can set a new course for our lives by returning to that pivotal point, facing the same decision and making the right choice—and karmic cycles give us these opportunities—we may find ourselves creating anew after the old patterns.

When we repent, we feel remorse and ask God for his forgiveness. We truly desire to atone for our past errors. We surrender our sins and negative karma by laying them upon the altar.

Saint Patrick speaks of the importance of confession as part of the process of repentance: "Therefore, take heart and recognize the mighty purpose of confession. Recognize it in this hour: that every man's sin, whether recent or ancient, does accrue to him and therefore prevent the full covenants of God from manifesting. Why is this so? It is because God has made covenant with his beloved Son who is your own Christ Self, who is worthy of every offering and of the fullness of the science of Being.

"This offering the Christ, by his grace, does bestow upon your soul when the soul is ready and able to receive it, clothed upon with that wedding garment. Thus, you who have gained the wedding garment, if the garment becomes stained, do confess your sins in a sealed letter to Almighty God, to the heart of Christ, and let it be burned. And if you desire that the Mother of the Flame should know this also to pray for your salvation, you may write to her as well in a separate letter.

"And, therefore, beloved hearts, understand that confession, remission of sin, repentance therefore does once again restore you to that alignment with the chalice of being who is Christ. For Christ is the crystal chalice, Christ is the Holy Grail, and the light that is poured therein does become the nectar thou dost quaff.

"Beloved hearts of living flame, therefore, not once in a lifetime but daily submit the past and the present into the sacred fire that the call might go forth and be answered as though it were the call of your Lord. And truly you are his vessel, his representative, his instrument and his messenger as you keep your soul unspotted from the world.

"Blessed hearts, it is efficacious to the spiritual life to understand the meaning of this confession. For truly, in the crystal clarity of the mind that does fast and pray weekly and cast those sins in the sacred fire, there does come the presence of holy angels and the recognition of the voice of Christ and the inner independence in the I AM THAT I AM."[13]

Patrick suggests that we write our confession in a letter to God. It is good to put down in black and white exactly what we desire to surrender. It helps to objectify it so we can see it as something separate from ourselves. As we consign this letter to the physical fire, we make a conscious decision to put the things we have written into the flame. The angels will take the etheric matrix of the letter to the masters, who can work with us to assist in our healing and in balancing the karma.

Next, we invoke the spiritual flame to consume these things we have confessed. We give our prayers and our violet-flame decrees and call for the transmutation of any burden we may have placed on any part of life. If it is possible, make restitution to a person you have wronged. Ask forgiveness of anyone you have wronged, and seek to undo any harm you may have caused.

El Morya tells us: "If you are outside of the Law, whether human or divine, you must quickly confess your sins to the appropriate persons, make rectitude, correct such states and come into alignment. For the sin not confessed, the illegal posture not acknowledged, though none may know about it, does prevent the karma from descending and therefore does prevent the expiation of that karma—*even if you give the violet flame decrees daily.*

"The making right of all things with all persons in embodiment or elsewhere is most necessary, for the alignment with my heart or with the embodied messenger cannot be strong when there are those deeds, actions and records not in keeping with the Law."[14]

Finally, having made our confession and received forgiveness, let us not forget the words of Jesus: "Go and sin no more."[15]

SPIRITUAL EXERCISES

Write a Confession Letter

As you seek to answer Jesus' Call to repentance, it can be very valuable to write a confession letter including everything in your life up to the present that you wish to confess and put into the flame. This is a letter from you to the Master. No one else will read it.

In writing a confession letter, it is important to be specific. As you write the letter, specific incidents may come to mind. Write them down, not in great detail, but enough to identify the sin of omission or commission.

Jesus tells us: "It is a joy and a cause for rejoicing to cast into the sacred fire all that is not worthy of permanence in God. 'This, not that.' Thus, sort the memories. Thus, sort the records and the past, and therefore retain that which is worthy to be made a permanent atom in your being and in the kingdom of God's consciousness."

This letter might take a few hours to complete, or you might come back to it periodically over the period of a week. When your letter is finished, burn it in the physical fire as you consign its contents to the spiritual fire. Consciously surrender all attachment to these things and the former state of consciousness that led you into these detours from the Path.

Then, invoke the sacred fire. Call for the flame of forgiveness. Ask forgiveness of God and your fellowman, and send the flame of forgiveness to all you have ever wronged and all who have ever wronged you. Send the violet flame into the situations to transmute the burden placed on you or another. Call to Astrea to clear the records and cut you free from these momentums. Call to Archangel Michael to protect you and seal your determination not to repeat the mistakes of the past and to set a new course for your life.

This ritual is one you may wish to repeat from time to time. When you write a new letter, you do not need to include incidents that you included in a previous one. They have already been surrendered and cast into the flame. However, do include anything that has happened since the last letter and anything that has surfaced in memory that was not in a previous letter.

Ritual of Forgiveness

Forgiveness is an important part of the ritual of repentance. It is a quality of the violet flame and a key to the age of Aquarius. We seek forgiveness for our own karma and burdens we have placed on others, and we also need to forgive those who have burdened us. In the parable of the unmerciful servant[16] Jesus taught how important it is to forgive others. We also need to forgive ourselves and to be able to accept God's forgiveness when it is extended to us. Do not believe the lie that you are unworthy of being forgiven. As you forgive others, so you will be forgiven.

1. Think about those you need to forgive, and allow them to pass before your mind's eye. This includes anyone and everyone you may need to forgive—members of your family, friends, co-workers, the ascended masters, the Father-Mother God, and, most especially, yourself.

2. Ask your Holy Christ Self to bring to your awareness anyone you may need to forgive from this or any past life. You may even become aware of an ancient record from Atlantis or Lemuria that is ready to be transmuted. Your Christ Self will bring this to your outer awareness if you ask.

3. As these people or situations come to your awareness, consciously send them forgiveness. Send the violet flame as an action
of forgiveness to the people involved. Use the decree "The Law
of Forgiveness" or other violet flame decrees to reinforce this
action. See this violet-flame dissolving any resentment, anger or
non-resolution you may have over these situations.

4. Kuan Yin asks us, "Call upon the law of forgiveness. See yourself drenched in a holy unguent of purple fire, in a balm of violet ray. See yourself receiving that mercy in proportion as you
give it, for it is the Law that you will reap mercy only as you
sow mercy."[17] Use this visualization as you give the following
decree invoking the flame of forgiveness:

THE LAW OF FORGIVENESS

Beloved mighty victorious Presence of God, I AM in me, beloved
Holy Christ Self, beloved heavenly Father, beloved great Karmic
Board, beloved Kuan Yin, Goddess of Mercy, beloved Lanello, the
entire Spirit of the Great White Brotherhood and the World Mother,
elemental life—fire, air, water, and earth!

In the name and by the power of the Presence of God which I AM
and by the magnetic power of the sacred fire vested in me, I call upon
the law of forgiveness and the violet transmuting flame for each trans-
gression of thy law, each departure from thy sacred covenants.

Restore in me the Christ mind, forgive my wrongs and unjust
ways. Make me obedient to thy code, let me walk humbly with thee
all my days.

In name of the Father, the Mother, the Son and the Holy Spirit,
I decree for all whom I have ever wronged and for all who have ever
wronged me:

Violet fire,* enfold us! (3x)
Violet fire, hold us! (3x)
Violet fire, set us free! (3x)

I AM, I AM, I AM surrounded by
a pillar of violet flame,*
I AM, I AM, I AM abounding in
pure love for God's great name,
I AM, I AM, I AM complete
by thy pattern of perfection so fair,
I AM, I AM, I AM God's radiant flame
of love gently falling through the air,

> Fall on us! (3x)
> Blaze through us! (3x)
> Saturate us! (3x)

And in full faith...

* "Mercy's flame" or "purple flame" may be used here.

Saint Patrick calls us to confession and forgiveness on a daily basis. A very good time for this is at night before you go to sleep. Review your day, confess those things that were a compromise of your path and call upon the flame of forgiveness.

Pray Fervently to the Heart of Jesus

In this dictation Jesus gives us two mantras we can use. Give them with the full fervor of your heart as you pray to Jesus in answer to his call: "I have called you. And may you know that it is your turn to call, to call and to call again to me, crying out:"

> O Jesus, come into my temple!
> O Jesus, my Lord, receive me as thine own.

You can also give these mantras as you walk from place to place or at any time during your day.

FOR YOUR JOURNAL

How Will *You* Answer Jesus' Call?

"I Call you to repentance."

What does this Call mean to me?
What will I do to answer this Call?

CHAPTER 15

*"The Call of love"—the "outreaching of
your heart, your hand and your speaking
of my Truth… to all who have been
a part of me and my life."*

The Call of Love
In Preparation for the Wedding Day
Your Marriage to Jesus Christ

My beloved brides, I receive you to my heart in preparation for the wedding day. I come to you as you have come to me. And in this hour love suffuses our hearts as my Sacred Heart enfolds your own. And in this moment in the bridal chamber we prepare your soul for the entering in, which shall surely take place as you weave and continue to weave your wedding garment. Gifts of the violet flame given to you are also for the weaving of this garment. It is called the deathless solar body.

And you also recall the parable where the one came in to the marriage feast having not the wedding garment and that one was cast into outer darkness.[1] For, you see, your wedding must take place in the etheric octave, and to be in that octave you must have the appropriate soul apparel—the wedding gown and the bridal veil.

These garments, beloved, are the garments you are to perfect. For as you have been told, there are rents in your garment caused by all manner of intrusions, tears that come from encounters on the astral plane or the violent misuse of the light, from the rhythms of Antichrist and all manner of attacks upon your soul.

I, Jesus, desire to assist you in your preparations, for the wedding date is set and I, your Lord, expect you to be in that secret chamber at the appointed hour.

Indeed it is a boon—the gift of Omri-Tas, his presence and flame, of Saint Germain, the Maltese-cross formation and their multiplying of your calls to the violet flame [by the violet flame sea].[2] Surely you shall have the wisdom and the rejoicing in me to use this violet flame industriously so that the garment might be complete and strengthened and no more subject to the tears of the lower octaves.

It may be a bit difficult to visualize but nevertheless, beloved, you must call forth the armour of Archangel Michael and the seraphim of God, not only for the protection of your soul and your four lower bodies but also for the protection of this garment—[the deathless solar body] as both the undergarment of humility and the outer garment of honor.

For is not honor born of humility?

For when one comes to comprehend the honor of God, is one not humbled before the great light, the dazzling white light of the presence of the cosmic honor flame?

Honor, then, is an homage that you pay unto the living Christ that I AM and unto your God. It is the honoring of the light that is unsullied and untainted, the light that is the strength that holds together the Matter cosmos.

Honor is a strength beyond other strengths. Honor is purity. Honor is the majesty of God. It is the single-eyed vision and the adoration of the one true God. Honor is oneness. It is wholeness.

One cannot enter into its precincts without the ultimate understanding of humility, for humility is before God and before the living flame. It is a self-effacement for a purpose: that the lesser self be sealed and the Greater Self appear. It comes down to the saying I gave to your Catherine, "I the All: thou the nothing—I the All: thou the nothing."³

Thus, as you say it unto me, you say, "O Jesus, my Lord, thou the All and I the nothing. Thou the All and I the nothing!" And as you say it, beloved, my Christ Presence becomes my allness in you, and the mortal self disintegrates and the True Self is manifest. It is a yin and yang action of Alpha and Omega.

> O Jesus, my Lord, thou the All of me: I the nothing.
> Take my nothingness, O my Lord, and let me be the allness
> of thyself. Be the Christ in me, my Lord, and I shall be wor-
> thy—worthy to be thy bride, as thou art the Lamb and
> thou art worthy before the throne of God.

So it is, beloved, the transformation of self by the displacement-replacement. The honor of God it is.

In the sanctuary of love I commune with your heart—first with the heart, beloved. Now feel my sacred heart, for I desire you to probe with me the elements of heart that require healing, transmutation.

I give you to see now fractures in the mandala of the heart, violations of the twelve petals of the heart. I allow you to see the imbalance of the threefold flame and records of the past that show you clearly how in choices made you have reduced rather than increased that flame. I show you this in love, beloved, for love imparts truth and vision.

Having the vision now, as I show it to you, of your Holy Christ Self, you can see how much you are mirroring of that Self and how you can mirror more by meditating on the elements of the Christ Self and Christ flame that are wanting in the mirror of self.

I hold you, beloved, I strengthen you as you look and see. Let it be an objective and scientific study of who and what you are today and all that you can be tomorrow.

O my Holy Christ Self—thou the All and I the nothing—be thou myself as Holy Christ flame burning on the altar of my heart for my Jesus, my Bridegroom, my Lord!

Sweetness is indeed the taste of the living Christ flame. Taste, then, the essence of myself. Know it is the portion also of your Holy Christ Self.

Thus know me as your sweet Jesus but know me also as your counsellor, confessor and chastiser. I also come for the taming of the shrew of the lesser self, called the wretch.

Yes, beloved, this is a shadow, a shriveled-up form, a garment no longer worn but yet remaining in your closet. I strengthen you to take it out and see it. See this part of the not-self, the not-so-nice part [of you]. You take it. I hand it to you now and bid you cast it into the violet flame. Be done with it! And see how the flame rejoices to consume it!

O what gifts of wonder of the violet flame I did impart to my disciples and others of you in various ages, as you have been in the violet-flame temples of Atlantis! No wonder you are so happy to give the violet flame [decrees] in this embodiment! You have longed for [the violet flame], thirsted for it, sought it in the drinking of Communion's wine and the partaking of the bread. You have waited for the dispensation [to come] to you again and it has come, and you have become the devotees of the seventh ray.

May you also become brides of the seventh-ray hierarch, Saint Germain. May you become brides of the Holy Spirit, as Mother Mary did become the bride of the Holy Spirit.

Yes, beloved, when all of Chaos and Old Night and Armageddon threaten without like a violent winter storm, is it not good to commune in the secret chamber of the heart and to know a compartment of eternity that shall one day be the vastness of interstellar space for thee and me alone and for thee and thy twin flame?

Seek the marriage to the Christ! All other things shall come to you. Seek the sacred heart! Seek my blood and my body. Seek me everywhere!

Each time you find a corner of self where the rays of light now penetrate and you find the skeletons in your closet, so visualize my face and body, my presence there.

Remember the initiations I underwent in my final incarnation that you might know the pattern, the preparation of the soul through the violet flame [for her own initiations]: the forgiveness of the waters of the human consciousness as they become the wine, the sanctification of marriage as a sacrament in the Church and as the wedding of the soul to her Lord. Remember the path and the initiation of the alchemy of supply and the multiplication of the loaves and fishes by the power of Alpha and Omega.

Remember all of these footsteps while you are yet able to balance heart, head and hand by violet flame. [For this is the goal and the mandate of your soul's physical incarnation.] Remember the point of entering into congruency with the perfection of your inner blueprint by that divine direction.

Remember, then, the transfiguration as the soul enters into and receives the impression of the perfect pattern [of her Holy Christ Self] to be outpictured. Remember the crucifixion, for Christ in thee must yet be crucified. Yes, remember living in the heart of the earth in the presence of resurrection's flame as I did. Remember the resurrection. Remember the forty days of profound inner temple instruction [following]. Remember the ascension.

These are the key initiations and there are many in between. Resist them not, resist me not! Resist not my footprints in the sands! Resist me not, beloved.

And surely know the confession of the soul and the holy sacrament [of penance]. Know the baptism. Know the Communion. Know that thou canst be a part of holy orders and yet maintain the rites of marriage and family in the holiness of God. Remember the soul's appearing with first breath and the soul's departure with the last.

The consecration of these rituals, beloved, becomes a part of the larger spiral [that is your soul's bonding to my sacred heart] and is there as matrix complete when you are received as my bride and the bride of the Christ of you.

This moment of the fusion of hearts is a moment that comes after the final exams, as it were, of your life's record, your going out of the way and coming in again, going out of the way and coming in again, until finally all desire to go out is purged from you and your sole and principal desire is to remain bonded to my heart and never, never again to violate that sacred vow of our union. For this calling I did descend to rescue your soul, who had broken the tie to my heart.

I am come, beloved. Do not tarry and tarry again [in the outer way] unto future ages down the halls of eternity. Take [the initiation] in this hour. O take it! Take it and work so much good by my sacred heart become thy heart.

Surely this is the key to your becoming a candidate for the ascension. Surely thou canst not ascend without the prior bonding to that heart. Know it early, that all the days of thy life thou might impart to many the flame of love that is the bonding of our union.

I woo you to the bridal chamber that you might bear in your being and life that special love that all recognize and know as my love. When you are bonded to my heart you also have the Holy Spirit, whose gifts you can increase and multiply.

I desire you to be, as it were, salesmen for God,[4] for the path of

Christic union, for love itself. The world has not tasted the sweetness of this love, and souls who have lost it so long ago cannot remember the taste.

Let them know it through you, beloved! Let them know it! Let them know a love that rekindles a desire within them to also go and get that love, to seek me and find me even when I play hide-and-seek with them to test their real desiring to see if they will be deterred by an easier search and the finding of some lesser manifestation.

Inspire them to seek true love, the true love of Christ. Inspire them by your joy and patience, your meekness as well as the emboldening power of Elohim upon you taking wise dominion over the territories of the earth body in the sense of the territories of the mind and the heart and the domains of consciousness as compartments of being.

Yes, beloved, let my love in you be the irresistible force of cosmos that draws souls who can be drawn in by no other way but by my love. For having been beaten and bruised in so many circumstances, having had their loves betrayed again and again, these need the comfort of my love in you.

I the All of love within you: thou the All of love in me. Let this be the magnet of the Central Sun and your offering of gratitude upon the altar of God that you might now know and be and enter the golden cycle of the sun!

Oh, such a precious meeting of hearts in this place has come about! May you, as a nucleus of lightbearers worldwide, become the mandala of my sacred heart—the pattern, the form, the oneness, the heart of the mystical body.

O know this love tryst, beloved, and hasten to the altar of the marriage of thy soul to Christ!

This is my voice [in which I speak] to you, this is my message as I speak in the tenderness of the Divine Mother and the quietness of the Father, who does oversee the preparations of your soul.

I am your Jesus if you will have me. And if you will, I counsel you, drink, drink, drink quickly the elixir of violet flame for the dispelling of forgetfulness, for the remembering of all that we have been together since the beginning of our going forth from the Central Sun.

I call to all of those who have been a part of myself and my life. I call them through you and I call directly to their hearts. I call and I call and I call again! It is the call of love.

May the many who have not received me who once knew me be reached by your outreaching of your heart, your hand and your speaking of my truth.

Thou dost know and have my truth, beloved. Truth is an activating force of the Holy Spirit in your life. Let it take you where it will take you and move you as it will move you! Let it speak through you or be silent. Let it testify of me.

I am the witness of the God of love. May you be the witness of my flame, offering salvation by a path of rigorous discipleship in the rituals of love unfolding and becoming Love.

O Holy Spirit, O the allness of God, descend upon each one according as the Holy Ghost is wont!

I, Jesus, stand in the temple of the Central Sun even as I am here. And I establish, therefore, an arcing [of light to] your being that you might see and glimpse and remember the great cathedral that is called the Temple Beautiful. I assure you, beloved, that on your wedding day you shall be beautiful in the Temple Beautiful.

I seal your vows and send you back to life's journey with all of the zeal of the love we share forever and forever and forever.

Amen! ["Amen."] 🍇

October 14, 1991
New Orleans Airport Hilton
New Orleans, Louisiana

Let my love in you be the irresistible force of cosmos that
draws souls who can be drawn in by no other way but by love.
JESUS

The Call of love is Jesus' call for us to prepare our souls for our wedding day. He tells us that he desires to assist us in preparing for this initiation. He says, "The wedding date is set and I, your Lord, expect you to be in that secret chamber at the appointed hour."

How to Prepare for Our Wedding Day

Jesus tells us that to prepare for our wedding day—the alchemical marriage of our soul to the heart of our Holy Christ Self and to the Sacred Heart of Jesus—we must go deep within to find those elements of self that need healing and transmutation. We must also weave our wedding garment, our deathless solar body. Our souls must be clothed in this garment of light for this wedding ceremony. Many ascended masters have spoken to us of this wedding garment and the process of weaving it.

Serapis Bey in his *Dossier on the Ascension* teaches that the parable of the wedding garment relates to the deathless solar body. Sanat Kumara tells us that the deathless solar body is woven as we recite mantras, songs and decrees with devotion.

The Goddess of Light gives the following beautiful description of the deathless solar body: "The soul is the feminine aspect of your being. The soul is the bride waiting to unite with the Spirit and the hand of the Christ. And so, whether you occupy a male or a female form for the purposes of polarity in this world, know that the wedding garment is woven out of this very matrix that I place here by the scepter of my authority. And that wedding garment is like that precious swaddling garment that Mary placed around the Infant Child. It is a garment of light that the soul must wear. You see, you have been given coats of skin, four

lower bodies as the garment of consciousness for you to tarry in
time and space in Mater to gain self-mastery. But when that
mastery is won, the coats of skin must give way to that higher
light body, that deathless solar body consciousness of the Son,
and the only begotten of the One, of the Father-Mother God....

"As you invoke your own deathless solar body, call, then, for
the convergence of that pattern upon your own aura. Call, then,
for the filling in of the pattern with skeins of light, with the veils
of the Mother, with the weavings of the soul and the virtues of
your causal body. And see how, although the pattern is the same,
not two among you when you come before the Lords of Karma,
will find that you have woven the same wedding garment. For
each garment will bear the design of the flower of your soul identity, the symphony of your twin flame, the keynote of your life
and the seal of your divine plan fulfilled."⁵

Gautama Buddha describes the deathless solar body as "the
soul's garment unto eternal life." He explains that it "is composed
of an infinite number of stitches, and, if this were physical, it
would be a very thick knitting, inches thick.... The sphere of light
of the base chakra provides the yarn for this knitting, and it is fully
abundant unless squandered in unholy and ungodly action....

"By action, by word, as you go about the business of the
Father-Mother God, you are weaving and knitting that garment;
and the astral that was, disappears. It is displaced, for this body
[the deathless solar body] is light. It has infinite strength,
resilience, mother-of-pearl radiance. Know and see the beauty of
this garment. Treasure it. It is the weaving of many lifetimes.
Some weave slowly, some fast. Some return to their knitting in
every spare moment. Some set it aside for years."⁶

The Maha Chohan tells us of the experience of wearing this
garment: "You will know when the soul is weaving the wedding
garment by the feeling of comfort around your form that is like
unto a swaddling garment placed on a newborn child. It is a feeling of being in the warmth of God, in the bunting of the new
babe. It is the feeling of the flow of light around the aura of the
head. It is the feeling of being clothed upon and no longer stand-

ing naked, finding oneself in the consciousness of sin and running for the fig leaf consciousness."[7]

The Soul and the Alchemical Marriage

El Morya explains that the soul is the non-permanent aspect of the self: "God is a Spirit, and the soul is the living potential of God. The soul's demand for free will and its separation from God resulted in the descent of this potential into the lowly estate of the flesh. Sown in dishonor, the soul is destined to be raised in honor to the fullness of that God-estate, which is the one Spirit of all life. The soul can be lost; Spirit can never die....

"The soul, then, remains a fallen potential that must be imbued with the Reality of Spirit, purified through prayer and supplication, and returned to the glory from which it descended and to the unity of the Whole. This rejoining of soul to Spirit is the alchemical marriage, which determines the destiny of the self and makes it one with immortal Truth. When this ritual is fulfilled, the highest Self is enthroned as the Lord of Life, and the potential of God, realized in man, is found to be the All-in-all."[8]

The messenger explains that the soul, although born in mortality, can become immortal through the alchemical marriage: "We can think of the soul as a glisteningly transparent sphere that is constantly evolving—or devolving. The soul is the mortal part of ourselves that can become immortal—that must become immortal if she is to survive. To achieve immortality, the soul must be fused, or bonded, to her Higher Self, who is her Holy Christ Self. Yes, until this bonding takes place, the soul is impermanent and, therefore, can be lost. This is why souls who are not tethered to their Higher Self are in jeopardy on planet Earth."[9]

Our soul is the feminine aspect of our being in relation to the Spirit, which has the masculine polarity. Thus, we often refer to the soul as "she." The soul resides in the seat-of-the-soul chakra and prepares to become the bride of Christ.

The ascended masters tell us that our souls are child-like and need nurturing, protection and guidance from our Higher Self. However, the human ego also seeks dominion over the soul. It becomes the unloving parent, preventing our Higher Self, our heavenly Father-Mother, from leading the soul.

The soul is not whole, due to many past experiences and choices, including traumas, violence and abuse—mental, emotional or physical. The soul has wounds and scars that need healing. The Goddess of Wisdom tells us that fragments of the soul may even have become lost: "In some cases, the soul, its forcefield, has been split by very intense fears of the past—traumatic experiences wherein you might say the soul has been driven underground, far into the depths of the subconscious like a frightened child. The soul must be called back."[10] These fragments of our soul remain there until we consciously work on healing these past traumas.

As we diligently give the violet flame and direct it into the records of pain, the parts of our soul can be healed and drawn back to the seat-of-the-soul chakra.

The Path of Love

In this dictation Jesus speaks often of love. He Calls us to a path of love, to reach out to those who have been a part of himself and his life. He desires that his love burn in us as a sacred conflagration and that, on fire with the love of God, we reach out to enflame other souls with this divine love that has consumed us.

In order to fulfill this request and to be the fullness of the love that we have received, we must first be able to love and compassionately embrace our own souls. We must feel worthy and be able to receive God's love for us—then we can share this love with others.

The messenger offers eleven keys to giving and receiving more love. Day by day, as we work on unlocking our own hearts and the hearts of others, we become the instruments of Jesus as we are increasingly able to answer his Calls. As our hearts unfold, God fills our chalice with more of his light, more of his love, blessing us and, through us, others.

1. **Be open to exploring the roots of your inner pain and your sense of guilt.** We can only get so far on the spiritual path

without digging deeply into our psychology.

2. **Let go of the past.** If you continually revolve the past, you aren't free to move on.

3. **Forgive.** First, last and always, forgive, forgive and forgive.

4. **Use the violet flame to transmute burdens of the heart.** Sometimes you may feel burdened without knowing why. It may be because your burdens rise up from your unconscious mind to reveal events of past lives. When this happens, it indicates that the Maha Chohan is opening a crack so that you might understand past karma and how you can balance it today.

5. **Increase the magnet of your heart by activating joy and gratitude.** Joy goes hand in hand with love. Joy is contagious, and it's magnetic. If you have joy, you can give and receive more love.

6. **Establish heart perspective.** Practice seeing, thinking, doing through the heart.

7. **Stretch a little bit every day.** Saint Germain says that if you want to expand the love in your heart, then "go out and find those who need your love and give cup upon cup of love's elixir to all who will receive your love."[11]

8. **Establish vertical versus horizontal relationships.** So many times we try to connect horizontally, directly from person to person. In order to have a deep and truly satisfying connection with anyone, we have to move vertically—through the nexus of our Higher Self and their Higher Self. When you reach out to another, you are really giving your love to God—because you are serving the God who lives within them.

9. **Guard the heart against forces of anti-love.** The heart is extremely sensitive to all types of vibrations. Don't let it be bombarded by dissonant sounds or discord. Protect the heart by giving decrees to Archangel Michael.

10. **Cultivate softness.** Softness is ultimate strength. Softness is a nurturing, giving attitude. Rather than reacting to another's anger or emotions with more anger and emotions, softness is responding from a position of centeredness—from a heart perspective.

11. **Love and nourish yourself.** Jesus said: "Thou shalt love thy neighbor as thyself."[12] How can you really love your neighbor if you don't first love yourself?[13]

Djwal Kul tells us: "Love is something that does not stand still but must be practiced. We can affirm that God is love. Then we must turn around and be that love in action by being our brother's keeper."[14]

SPIRITUAL EXERCISES

Meditation on the Christ Self

The messenger teaches the nature of our relationship with our Christ Self and gives a meditation and visualization for the forming of that Christ within us: "The apostle Paul was the first mystic who recorded the concept of the indwelling Christ being formed in us. He wrote in Galatians, 'I travail in birth again until Christ be formed in you. I live, yet not I, but Christ liveth in me.'[15] Paul proclaimed the Christ within as the inheritance of all Christians....

"If you have a Holy Christ Self, then why does Christ need to be formed in you? The Holy Christ Self is above you in higher planes. When you visualize Christ being formed in you, see this as points of light coming together in concentration, originally dispersed and vapory with no form or shape. As you begin to know who is Christ and what is Christ, his attributes, his works, his words, as he lives daily, there is forming in you your concept of Christ, your image of Christ, the Christ whom you adore and whom you worship, the Christ who is your brother and teacher and friend.

"And so each day that Christ is being formed in you, becoming more concentrated as light until the very presence and outline and truly the form of your Holy Christ Self is duplicated here below. Paul said that Christ lived in him, and he discovered that when Christ lived in him, he no longer lived in himself. He said,

'I live, yet not I, but Christ liveth in me.' And so he was no longer 'I, Paul.' He was 'I, Paul, one with the Christ.' "[16]

Use this meditation and visualization to assist you in drawing down the light of your Holy Christ Self.

Give Jesus' Prayers

Jesus gives us two prayers in this dictation. Say these prayers as you enter deeply into the sense of oneness with him.

> O Jesus, my Lord, thou the All of me: I the nothing. Take my nothingness, O my Lord, and let me be the allness of thyself. Be the Christ in me, my Lord, and I shall be worthy—worthy to be thy bride, as thou art the Lamb and thou art worthy before the throne of God.

Jesus tells us as we give this prayer that "my Christ Presence becomes my allness in you, and the mortal self disintegrates, and the True Self is manifest. It is a yin and yang action of Alpha and Omega."

> O my Holy Christ Self—thou the All and I the nothing— be thou myself as Holy Christ flame burning on the altar of my heart for my Jesus, my Bridegroom, my Lord!

Replace Your Unreal Self With a Visualization of Jesus

Jesus tells us to seek him everywhere! And he teaches us, when we are confronted with an aspect of our unreal self, to replace it with a visualization of himself. He says: "Each time you find a corner of self where the rays of light now penetrate and you find the skeletons in your closet, so visualize my face and body, my Presence there."

Weave the Wedding Garment

Jesus asks us to pursue two specific actions with the science of the spoken Word in order to weave our wedding garment. The first is the action of the violet flame. Try not to miss a day of giving your violet-flame mantras for the weaving of this deathless solar body. It is also the most practical and efficient way to stay ahead of your karma!

The violet flame is the most physical of all flames. When we invoke it, transmutation goes on at all levels. The violet flame not only expel toxins lodged in our physical organs but also transmutes the karmas and traumas of our present and past lives recorded in our etheric, mental, emotional and physical bodies.

Jesus also asks us to visualize and call for the armour of Archangel Michael and the seraphim for the protection of the deathless solar body. You can include this call and visualization with your daily decrees to Archangel Michael (see page 43).

For the action of the violet flame, you can use the decree "I AM the Violet Flame" (see page 71) or any of the many violet flame decrees that the masters have given. Here is another one, "Radiant Spiral Violet Flame." Use the preamble and ending from "I AM the Violet Flame" with this decree.

RADIANT SPIRAL VIOLET FLAME

Radiant spiral violet flame,
    Descend, now blaze through me!
Radiant spiral violet flame,
    Set free, set free, set free!

Radiant violet flame, O come,
    Drive and blaze thy light through me!
Radiant violet flame, O come,
    Reveal God's power for all to see!
Radiant violet flame, O come,
    Awake the earth and set it free!

Radiance of the violet flame,
    Explode and boil through me!
Radiance of the violet flame,
    Expand for all to see!
Radiance of the violet flame,
    Establish mercy's outpost here!
Radiance of the violet flame,
    Come, transmute now all fear!

And in full Faith I consciously accept this manifest, manifest, manifest! (3x) right here and now with full power, eternally sustained, all-powerfully active, ever expanding, and world enfolding until all are wholly ascended in the light and free!

Beloved I AM! Beloved I AM! Beloved I AM!

FOR YOUR JOURNAL

How Will *You* Answer Jesus' Call?

"The Call of love"—the "outreaching of your heart, your hand and your speaking of my Truth... to all who have been a part of me and my life."

What does this Call mean to me?
What will I do to answer this Call?

CHAPTER 16

*The Call to prepare for the initiation
of the descent into hell.*

The Descent into Hell

I AM the Bridegroom, yet I come not in the midnight hour[1]—happily for thee.

Beloved ones, I have chosen to come in this quadrant of the day of Thanksgiving[2] that those who have authored the day with their early celebrations might know that the finisher of their faith[3] does remain. For those that are first shall be last, yet those who are last are first.[4] Thus enter ye, the firstfruits, and fulfill unto the last.

I come to plant my shepherd's crook in your desire body and in the astral plane of the earth. Yes, beloved, you must also pass through the astral plane and the astral sea. Better do it while you have physical body that you will not be required to tarry there after the body is no more. For when you have physical form you have the option of anchoring the full mind of Christ. But then the attainment is set. And therefore, let him that is filthy be filthy still; let him that is pure know purity still at the hour of passing.[5]

Many opportunities have been given to you to balance karma in this life. And [you have been given] a path so clear it is as the clear stream of the River of Life. Now count the blessing of God-harmony, God-gratitude and God-justice. These three, beloved, are the sign of the conquering of the astral plane.[6]

Yes, happy are ye when you meet the Bridegroom, who shall receive you as his own and therefore take you down the spiral staircase that does lead to the very depths of the subconscious and the unconscious. Therefore with thy Bridegroom, the Bridegroom who does come this day in the person of myself, conquer death and hell while the hour is yet with you, while the breath of the Holy Spirit is with you and while the fire can be increased in the heart.

Know well the teachings of Phylos: All progress does cease at the hour of the passing of the soul from this body.[7] Thus you will wait and wait again and perhaps seek to serve penance in some level of the astral plane or the etheric if you have well prepared.

But, beloved, how many more thousand times does the victory count in the physical octave? I can scarce tell. Therefore know the truth and let the truth make you free. And know that the sword of truth is the flame of truth in action. No greater defender is there than Pallas Athena for the truth of your immortal being.

Therefore, be willing to probe and ponder self, to wrestle when you see the tip of the iceberg and know that much remains in the unconscious. Be willing to grapple and deal with these things.

Why do I speak of it?

Because of much self-indulgence and willingness to dwell in dreams of unreality and spells that are cast upon you by those who know that the way to detour a keeper of the flame is to take that one upon fanciful thought, thinking, feeling, fanciful daydream-ing—dreaming of things that might be, that one will do someday, whiling away the moments, the seconds and the minutes that are cups that could contain infinity.

Knowing infinity takes only sixty seconds, but what is the preparation for the sixty seconds, beloved?...

Make up, then, for lost time, for this is an hour when many lightbearers must be ready for the descent into hell. I have waited long enough for your preparation. Therefore if you are not pre-pared, prepare quickly, for I shall take you with legions of the seven archangels. Many are required in this life to descend to lev-els where you would not ordinarily abide, for there you have left records and the worst of your karma and those things that must be transmuted else they shall shortly come to pass as outpicturing calamities in your life....

Pray every day that the LORD shall give you the resurrection and the life. Pray every day for the armour of Saint Michael the Archangel and Holy Justinius whereby you shall descend that stair-case with me. We may do it again and again and again, ten thou-sand times, year in, year out.

Will you weary? Will your hands become dried and cracked? Will your nails separate from your fingers as you approach the heat of hell itself?

I tell you, beloved ones, be willing to descend into your own unconscious and subconscious but [be] clothed upon with the Sun of the mighty I AM Presence. This you can and shall do and by it have a glorious resurrection, a *glorious* resurrection, I say—not merely "a better resurrection"[8] but a glorious one.

Walk the earth, therefore, conquerors of death and hell. And to know the difference between absolute Evil and absolute Good, beloved, truly enter in to the sacred fire that does consume the sympathy with self of the human consciousness.

O beloved, trace the feelings. Ratify those that are the desiring of God. The joy of your soul and of God's desiring is that you should be the Christ as I AM.

Hurry, then. Hurry, then, to make your peace with God. Let no disruption or eruption from deep within steal from you the great love tryst with your own Christ mind.

And remember you are tested day by day to see if you will be moved. For when the hordes of hell bark at you and howl, when they come with their flinging of hot mud as [they did] against Gautama, when these temptations come, beloved, and they try one last try to steal you from the altar of God, then I say, take your stand and remember that the God Presence will descend upon you in that hour. The mantle of the Great White Brotherhood shall be upon you and the mantle of the messenger, who walks in my footsteps, standing with those who are lost—the sheep who have gone astray or those who have been captured by the wolves....

Through [the true and living guru-chela relationship] which we have established, beloved, you may know me as Master and I may call you disciple; and you may have my direct love, my own heart, my Body and my Blood. Yes, beloved, this *is* the living Church, for the ascended masters move among it, and the chelas and the disciples have touched the hem of the garment of God.

Where others, beloved, do not invoke the violet flame or give the decrees you give and as all the children give also, we use from your reservoir of light, as we know you would have us, those energies that are needed by many hearts of goodwill who yet know not how to pray and draw down truly the fire of God. This is indeed a dispensation.

Many of you are tied, by your own volition and consent at inner levels, to individuals of great light who yet have but fragmentary prayers of the old dispensation. And you have offered to sustain them in their great and mighty work across the earth by your constant decree vigil. Sometimes when you do not have time to come to the court and you feel heavy and burdened, know that your light has gone to these and it is time to renew your cups and draw down more fire of God.

The key to that fire, beloved, is also the flame of devotion and adoration spoken of this day by the messenger. The love tie to God gives you a great magnet whereby you can draw more and more and more light. And as you learn the mastery by the sacred breath of that light and fire, beloved, so you shall know an increasing light in the aura.

Watch, then, how the ovoid of light does expand and expand and how you are able to give more and how you must defend more that very light and maintain your position on the Path and your vibration....

You shall know the hosts of the LORD. Most of you have prepared diligently with the almost unceasing use of the Archangel Michael decree and song tape, the Archangel Michael Rosary and also the tapes of beloved El Morya. This has put you in the position, beloved, where it is safe for me to guide you to the depths. And when you go there, beloved, and when we work together with the assistance of mighty angels, you shall be cut free, unless of course you go back to the ways of your own self-indulgence of emotional and astral levels.

You are a creator and a co-creator. As you can uncreate, so you can re-create the former conditions. Therefore, guard the flame, guard the consciousness and take the extra moments you have to seal yourself in the mighty power of God.

Let freedom of religion know the new birth, for the signs of the times and the signs in the heavens portend it—passing through severe persecution and on to an unprecedented freedom. This is the hour to fulfill astrology as you fulfill prophecy—in action, acting quickly and seeing an opportunity and making the most of it.

Thus, sometimes the Call is an act, beloved. Action itself will enable you to be the fulfiller of your destiny rather than to watch the astrology and simply think it will happen because the portent is there.

The portent, beloved, is like the potential. The Christ-potential is always with you. What you make of it and what you do with it from dawn to dusk, through all your waking hours and then out of the body at night is all the telling.

Nothing is guaranteed by potential. Nothing is guaranteed by astrological portent. These are signs of the times. Nothing is guaranteed by positive or negative karma but what you make of it in the nexus of time and space while you have breath and life and body and mind and reason and experience.

Yes, beloved, the hours fly swiftly. The sands descend with regular time. Enter in to the time frame and beat the Fates.

Know that eternity in sixty seconds. Yes, beloved, it can be done. Let the preparation begin....

All is well, beloved. All is well. Enter in now to the love of the Christ, the Holy Christ Self, who does now acquaint you with the flame of peaceful love and loving peace.

This is a day of peace and a day to contemplate the preservation of America at every level of being. You may do this by preparing your four lower bodies, your soul and your spirit, your mind and your heart that you might be the incarnation of the Word, I AM THAT I AM, and therefore make possible that which might have been the impossible on behalf of millions.

God shall honor the single Christ who is born among you—or the many [Christs]. It is your choice, beloved. See that you do not neglect your physical Christhood. 🌿

November 28, 1991
Thanksgiving Day
Royal Teton Ranch
Park County, Montana

> *Now count the blessings of God-harmony, God-gratitude*
> *and God-justice. These three, beloved, are the sign of the*
> *conquering of the astral plane.* JESUS

Jesus calls us "to prepare for the initiation of the descent into hell." Clothed upon with the armour of Archangel Michael, and prepared with the circle and sword of Astrea and the violet flame, we are ready to answer the call of the Master and go with the legions of the seven archangels into levels of the astral plane. Jesus explains that this preparation is important because "many are required in this life to descend to levels where you would not ordinarily abide, for there you have left records and the worst of your karma and those things that must be transmuted else they shall shortly come to pass as outpicturing calamities in your life."

Christianity teaches that between his crucifixion and resurrection, Jesus descended into hell, where he preached and brought salvation to souls imprisoned there. The apostle Peter stated that Jesus "preached unto the spirits in prison."[9] The tradition of Jesus' triumphant descent into hell is affirmed in the Apostles' Creed, the statement of the fundamental tenets of Christian belief that, in its earliest form, can be traced back to the second century. The Catholic version of the creed states that Jesus "was crucified, dead, and buried. He descended into hell; the third day he arose again from the dead."

The Elohim of the third ray, Heros and Amora, explain that Jesus' "descent into hell" was a descent into levels of the astral plane of planet Earth. "You have been told by the messenger that there are thirty-three levels, descending in vibration, of hell, just as there are thirty-three levels of initiation moving into the higher etheric octaves unto the ascension.

"I unveil for you, then, a labyrinth of the layers of hell upon this earth, and as they proceed downward, it is almost as though you would travel through the catacombs. Those of you who have traveled through the catacombs in Rome and have had to understand how the Christians could survive there must also know that these faithful ones (many of whom have been waiting in the etheric octave in the resurrected state until you should also come to that place on the path of your soul's initiation in the resurrection flame) were simultaneously undergoing this initiation of the descent into hell; yet some of them spent the remainder of their lifetimes in the catacombs in those conditions of darkness and cold.

"Know, then, that this descent into hell by the Lord Jesus Christ was a descent into every one of the thirty-three levels, and he did preach the rebuke of the living flame of Truth unto all who dwelt in them. Whatever the station or state of consciousness he found them in, the Lord did preach his message into the very teeth of their viciousness, into the very darkness and depths thereof."[10]

Physical and Astral Planes Overlap

The ascended masters teach that, while the astral plane is a level of being beyond the physical, it does overlap with the physical plane. The messenger describes the levels of the astral and explains what is found at these levels: "So we can see that it is possible in a portion of our lives to overlap and occupy the first level of the astral plane—worlds of illusion, rock music, sensuality and drugs. Deeper and deeper into that darkness we can descend to level two, three, four, five, six, seven.

"And when we get to level seven, we are on that border where we can, then, tread in the levels of death and hell that relate to the Atlantean compound.* It is very dark at level eight, and it continues in blackness in continuing gradations to the very bottom where lifestreams who have committed crimes against humanity wait out their cycles prior to their appearance before the Court of the Sacred Fire and the twenty-four elders.

---

*a level of the astral plane where recalcitrant souls from the time of Atlantis were detained in order to prevent their reembodiment for a certain cycle of time.

"I have seen, through calls I have made for the binding of certain individuals who have been perpetrators of evil against mankind, that they have been in that thirty-third level. And because their time was up and I made the calls to God, they were bound and taken out of that level where they had been in and out of embodiment for many, many lifetimes and since they passed on in their life in the twentieth century."[11]

Transmute All Ties to the Astral Plane

The messenger teaches that we must be determined to reach the etheric octave at the time of our transition. And we must also make the calls while we are yet in the physical octave to transmute with the violet flame any karma that would hold us and bind us to the astral level:

"If you transmute your karma made with the astral plane, with people who live in the astral plane and are of it, then, you see, you don't have the ties and the obligations to enter that plane in order to pay your debts. It is far preferable to pay those debts while in physical embodiment, because when you are out of embodiment it is much easier to get lost in the astral plane while you are attempting to balance karma there. The Catholic teaching is correct. There are such levels as limbo—first and second and third levels of gradations of hell that are of less intensity. Going there is not a guaranteed return. So while we have life and breath, we want to serve to set life free, do our violet flame and Astreas, and withdraw our energies from that level."[12]

The messenger explains that "it is the mission of the messenger and all who follow the path of Christic initiation in the footsteps of our Lord to 'descend into hell,' i.e., the astral plane, with Jesus to rescue souls of light, to rebuke and preach repentance to the fallen ones and to call for the judgment and the binding of those who remain in the death consciousness—avowed destroyers of life."[13]

Archangel Michael cautions us to have on the whole armour of God if we are going to deal with these levels of darkness. "Thus, you must be wise and realize that merely because you have a tube of light and the action of my blue flame and sword is no guarantee that if you descend into hell and do play with the fires of hell and say, 'I am immune,' you will not be caught up in a situation in which you will find yourself ill-equipped to deal with the forces unleashed against you.

"Therefore, the wise seek the holy mountain of God and the Holy of Holies of their own I AM Presence, and they remain on guard. This is the very first lesson of the angels of our bands and you who would desire to serve with us at inner levels. You have heard the statement, 'Fools rush in where angels fear to tread.' Until you know solidly how to invoke spiritual protection in the physical/astral/mental/etheric planes and to be certain that you have on the armour of the angels of the first ray, do not so lightly go into places of darkness."[14]

This is why it is essential for the lightbearers to invoke the protection of this mighty archangel by giving his decree daily. (See chapter 2.) As you give this decree, visualize Archangel Michael standing before you. See in your mind's eye his sword of intense fiery blue flame protecting you and cutting you free from all unwanted astral substance. See yourself clothed in the armour of the angels.

Saint Germain encourages us: "You must believe in yourselves. And you must believe that God in you can bind and conquer death and hell. That is the equation. And if you believe it with all your heart and mind and soul, the fallen angels will not be able to move against you. Yes, that is the equation. Try believing in yourselves; for every son and daughter of God who believes in God and believes in himself can have the victory."[15]

Be Willing to Descend into Your Own Unconscious and Subconscious

As part of our preparation for the initiation of the descent into hell, Jesus asks us to descend the "spiral staircase" that leads to our own subconscious and unconscious. These layers of our own being must be cleaned out so that there is no point of vulnerability, no magnet within us of like vibration to these levels where we must accompany Jesus.

Lanello speaks of this process of descending the spiral staircase of our own being to do this inner work: "The Holy Spirit is the great multiplier, beloved. Therefore, understand that when your heart is a well of living fire, the multiplication of that fire is also infinite. But if there be lurking somewhere in the folds of the garment of the unconscious, indeed, a force of anti-love neglected, left there long ago, which you have since sought to transmute but you have not—if this be the case, beloved, there is also a multiplication, by your tie to the Great White Brotherhood, of that substance.

"Thus, I must warn you, before you make your first mark on the journal of 1993, that you are in a karma-making situation when you fail to pursue the inner resolution of that original ancient point of anger (and all the other Martian manifestations) that divided you from your God. It is one thing to recite these conditions of consciousness that they might be bound through your decrees, but it is another to truly desire it—to go after them and to exorcise them.

"Yes, be the deep-sea diver! Go down to those levels and ask to be taken this night not to retreats but to the caverns and canyons of your own subconscious and astral body and the unconscious, beloved. For this is the place that you must now revisit, the place where you who have remained here in the community have the strength to go.

"Yes, you have the strength to descend with accompanying seraphim and members of the bands of seven archangels and to call for the exorcism of those points of darkness, neglected, long-forgotten, that still weigh you down as though you were yet carrying a burden on your back that you carried ten thousand years ago. And indeed you are, but you have forgotten that you yet carry that burden.

"Well, I wish to quicken the memory. And I wish you to offer the prayer and use this call, beloved."[16] (See Spiritual Exercises for the prayer given by Lanello.)

Human Sympathy and Divine Compassion

Jesus desires us to "walk the earth, therefore, conquerors of death and hell. And to know the difference between absolute Evil and absolute Good, beloved, truly enter into the sacred fire that does consume the sympathy with self of the human consciousness."

Sympathy with the self is the attitude that allows us to live with our imperfections or indulgences. We feel sorry for ourselves, so we have an ice cream or do something to make ourselves feel better. We realize we have a problem, but we say, "Poor me, what can I do?"

We always need to have compassion for ourselves, and realize that even though we may have human imperfections, we should not indulge these things. We need to love ourselves, but at the same time maintain the constant determination to come up higher and transcend our limitations.

We also need to have compassion for others while not indulging in sympathy. The ascended masters have often counseled their chelas to learn the difference between human sympathy and divine compassion. When we become involved in sympathy and feeling sorry for ourselves or for someone else, we are, on a certain level, accepting human imperfection and, therefore, reinforcing it and giving light to it. This kind of sympathy does not have the strength to help us or another person rise above their negatives or the burdens they carry.

True compassion comes from the heart, and brings the strength of the Christ to contact the point of the Christ in another person and help him or her overcome any negative conditions.

SPIRITUAL EXERCISES

Give Lanello's Prayer to Descend the Spiral Staircase

Lanello has given us a prayer to help us transmute the records of anti-love buried deep within our own subconscious/unconscious. He asked us to give this prayer for thirty-three consecutive days and to call for his assistance in doing this inner work, so important to our Path.

Prayer to Descend the Spiral Staircase

I call now to my beloved Lanello, my mentor of the Spirit. I call to El Morya, Archangel Michael and the Lords of Karma, my own Holy Christ Self and I AM Presence and all who assist me on my way.

Take me now, O holy ones of God, down the spiral staircase into the depths of the subconscious, the electronic belt, the astral plane and the unconscious. Take me there, O God! With covering cherubim guide my feet, guide my heart and mind.

Therefore, I ask for the armour of seraphim and Archangel Michael and the helmet and shield of the Lord and the sword of blue flame. And I ask to be guided by the Maha Chohan as to what I may be delivered of, and I would perform that exorcism under the living Christ Jesus, my Lord.

I call, then, that day-by-day for thirty-three days I shall achieve the undoing of those substances that dwell within me that will not speed me on my way to a glorious God-freedom that I seek but will only hold me back.

And, therefore, O God, I surrender that portion of myself that helps neither you nor me. I ask that I might be cut free from all individuals that I have ever been a part of where the will of God dictates that I ought to be cut free. I ask to help those I may help and to remain tied to those with whom I should remain tied according to the will of God. And I call for the balancing of all karma by the violet flame.

It is my deep desire, O mighty I AM Presence, that I might be delivered of excess baggage now, that I might become a better servant of the Lord Sanat Kumara and that I might be free to help others—free of the schisms in my own psyche, free of all encumbrances of the human consciousness, so that I need not withhold the perfect gift to anyone, friend or foe or stranger, who does knock at my door.

I commend this prayer to the heart of God for adjudication. And I pray for the dividing of the way of the Real and the unreal within myself that Victory might have his day through me.

As a humble pilgrim on life's way, I seal my prayer this day, O God. God, help me! God, help me! God, help me![17]

Invoke Protection from Archangel Michael Daily

The Spiritual Exercises in chapter 2 include one decree to Archangel Michael. Many disciples of Jesus give this decree for twenty minutes or more each morning. It is a wonderful ritual for beginning each day with the archangels and ensuring that we have their ongoing protection.

Here is a short decree to Archangel Michael that is ideal to give when you are traveling. Visualize the presence of Archangel Michael on every side of you as you give this call.

TRAVELING PROTECTION
Lord Michael before, Lord Michael behind,
Lord Michael to the right, Lord Michael to the left,
Lord Michael above, Lord Michael below,
Lord Michael, Lord Michael wherever I go!

I AM his love protecting here!
I AM his love protecting here!
I AM his love protecting here!

Give Pope Leo XIII's Prayer

"One day when Pope Leo had finished Mass, he stopped at the altar as if in a trance. Later he explained he had overheard Satan speaking to Our Lord. Satan requested 75 years to attempt to destroy the Church. The Lord said, 'You have the time; you have the power. Do what you will.' The pope understood that if the devil had not accomplished his purpose at the end of the time limit, he would suffer a crushing defeat. He also understood that through prayer and sacrifice and living good Christian lives, we could offset the power of the devil and his human agents. Thus, Pope Leo composed a prayer to invoke Archangel Michael's intercession, which was said at the conclusion of Mass for 78 years. This practice was discontinued after Vatican II. Pope Leo XIII's prayer, revised and updated by the messenger for students of the ascended masters, is included in Archangel Michael's Rosary for Armageddon."[18]

Before giving this prayer it is important to call to Archangel

Michael for your protection. Give the "Traveling Protection" decree or other decrees to him.

Saint Michael the Archangel, Defend Us in Armageddon

Saint Michael the Archangel, defend us in Armageddon. Be our protection against the wickedness and snares of the devil. May God rebuke him, we humbly pray. And do thou, O Prince of the heavenly host, by the power of God, bind the forces of death and hell, the seed of Satan, the false hierarchy of Antichrist and all evil spirits who wander through the world for the ruin of souls. And remand them to the Court of the Sacred Fire for their final judgment [including: ___(insert optional personal prayer here)___].

Cast out the dark ones and their darkness, the evildoers and their evil words and works, cause, effect, record and memory, into the lake of sacred fire "prepared for the devil and his angels."

In the name of the Father, the Son, the Holy Spirit and the Mother, Amen.

Give Archangel Michael's Rosary for Armageddon

Archangel Michael's Rosary is a service of prayers, decrees and hymns to invoke the assistance of Archangel Michael, the hosts of the LORD and the nine choirs of angels for the resolution of personal and planetary problems and for the binding of the forces of evil attacking the children and youth of the world. Contact The Summit Lighthouse to obtain a booklet of this rosary either alone or with an audio recording of the messenger leading students of the masters in this service.

FOR YOUR JOURNAL

How Will *You* Answer Jesus' Call?

The Call to prepare for the initiation of the descent into hell.

What does this Call mean to me?
What will I do to answer this Call?

CHAPTER 17

"I Call you to the heart of God."

The Christmas Rose
"I Call You to the Heart of God"

Yes, I AM come. And in this hour of my coming I enfold the earth in the rose of my heart. Let its petals reach to your innermost being, for I touch all who keep my flame of love. Therefore may you be as kindling wood!

So receive the flame of the Christmas Rose and know, beloved, that without compassion there is no saving of the soul that is lost, there is no wherewithal within you whereby you might reach out and convey the current of love that will rescue some poor wretch caught in the briers of the astral plane, perhaps by no fault of current karma but of the ancient struggle of the forces of light and darkness.

Be assured that some who are caught in the brambles, beloved, may be noted as the tireless warriors who go forth to slay the fallen ones that others might form rings around the Central Sun, chorusing paeans of praise to my heart and the heart of God. Therefore, beloved, point not the accusing finger at the one who is soiled for the very fray.

Yes, the battle goes on at many levels, and the best of the sons and daughters of God descend on Christmas Day for the binding of the fallen ones and the seed of Satan whose hour is come: for it is Christmas.

Yes, beloved, I wish you a very, very holy Christ Mass in this hour. And I come to celebrate with you the birth of the one Christ in your heart, one by one by one. I come to adore the body of God that is one, yet individualized.

And I am seeing with the full power of my being the emergent Christ of yourself/myself, for we are one. And all life is one and God is one! Though there be a billion times a billion rays of light of that Christ, there is but one.

I come to celebrate that birth or perhaps its new conception and ongoing gestation. Whatever your level on the Path, beloved, I take my rod, even as the rod of Aaron become the rod of Joseph, [and I measure your progress this day].

Yes, the rod, beloved, it is the measuring rod.

Where are you this day?

Where is the line that denotes progress?

For the lines increase from birth unto transition.

I desire to see you come to the full turning of that rod, which in my hand becomes the shepherd's crook, great symbol of the raised sacred fire of the Kundalini. I desire to see that budding at the base of the brain and continuing to the point of the third eye. It is a challenging road, beloved, for the fire does bring to the surface those things that must be cast into the flame, consuming as it rises, rising as it consumes.

Thus, measure your rod, beloved, and know that the rod of Aaron does portend the hour when you take dominion in your Christed being of all things in the earth; and with my beloved Mother you place the moon beneath your feet and you are no longer pulled this way and that by the emotional body of the mass consciousness or the tides of the sea. And when there is no more night and no more tide, you will behold the tideless sea.[1]

Therefore the stillness of the desire body! Therefore the empowerment by the desire body within all of the chakras!...

Yes, beloved, step-by-step here in physical embodiment you nourish, you water our garden and you increase the light-manifestation in yourself for the supreme purpose of having that wherewithal to extend to others. Let the sacred fire be contained.

Be the observer, then, first of yourself, of the inbreath and the outbreath. Let there be the balancing and calming of the forces, the observing of the breath, the observing of the mind. This is to sense yourself in the very heart of your Holy Christ Self. And this Holy Christ Self does descend upon you in moments of joyous devotion, in the hours of Armageddon when you wage supreme warfare against the demons and discarnates, who are of the Antichrist.

Yes, beloved, being the observer and maintaining the point of inner poise may be accomplished this day by you, but on the morrow it will be a new level and a new challenge, greater by far than the last. This is how it will be until you shall have attained absolute union with the absolute God.

The testings come but, oh, what joy to know that up that spinal stalk, up that ladder, you can achieve greater and greater adeptship within these four lower bodies, therefore joyously demonstrating to many that the path that is followed does bring joy and mastery and is not the *via dolorosa*. It is not a sorrowful way!

But that [path] does not exclude the pain and the trial of overcoming. It does not exclude the wrestling with the lesser self and the hordes of hell. All these things come to pass.

But what? You have the entire Spirit of the Great Brotherhood to reinforce you, and cosmic beings all the way back to the Great Central Sun. No test is given without a mighty force of angels to reinforce your will and your determination.

Blessed hearts, *engage your teeth* in the struggle and surmount it and know the supreme bliss of union. This union you can accomplish daily—*daily*, I say! Do not postpone it!

The bliss of union with the Godhead through your mighty I AM Presence can be touched and known by each and every one of you daily. And the time for the cutting off of the day and the entering in to the heart of God without fail is just before you retire and close your eyes to dream the dream of God's love, to journey to temples of light higher and higher in the etheric octave, even before you make your ascension.

Doors open to you as you build upon a foundation and do not lose what you have built as children do who play and build their towers and knock them down. This tower that you build must be sturdy. It must be well designed and well sealed.

Know, then, that once a day you must stop the cycling [and recycling of the mind], the turning and the turning and the turning, else you will find yourself winding a coil of the stresses and tensions of life around your spinal cord. For that momentum must [one day] be collapsed by your entering in to the heart of eternity....

In this hour, then, contemplate the assimilation of my Word as my Body and my Blood, of my Word as Alpha and Omega, the beginning and the ending of the cycles of your being.

Yes, beloved, it is an hour to contemplate that in this finite plane there is a beginning and an ending. There is a *b.* and a *d.* on every tombstone, but you are not confined within that frame of time.

Time is the friend and the enemy. Use it wisely and you will break its shackles and be eternal. Use it poorly and you will be buried with the corruptible form and find yourself in the astral plane.

Make use of the hours and break their chalice. Let the hour become infinity in those moments when you enter God undisturbed in the quietness of your room, as you sit upon your cot and contemplate the source of being.

This is the key I give you to meet all challenges of the day and of many lifetimes. To know that communion, beloved, is to remember the bliss and the Law of the One, to be stripped of all wrong desire and inordinate seeking for those things that are not of God.

When you desire God and know God, very little else concerns you. It is the absence of God Self-awareness that takes you into the byways and blinds you to this and that pull—pulls from the astral sea, pulls from the lunar vibration.

Yes, beloved, I have come to Call you many times. Many times have I come. But on this day I simply Call you to the heart of God. And I ask you to pause and discover in a very real measure that oneness, that you might never again be moved from the bedrock of your divinity.

In this octave, O beloved, be that God and be not satisfied until you touch that God! You will know that God has touched you when you feel the suffusing glow of compassion and the joy that transcends all adversity and every means used against you by those who are caught in the web of the astral sea.

They have many ploys. But if when they knock, you simply say, "I am not there, I am not here," [you give them no point of entry]. Therefore, you do not answer the door, you do not answer at all, because they are not knocking on the right door.

When they rise to the level of the door to the kingdom of God and you are in that kingdom, you may then challenge the spirits, test them to see whether they are of God[2] and dismiss them. For even fallen angels will attempt to mount to your throne of oneness in the Godhead.

Yes, beloved, I do not speak mere words. I speak to you of a mystery and of a path and of a searching and of a finding.

I speak to you of pursuing God until you are wrapped in God, you are bathed in God, you are chewing morsels of God consciousness, you are sipping nectar of God. I am speaking of an experience that you must have by your own seeking, your own pursuit, your own determination that you will not rest until you have this bliss!

Yes, beloved, it does require the giving of that love that God has first given to you, multiplying it by the flame that God has placed in your heart. It is being willing to go wherever I call you, to perform whatever task, to do it in the LORD's name—to do it, beloved, for you know it is a means to an end and you know that I reward and that my reward is with me and that I come quickly[3]—very quickly, when you meet the requirements of the Law for the harmony of your own being.

It is for this bliss and this contact—known in all levels of being, yet desired—that one thirsts. It is for this, beloved, that pilgrims and saints and holy men and women have given their lives, have laid down their lives, have become martyrs, have been unwilling to stop until by absolute determination to fulfill the work of the Son, they entered into the Word of the Father.

Do not stop short of this sipping of the nectar of God each day. For often it is right there, ready for you to take, but you close your book and enter into something mundane, scarcely noticing my angel already extending the cup and yet having to withdraw it, for you have taken your attention from the Godhead.

I speak of empowerment again and again. I speak of love as the true empowerment. There is none other except that which is taken inordinately for selfish gain. True power is love and love is the power that quivers a cosmos, whereby the voice of a child so endued can be heard on distant star....

I am Jesus, your brother, your friend, your teacher, avatar of the age, desiring so to strengthen you that you might be unto the many what I have been unto you. Keep on keeping on, beloved, for your track is direct to the star of great, great hope.

I seal you in this hour that you might rejoice yet more hours this day in what it really means to be the Christmas Rose.

I bestow upon each one of you the kiss upon the forehead of the Christmas Rose. To the little child within you, to you yourself, in each year of your life on each birthday, [I give the kiss of the Christmas Rose, and] I seal you, each and every year unto the present, beloved.

Know that my love is sufficient unto you to resolve every unresolved problem—a spiritual problem, a problem in the psyche or in your psychology, a problem of the mind or the heart or the desires. This kiss, beloved, is there for you to accept and, with it, to accept the healing of the experiences of that year of your life.

Those books that the messenger has recommended to you I recommend also. They will assist you to travel through some of the labyrinth of the subconscious. But you need not travel through all; for by and by in the records of the former self of this and previous embodiments, you will come to the key, beloved, you will discover what it is! And in that mighty key that is your own Christhood, that mighty key, beloved, you will collapse all the rest! And you will not need to journey any longer.

Do not make the mistake of thinking that you have arrived at the key. For you may have the key in your hand, beloved, but unless it is in your heart, unless you truly have become that person that is truly you, you must continue and continue.

For the real discovery will result in the assimilation of my Body and my Blood.

Take, eat. For this is my Body. This is my Blood. 🍇
[Holy Communion is served.]

December 25, 1991
Christmas Day
Royal Teton Ranch
Park County, Montana

When the heart is pure, all other levels of being can be purified. Therefore, let the heart be pure and true and loving, bearing the cosmic honor flame. Let the heart be the open door whereby the Holy Spirit will come upon you. Let the heart be the open door to the tired, the poor, the huddled masses yearning to breathe free. JESUS[4]

In this dictation Jesus sweetly enfolds the earth in the rose of his heart. He asks us to "receive the flame of the Christmas Rose and know, beloved, that without compassion there is no saving of the soul that is lost."

Our Lord embodies the flame of compassion and loving kindness that is the signature of his guru, Maitreya. And on this day he simply calls us "to the heart of God."

All the masters have spoken to us of the path of compassion. Lanello is a master known for his magnanimous heart, and he explains this path as a very practical one. "And where you see any son of light spearheading a cause, I say: Help him, encourage him and offer that cup of light—not neglecting the cup of cold water, the food, the refreshment and the care. Providing physical needs is an essential part of the experience of love. Therefore, beloved hearts, recognize that when your bodies and minds have needs, these are supplied in the truest sense of love that need not be a descending spiral but one that uplifts and exalts and comforts by the eternal covenant of compassion.

"The covenant of compassion is the key to victory. When you call for my mantle of victory in this year, O beloved, remember that it is won by the covenant of compassion. Those toward whom you are compassionate can be victorious because they know that you love them.

"Love someone today. Love someone each day with the kind of love for which the soul is yearning. For the world will offer its loves, but the soul remains hungry and weary and crying—crying out for the tenderness that understands it and does not merely take care of the creature comforts. When you give a meal or when you give physical aid, it is received in joy because the spirit that flows with it reaches the soul, and the soul is at peace and no longer under the strain of world distress."⁵

Mother Mary advises us: "Learn compassion by looking through another's eyes, by walking in another's footsteps, by entering the heart and the mind for a moment, for a while, of father, mother, brother, sister or little child."⁶

I Call You to the Heart of God

The Master desires that we truly *experience* the love God has for us. This is easier for some than for others. We know, however, that God has placed a flame of love within us, in the secret chamber of our hearts. If we take some time every day to place our attention on this living flame, we can accelerate the feeling of love in our being. It is a simple equation but sometimes not so easy to fit into our busy schedules!

Jesus asks that we "pause and discover in a very real measure that oneness" with God's heart that we "might never again be moved from the bedrock" of our divinity.

Jesus' Keys to Enter God's Heart

Jesus gives us many keys to enter God's heart. Here are a few:

1. **Consciously enter into the heart of God each day.** "The time for the cutting off of the day and the entering into the heart of God without fail is just before you retire and close your eyes to dream the dream of God's love, to journey to temples of light higher and higher in the etheric octave." See Spiritual Exercises, chapter 3, for an example of a call you can give to be taken to the temples of light.
2. **Use your time wisely.** Jesus says: "Make use of the hours.... Let the hour become infinity in those moments when you enter undisturbed in the quietness of your room, as you sit upon your cot and contemplate the source of being."
3. **Seek God with determination.** "Pursue God until you are

wrapped in God, you are bathed in God, you are chewing morsels of God consciousness, your are sipping nectar of God. I am speaking of an experience that you must have by your own seeking, your own pursuit, your own determination that you will not rest until you have this bliss!"

4. **Become God in action.** To enter the heart of God "requires the giving of that love that God has given to you, multiplying it by the flame that God has placed in your heart. It is being willing to go wherever I call you to perform whatever task, to do it in the LORD's name."

Jesus tells us that we will know we have succeeded in this quest to enter the heart of God "when we feel the suffusing glow of compassion and the joy that transcends all adversity."

Expanding the Light of the Heart

As well as extending the flame of love in our hearts to others in practical service, we can also expand that flame and radiate love to others in our spiritual devotions.

Saint Germain reminds us: "Each acknowledgment paid daily to the flame within your heart will amplify the power and illumination of love within your being. Each such attention will produce a new sense of dimension for you, if not outwardly apparent, then subconsciously manifest within the folds of your inner thoughts.

"Neglect not, then, your heart as the altar of God. Neglect it not as the sun of your manifest being. Draw from God the power of love, and amplify it within your heart. Then send it out into the world at large as the bulwark of that which shall overcome the darkness of the planet....

"Remember that as long as you face the light, the shadows are always behind. And the light is there, too, to transmute them all."[7]

Saint Germain has written "I AM the Light of the Heart," a beautiful prayer to celebrate the divine flame within our hearts and to radiate the love in our hearts out into the world. (See Spiritual Exercises.)

Saint Germain has also given us his Heart Meditation as a

means of entering the secret chamber of our heart and communing there in the heart of God. This self-clearance is invaluable for those who seek to accelerate the balancing of the threefold flame and to expand the love and compassion of God through their hearts. (See chapter 10.)

The Healing of Our Psychology

Jesus concludes his "Call to the heart of God" with a gift of healing to the soul and the inner child of each of us: "I bestow upon each one of you the kiss upon the forehead of the Christmas Rose. To the little child within you, to you yourself, in each year of your life on each birthday, I give the kiss of the Christmas Rose, and I seal you, each and every year unto the present, beloved.

"Know that my love is sufficient unto you to resolve every unresolved problem—a spiritual problem, a problem in the psyche or in your psychology, a problem of the mind or the heart or the desires. This kiss, beloved, is there for you to accept, and with it, to accept the healing of the experiences of that year of your life."

Jesus also commends us to the study of psychology as a means to navigate "some of the labyrinth of the subconscious" and thus find the key of our own Christhood. The ascended master Kuthumi is a master psychologist and also has offered to assist us in working with our psychology.

He says: "Thus, I come, the joyful student, to announce to you the most precious dispensation, which comes from Maitreya, placed upon me by him with all diligence and the same concern for the step-up of your lives. This dispensation is my assignment to work with each one of you individually for your physical health and for the healing of your psychology, that we might swiftly get to the very cause and core of physical as well as spiritual and emotional conditions that there be no more setbacks or indulgences and surely not two steps forward and one step back.

"Thus, from this hour, if you will call to me and make a determination in your heart to transcend the former self, I will tutor you both through your own heart and any messenger I may send your way."[8]

There are also times when outer assistance can be very helpful in dealing with issues in one's psychology. Mother Mary explains the importance of being willing to accept help when it is needed: "Blessed hearts, many who come to this Community are perhaps 'diamonds in the rough' who have not had the perfect tutoring of the soul or the background in all of the proper manners and behavior. Some have had a fragmented development of the psyche in childhood, and they have a difficult time in dealing with that which is in the subconscious that they do not understand at all. Some do not even know when they need counseling or when it is necessary to have therapy.

"Therefore, those who have the loving heart and the wise heart must be alert to this need so that those who do require assistance do not give up the Path before they have had the opportunity to make a go of it through the understanding of wise counselors who will show them how to unwind the various experiences of the past and how to unwind from the coil of being those momentums that have resulted from fragmented situations, especially at the emotional level, from early childhood on.

"Of course, beloved, there is no replacement for the violet flame in this area. And those who have such problems must beware of extreme self-indulgence and spiritual pride and the sense that says, 'I can go it alone. I can do this myself. I do not need anyone's help.' This is a most dangerous state of mind, beloved, for our Father has created life so that all parts of life are interdependent. It is the very law of the harmony, of the chemistry of a cosmos. No one individual manifestation of God in this level of soul evolution and octave could possibly contain all of the elements necessary for the full integration of that God within the personality."[9]

Thus, when we have a problem that is of long duration that becomes a stumbling block on our path, it is often very beneficial to seek counseling or therapy, as Jesus says, to help us navigate the labyrinth. Problems such as low self-esteem, anger or depression often have causes lodged deep within the psyche, and there is often something we need to learn at a conscious level in order to rise to a higher level. While the spiritual work and the violet flame can be very useful in dealing with these situations, unless we can learn the lesson and make a conscious change in direction, we may unwittingly re-create the original causes.

If you do look for a counselor or therapist, ask the masters to guide you to the right person and to work through that person to assist you.

SPIRITUAL EXERCISES

The Messenger's Meditation on God in Your Heart

"Feel the vibration of God in your heart. Visualize the three-fold flame. The apostle Peter spoke of the hidden man of the heart, your beloved Christ Self. You can visualize the Christ Self in the secret chamber of your heart, and suddenly the chamber becomes the size of the altar, and the dimension is such that you may enter in and kneel before the high priest of your temple.

"Let us visualize beloved Jesus overshadowing us, his arms around us, standing taller than we are—his Electronic Presence enfolding us in the all-power of love, the all-power of wisdom, the all-power of the will of God itself. Let us for this moment enter the very body of Christ in this manner and then enter into the heart of hearts, communing there in glory.

"As we say the name of God, it is an affirmation that draws the light of God into the interior castle of our being. And there we begin to hear the sound of angels singing the song of glory and of Home and of triumph here—here in the very heart of earth, here in the Matter spheres, here where we dwell for a purpose—that God's kingdom within us might manifest here truly as the triumph of the Father with the Son through the Holy Spirit. In the name of the Mother, Amen.

[Here repeat aloud the mantra: "O God, You Are So Magnificent!" with great feelings of love and devotion to the I AM Presence.]

"Kneel before the living God in the person of the living Christ at the altar of Being and offer your prayer and the command of light to 'Keep My Flame Blazing.' In this meditation, you are speaking directly, personally, face-to-face with the beloved Christ who lives in your temple:"[10]

KEEP MY FLAME BLAZING

Keep my flame blazing,
By God's love raising,
Direct and keep me in my rightful place!

I AM Presence ever near me,
Keep me mindful of thy grace;
Flame of Christ, ever cheer me,
In me show thy smiling face!

Give Saint Germain's "I AM the Light of the Heart" Decree

"As you recite 'I AM the Light of the Heart,' visualize light descending from your I AM Presence and Holy Christ Self to your heart, where it will be released according to the worded matrix of your decree.

"Then center your attention on your heart. Picture the brilliance of the sun at noonday and transfer that picture to the center of your chest, where your heart chakra is located.

"Now see thousands of sunbeams going forth from your heart to penetrate and dissolve any darkness, despair or depression, first within yourself and then within the people of the world.

"Project your love (which is really God's love) out into the world. See that love as intense fiery-pink laser beams that break down all barriers to the success of your relationships, your family, your spiritual growth, your career, your neighborhood or your nation."[11]

I AM THE LIGHT OF THE HEART

I AM the light of the heart
Shining in the darkness of being.
And changing all into the golden treasury
Of the mind of Christ.

I AM projecting my love
Out into the world
To erase all errors
And to break down all barriers.

I AM the power of infinite love,
Amplifying itself
Until it is victorious,
World without end!

Call to Kuthumi to Assist You in the Healing of Your Psychology and Physical Health

Make the following call and invite the master psychologist, Kuthumi, into your life for healing:

In the name of my mighty I AM Presence and Holy Christ Self, I call to beloved Kuthumi for the healing of my physical health and my psychology that I might swiftly get to the very cause and core of physical as well as spiritual and emotional conditions within my four lower bodies. Let there be no more setbacks and indulgences on my path. I send forth my gratitude for this dispensation and I ask that you tutor me through my heart and through any messenger you may send my way. In the name of the Christ I invoke the flame of God-determination to transcend my former self.

FOR YOUR JOURNAL

How Will *You* Answer Jesus' Call?

"I Call you to the heart of God."

What does this Call mean to me?
What will I do to answer this Call?

CHAPTER 18

"I call you to be those mighty electrodes
of your Holy Christ Self and your
mighty I AM Presence that the
earth might receive the light."

The Descent of the Crystal Fire Mist
From My Sacred Heart I Pour Out the Vial
Do Not Postpone the Day of Your Initiation

Lo! I AM come for the descent of the crystal fire mist into your heart! From my sacred heart I pour out the vial of the crystal fire mist.

O hearts of love, are you ready for this fire? ["Yes!"]

I pray, then, that you will understand that throughout this dictation the crystal fire mist shall descend drop by drop into the chalice of your heart. Drop by drop of sacred essence of my heart I place in your heart—crystal fire, ruby fire of my Body, of my Blood. This essence, then, concentrate or not, shall be suited to your preparedness.

Love is the key to my heart. Therefore meditate on love in this hour. Meditate on love in your heart/my heart. For I desire that our hearts should be one this day and I desire that you should meditate upon my Sacred Heart each day as you pray, as you offer the powerful decrees of the violet flame for world transmutation.

I ask you to meditate each day upon the Immaculate Heart of my Mother and therefore acknowledge her heart and my heart as one, as twin hearts offered for the salvation of the lightbearers of the earth and of all who will turn to face the Son of God and therefore receive the rays of light for a purging and a purifying and an action of the sacred fire whereby all might know the strength, the presence and the will to walk every step of the way home to God.

My beloved, would you be that wayshower? ["Yes!"]

I ask you, then, not to diminish, not to dilute this manifestation of my essence, which I pour into you this day.

You have come many miles—millions of miles and centuries. So, then, you have reached the moment that when you reach for the crystal fire mist, one does answer. I have answered the call; therefore this Easter conference has been named *The Descent of the Crystal Fire Mist.* You may wonder what is this mist, what is the fire and what is the crystallization of the God flame within you.

There must needs be, then, the purification by water and by blood, the purification by the sacred oil and the sacred bread. For I AM the bread of life, which came down from heaven.[1] I pray that you will eat of this bread and that you will know that the hour is coming—surely it is coming upon you as opportunity, beloved—to intensify and intensify again as the fiery coil of your being does reach for the upper chakras.

Thus, the intensification of the light, beloved, must be sought for and accepted by you. And there does come a time in your life, beloved, when nothing else will satisfy your hours, your moments or your days but communion with the Lord. These are the moments before your entering in, when the happiest occasion, even celebrated with lightbearers, will have something missing for you because you are about to experience the marriage of the Lamb, the true marriage, beloved, whereby you are bonded to my heart. Thus, I place drop by drop of the essence of the crystal fire mist within you that you might see this as the foretaste of that union.

You will knock, beloved, and the door will not be opened. And you will knock again and again and again and the door will not be opened. And you may be burdened by the weight of oppression and the depression of the world itself.

Know this, beloved: It is not because you are not in your right place. Being on the Path under the great teachers of mankind is where you belong. But you must remember that there is an ordered path. There is the dark night of the soul,[2] whereby you bear not only personal karma but planetary karma. There is a path of initiation whereby you come to the Presence of God in such an intimate interchange daily and hourly [that you] shine as the splendor of the sun, [the light] revealing, then, the remaining darkness and the ugliness of the human creation. And thus, you look at the absolute God, our Father-Mother, and the absolute misuse of the light in the misuse of the energy and consciousness of the Father and the Mother and you can scarcely abide betwixt these opposites.

Therefore, in preparation for the dark night of the Spirit, you must become balanced in body and soul and in mind and in heart. Not one of these can be missed. And the spirit itself, the spirit of a man, a woman and a child, must be strengthened, infired and emboldened. You must be ready for any challenge, any adversary, any condemnation and any burden, then, of darkness that does seem as a dark, dark night where there are no rays of light.

These moments and hours before the initiation of the crucifixion and before the ultimate bonding to my heart and the heart of your Holy Christ Self must be understood. For if you know them not, then you will not be able to interpret your own discouragement, your own disillusionment with yourself and with others on the Path. Know, then, beloved, that that very hour and moment when you feel dry as a dry hole in the ground where there be no water—in that hour of dryness, beloved, you must stand and still stand to prove the path of your chelaship.

It is an hour when all must count themselves as chelas of El Morya, who does lead you in this way of ultimate overcoming. Do not lose the way, beloved! And do not loose your hand from the hand of the messenger, who is here to stay at your side and to walk with you through the dark night and the glory of God— yes, the dark night and the glory, the dark night and the glory. And these alternating conditions of consciousness bring you to the place where they are oscillating with a mighty speed until finally you break loose and it is all the glory, beloved, and the darkness is behind you. Many hours and days and years will pass for some of you ere all of this take place in your being.

I come, then, with your beloved mentor of the spirit, El Morya, to counsel you this day. For there are those who, when seeing the abyss of their own human creation and the abyss of planet Earth and beholding death and hell itself, will step back and say, "I will not take the initiation of the dark night of the soul this day or this week or this month or this year, but I will tarry in my level of comfortability and insulate myself from these true initiations of the saints."

Yes, beloved, I come to give you a little push. For you must have that push and you must go beyond that certain level of life and life-style that you have set for yourself, even protected within the walls of this community, even outside as you dot the landscapes and the continents with your flames and presence around the world.

Whether in cloister or at work in the fields or the cities, whether far in time and space, all of you who are true chelas of the will of God are as near to me as my heartbeat and your own, save for this: when you put distance between yourself and myself because you wish to postpone the day of the initiation.

I remind you of the day that my [public] initiation began. It was there at the marriage feast in Cana of Galilee.[3] And there did my Mother come to make certain that I did not deny or forsake the opportunity for that initiation. Yes, beloved, I was not pleased to begin that day. Nevertheless, the blessed Mother Mary supported me. My dear Mother stood by and gave instructions to the members of the feast; and therefore they did bring the bottles of water, and therefore the miracles did begin in public.

And when that public manifestation [of miracles] began, beloved, it was the countdown to the crucifixion. But remember this also: it was the countdown to the action of the resurrection and to the ascension! Therefore, you see, not to take the first step is to be deprived of the last. And thus, there were those three years of the demonstrations of cosmic law, of the very science of the Word and the sacred fire of the Divine Mother that was released for healing. And did I not gain that experience in the East in that life[4] and in ancient embodiments and as recently as in the embodiment of Elisha, tutored by Elijah?

Yes, beloved, we do have our day. May you recognize your day and not postpone it! For here at Maitreya's Mystery School— the school of my own beloved Guru, whom I called Father—you learn the path of the adepts that you would otherwise have had to learn in the etheric retreats of the Great White Brotherhood but for this dispensation of this hour and this time.

As the pall of the astral sea rises and overtakes you, some of you forget. Therefore, lest you forget, I come to remind you that there is not a single chela, whether at Maitreya's Mystery School or beyond, in the precincts of the world, who does not have the very personal tutoring, instruction, sponsorship and intense love of my heart and the hearts of the ascended masters who have pledged themselves to you.

You may think you make no progress here or there. You may become discouraged. You may think you have not a friend in heaven or on earth. But I tell you, when you have enrolled as a Keeper of the Flame, pledged to keep the flame of life and of the Great White Brotherhood upon earth, *you do have that sponsorship.*

You can "thin" the sponsorship by breaking the laws of God and the code of conduct for a true disciple of Christ, a true bodhisattva of Gautama Buddha. But, beloved, you have the same means [for "thickening" the sponsorship] as do all other devotees in the world, the means of confession, repentance and penance.

Therefore, do not hesitate to come before the altar of God. Do not hesitate to receive that living flame. Do not hesitate to put all things in order in your life, to pay your debts diligently, human and divine, and to communicate with the messenger or the ordained ministers of this Church Universal and Triumphant.

Yes, beloved, I come to you. For there must not be a dilution, there must not be a dissimulation. There must not occur in your life the pulling back, the lessening of the decrees, the shortening of the hours of services the world around. For, you see, when you do this you are taking a step backward, you are decelerating. And when you deny your Lord the full cup of the fire of your heart, when you fail to give the fullness of yourself and your own body and blood to your Lord, your Holy Christ Self, then you shall not receive the return and the mighty, abundant gift that does descend, even as it does descend this day.

I counsel all who will hear me throughout the world: To hear only the teachings and the dictations and to fail to put in the hours of invoking the violet flame may well cost you your ascension. And you to whom I speak know well to whom I speak, and those of you who have not diluted your efforts also know well where you fit on this path of goal-fittedness.

Yes, beloved, I come to warn you that when the earth grows darker, as it is still growing darker, your auras must grow brighter and brighter and brighter in absolute defiance of that mounting karma that must be consumed by a world conflagration of the violet flame and of the sacred fire and of the descent of the crystal fire mist!

Now then, in the descent of the light of heaven, there must be electrodes in the earth, there must be those who hold the Omega balance in the earth. And therefore, you compel the lightning to descend, you compel the fire mist to descend, you compel the sun of the Great Central Sun! For you are able to receive them in your body and they do pass through your body into the earth. And you remain untouched and unharmed by this lightning and this crystal fire mist, for you have raised and accelerated your vibration to that level.

Yes, beloved, this is your calling in this hour. And to this calling I call you: to be those mighty electrodes of your Holy Christ Self and of your mighty I AM Presence that the earth might receive the light, the lightning and the fire itself for the rebalancing of the elements, for the purging of the earth body of pollutions at all levels of the four lower bodies of her evolutions, that the earth might receive what is meet for regeneration and resurrection and the coming of a great golden age.

Beloved hearts of light, here is the formula. It is this. If you, the lightbearers who have this teaching, will make your bodies the living temple of God—that the Father, Son and Holy Spirit might enter those four lower bodies, might occupy until your full God-mastery, might use you then—you shall see a regeneration and a resurrection of the earth, you shall see the coming of a new day and a golden age.

But if there be not sufficient individuals who understand the necessity of intensification, of passing through the dark night of the soul and the dark night of the Spirit, of passing through [those initiations] and then walking the earth as I did in my resurrected body until the age of eighty-one as I did move on to the East and remain in Kashmir—if you, then, beloved, are not willing to walk the earth in your resurrected body, as has been done before and may be done in this age, then how will we have a resurrection of the earth body itself?

We will not have it! That is the answer....

O come unto me, all ye who are heavy laden and who labor and continue to labor and to labor.[5] I will give you the rest and the re-creation in my causal body if you will accept that miracle of grace, if you will accept my Electronic Presence. I am so waiting to assist you, to heal you and to offer you the full and overflowing blessings of the immaculate heart of my Mother. You have only to open the valve, to turn the dial, to focus in consciousness, yes, to gain that God-controlled attention on me and my sacred heart for me to do these things for you.

Lo, when they tell you, "Go here and go there and go to the next place,"[6] I say, "Come, come unto me. Come unto me and I will give you healing and rest and surcease [from your burdens]." Be, then, replenished, rejuvenated and regenerated in this hour, beloved, for you have worked and served and toiled long.

Now come out of that spiral and let the next spiral of your service and your work be braided with my own light, my own energies of the causal body and of your own. Let it be braided with your Holy Christ Self as you say, "Abba, Father. Abba, Father."[7] Oh, may you say it, beloved, in your heart and know, know, beloved, that the call to the Father-Mother, the call to me is the call to the everlasting Guru, your own beloved Sanat Kumara, who has sponsored us all.

April 19, 1992
Easter Sunday
Royal Teton Ranch
Park County, Montana

*I am so waiting to assist you, to heal you and to offer you
the full and overflowing blessings of the Immaculate Heart of
my Mother.*   JESUS

Jesus comes to us with a beautiful gift: "Throughout this dictation the crystal fire mist shall descend drop by drop into
the chalice of your heart. Drop by drop of the sacred fire essence
of my heart I place in your heart—crystal fire, ruby fire of my
Body, of my Blood."

The Master releases his sacred fire to each of us as we have
prepared to receive it. He charges us with his sacred fire essence
so that we might take up the Calling "to be those mighty electrodes of your Holy Christ Self and your mighty I AM Presence
that the earth might receive the light."

Jesus asks us to allow the powerful currents of our mighty
I AM Presence and Holy Christ Self to flow through our four
lower bodies and chakras. He Calls us to be pillars of fire, the
dwelling place of the Father and the Son and the Holy Spirit in
the earth, perpetually releasing the infinite light of God to ener-
gize the planet and to hold the balance of light against the forces
of darkness.

Archangel Raphael also gives us a vision of what it means to
hold a light in the earth: "Blessed ones, thou art golden pearls in
the earth. Know thy worth, and increase the layers of your individual pearls daily by devotion. Thus, surround that point of
light (i.e., the soul) with a greater and greater momentum of
devotion. Then see and know that you are, each one, an electrode
in the earth for the healing of the earth body.

"And you know the principle of the light that, where there is
the devotee, there is the flame of God and there the ills of the
world rush into the flame. Therefore, keep that flame blazing as
sacred fire of the Divine Mother, as violet flame that you yourself be not overcome by the darkness that must pass through into

the vortex of the pillar of fire of your devotion. Keep the devotion spinning that there might be world transmutation."[8]

Thus, we see that our heart chakra is intended to literally be a transformer of negative energy—a whirling vortex of an intense violet fire that consumes personal and planetary karma as these contact the intense light of God in our heart! For this to happen, we must be willing to invoke the sacred fire daily and let the intensity of the fire increase.

Mother Mary tells us how great a service we can render if we choose to take up this calling: "And, therefore, by your call, Archangel Michael and the mighty archangels do *bind* that dweller as you stand fast and behold the salvation of your God in your very living temple and you become on earth an electrode of living fire like unto the LORD God above who dwells in the Holy of Holies in the heart of the I AM Presence. This is the goal of your walk with God.

"Let not lesser considerations take the place of this path, this understanding, this vigil. For you see, just as quickly as you gain this Mother-awareness, this Mother presence, you will find yourself feeding the multitudes, tending the millions. For the Mother flame of cosmos will flow through you as those rivers of living water,[9] and many, many will gain that same inner strength by your presence in the earth.

"These days are not far from you! Do not compare the path of the ascended masters and the Great White Brotherhood to any other path, East or West. Let no man take thy crown in this hour. Let no man rend the veil of the holiness and the oneness of thy life with the living Christ.

"Understand, beloved hearts, that this is the new dispensation of Aquarius. It does not require centuries, as in the past, to come into this union."[10]

Saint Germain says: "For you also are destined to be the instrument of the LORD, to take the teaching and to give it to others whom the LORD has appointed to be with you in a cell of consciousness preordained. Yes, you are destined—if you make the right choices—to be an electrode of cosmic light and energy and love, so that the lightning that cometh out of the East and shineth even unto the West[11] might be grounded in Terra through the Son of God appearing right within your very own heart."[12]

The Initiation of the Dark Night

We understand that in order to be an electrode for God, there are choices we must make. We must be willing to pass through the initiations that come to us on the path. Jesus tells us, "Do not postpone the day of your initiation." Even as the Master pours out the light of his Sacred Heart during this dictation, it is up to us to choose to receive his light. "The intensification of the light, beloved, must be sought for and accepted by you."

In this dictation Jesus reminds us again that prior to the ultimate bonding to his heart, we will pass through the initiations of the dark night of the soul and the dark night of the Spirit. The dark night of the soul is not only the return of our personal karma but also the bearing of a portion of planetary karma.

Jesus seeks to prepare us for this initiation and gives us signs to watch for as we face the challenge of returning karma: we may become discouraged and disillusioned with ourselves and others on the Path; we may feel as if God, the masters and the angels have deserted us; or we may experience alternating conditions of consciousness, oscillating between the burdens of this dark night and joy in the glory of God. Jesus explains that these conditions do not mean that we are in the wrong place. They are, rather, a very part of the initiation itself.

Serapis Bey aptly describes these feelings and the process we go through as our souls approach these advanced testings on the Path that lead to the bonding to the heart of our Lord: "As you know from the writings of Saint John of the Cross, the soul's approach to the Inner Christ is a painful process of desiring acceptance and yet hearing the word, 'Not yet, not yet.' Blessed ones, be not the soul who fears to try again and again to receive the love of her Lord. Your Lord loves you, and the closer you come to this sealing oneness, the more you will see of yourself that cannot enter into the Holy of holies.

"But your soul does pant after the living God.[13] And the soul reaches the moment where no other desire fulfilled can equate with being received by the Lord. In that moment, beloved, there is an aloneness and a loneliness that is indescribable, for no one else can experience with you the mourning of the soul who is separated from her God, yet almost entering in. That is why it does require special counselors, special ministering servants to counsel those who may become, in moments, despondent; for they are so very near to that alchemical marriage and yet not quite.

"Beloved ones, until the Divine Husband, the Bridegroom, has finally stretched forth the hand to say, 'O soul, enter,' one is in a state of fear that one has been rejected, one is not acceptable, one is not clean enough, one has not measured up to that level. In a human sense of the word, many have experienced the rejection of a human lover or the friend or the parent, to the ultimate sadness and agony. Beloved, this prepares one for the rounds and the many rounds one must make until, finally, the Bridegroom steps forth with outstretched arms to receive the waiting bride.

"You are indeed the waiting brides of Sanat Kumara. The full sealing cannot come in a day, but this is your self-sealing day. This is the day you determine that when your Bridegroom proposes to you, your mind is made up. You will accept. You will accept.

"Is not life a preparation for this moment? This is the hour of the sealing of your heart. Press your hands to your heart, to your heart chakra, and feel your hands press in upon the heart. And let your will be made known to your heart by the pressing in of your hands, saying:

O be sealed, my heart, this day in the heart of God!
O be sealed, my soul, this day, in the heart of God!
O be sealed, my mind, this day in the heart of God!
O be sealed, my desire, this day in the heart of God!
O be sealed, my inner vision, this day in the heart of God!
For I desire only to see my God, my God.
I will not fear rejection this day.
I will not fear that I am not ready.
Though I come in rags...

I know that my Bridegroom shall wait for me
Until I shall have woven my seamless garment."[14]

Meditation on the Heart of Jesus and Mary

Jesus tells us, "Love is the key to my heart," and he asks us
to meditate on his Sacred Heart and on the Immaculate Heart of
Mary. The messenger explains the science of this devotion as an
open door to our own Christ consciousness:

"Meditation on the Sacred Heart of Jesus and the Immaculate Heart of Mary has been the natural unfoldment of the devotion of the disciples of the West as they entered into mystical
union with the Lord Christ and through him into the understanding of God as Mother, God as Holy Spirit and God as the
Eternal Father.

"The mystics of the Church have entered into the oneness of
the heart fire, the threefold flame in the heart, because the fount
of living flame, as well as the full concentration of the resurrection and ascension of Jesus and Mary, is in the heart.

"Both Jesus and Mary maintain a tremendous focus within
their heart centers of nothing less than the Great Central Sun.
And the energy of the Great Central Sun anchored therein is their
offering, their anchor point of light, whereby through grace we
also may come into our awareness of the sun of even pressure
that is the Christ consciousness within our heart.

"Jesus and Mary have appeared to many devotees, and some
of these devotees have had their revelations recognized by the
Catholic Church. Others have kept their watch and their silent
communion through the heart....

"God has ordained these two witnesses to be our sponsors
for the expansion of the Christ consciousness, which is to be
anchored in the heart as its seat of authority. The heart is the
fount of life, and out of it come the issues of life.[15] The heart
becomes sacred when the Christ consciousness is elevated, the
carnal mind is dethroned and the heart is made to be the master
of the temple and the master of our life....

"We find, then, that the heart is the key to attainment—not

the brain or the nervous system or any other part of the temple. The heart extends and transfers all the energies available to us from the other chakras—the throat chakra, the third eye, the crown, the solar plexus, the seat of the soul and the base of the spine. The heart contains the record of all our initiations, all our overcoming. And meditation upon the heart, the Sacred Heart of Jesus...creates a figure-eight flow of devotion.

"The flow of devotion from our heart opens the door to Jesus' return devotion, as he is devoted to our Christ Self. By accelerating the momentum of the oscillation, we enter into communion with our Lord. Although this communion is a scientific and complex process, I have explained it simply, and our understanding of it need not be complex.

"When we send our love to Jesus, we send him all that we are. Our total consciousness flows to him. Therefore, though we may appear to be loving, our love becomes a cloak surrounding our anxieties, fears and doubts. These doubts and anxieties are all contained within our aura, as nothing is hidden from the Lord.

"Our energy is carried to Jesus and passes through his Sacred Heart. As he returns his devotion to us, he also returns to us our energy, which has now passed through the transformer of his being. Not only has it passed through that great transformer, but it has also passed through all the initiations, momentums and matrices that he has outpictured throughout his incarnations— not only the initiations of his final thirty-three years, but all his experiences since the day of his birth in the heart of God....

"Our energy is then pressed through a mold, through the cylinders, cones and geometric forms (microscopic in size) of the entire heartbeat and heart forcefield of the Christ. Thus, it has the experience of going through the fourteen stations of the cross with Jesus, and going through all his experiences—his presence in the womb of Mary, his childhood, his healings, his agony and his crucifixion.

"Jesus' experience becomes impressed upon our cells, the cells of our energy. And when that energy is returned from him, we put on increments of his Christ consciousness."[16]

The Presence of the LORD in the Earth

In another dictation, Jesus gives the following vision of our calling to be electrodes of light in the earth: "You see how those of us—I speak of yourselves—who remain in life here must be the instrument of prayer answered and prophecy fulfilled. Neither fulfills or answers itself, beloved. You are the handiwork of God, and here below you are the Omega, the Mother body. And that is the universal mystical body of God in the earth, as you have been taught.

"Where will the LORD appear if there is not an electrode of light, a mighty sphere of light of bodies who have said, 'We are thy Body and thy Blood, O Universal Christ of Jesus and the Great White Brotherhood! Here I AM, LORD! I can have no other.' "[17]

SPIRITUAL EXERCISES

Seek Balance in Body, Soul, Mind and Heart

Jesus tells us that in preparation for the initiation of the dark night of the Spirit, we must have balance in all four of these areas of our lives.

Take time to reflect on each of these four areas. Ask Jesus and your Holy Christ Self to guide you and speak to you as you consider these questions:

- What are your strengths and weaknesses in these areas?
- Do you have balance in each of the four?
- Which areas need strengthening?
- What could you do to achieve greater balance in each of the four?

Enter into the Messenger's Meditation on the Sacred Heart of Jesus and the Immaculate Heart of Mary

"When you meditate upon the Immaculate Heart of Mary,

you can visualize it as this spiral nebula of light, and you can see that light coming from her heart to your heart. You can see yourself entering into her heart and her entering into yours until, once again, the cosmic interchange occurs.

"The purpose of meditation is so that the cosmic interchange becomes closer and closer. Here you are, dissolving into the Mother, the Mother dissolving into you. The Electronic Presence of Mother Mary will be where you are. And this is a law of geometry—things equal to the same thing are equal to each other.

"Here is this mighty cosmic flow. It is moving, relentlessly moving as with the speed of light. It is a scintillating fire. It is so bright that, physically, you cannot look upon that light. The violet flame moving, then, in the very temple of being beneath and above the heart is the transmutation of all that would slow down that movement of that figure-eight flow from the Mother to the Great Central Sun and back again....

"Why, the whole vast cosmos is a panoply of the most magnificent and wondrous, perpetually changing manifestations. I have become it; it has become me. I have entered into the joy of millions of angels who spiral with these energies. I have given them salutation of the dawn. They have given me their salutation as I move on this cosmic highway of energy. I am completely fulfilled in this companionship of all of the hosts of the LORD.

"And the law here is that things equal to the same thing are equal to each other. And so, when, by your love and devotion you have become the same frequency as Mother Mary, Gautama, Lord Maitreya, your I AM Presence, Alpha and Omega, you cannot be kept from their energy or forcefield, nor can they be kept from you. And therefore, this is the path to oneness."[18]

Steps to Become Mighty Electrodes

These are steps Jesus recommends we take in order to become a fiery electrode of our mighty I AM Presence (the Father) and Holy Christ Self (the Son):

1. Keep the laws of God and the code of conduct for a true disciple of Christ. If you make a mistake, pursue the path of

confession, repentance and penance in order to strengthen the tie again. Put all things in order in your life and diligently pay your debts—human and divine.

2. Receive the living flame. Give prayers, invocations and decrees each day. Invoke the light of the Holy Spirit through the violet flame.

3. Preach and embody the Word and the Work—the cloven tongues of the fire of Alpha and Omega.

4. Raise up the light of the Divine Mother as the Kundalini, the sacred fire at the base-of-the-spine chakra, through purity, God-control, God-Self mastery and the science of mantra and yoga. Give the rosaries to the Divine Mothers, beloved Mother Mary and beloved Kuan Yin.

Expand the Flame in Your Heart and Strengthen the Tie to Your Holy Christ Self

The flame within your heart is a living flame and outpost of the divine right within you. As you give devotion to that flame it can expand, and you can strengthen your tie to your Holy Christ Self. As you give this decree, send forth that love to your Holy Christ Self and your mighty I AM Presence.

INTROIT TO THE HOLY CHRIST FLAME

In the name of the beloved mighty victorious Presence of God, I AM in me, my very own beloved Holy Christ Self and through the magnetic power of the sacred fire vested within the threefold flame of love, wisdom and power burning within my heart, I decree:

> 1. Holy Christ Self above me,
>   Thou balance of my soul,
>   Let thy blessed radiance
>   Descend and make me Whole.

> Refrain: Thy flame within me ever blazes,
>   Thy peace about me ever raises,
>   Thy love protects and holds me,
>   Thy dazzling light enfolds me.
>   I AM thy threefold radiance,
>   I AM thy living Presence
>   Expanding, expanding, expanding, now.

2. Holy Christ flame within me.
   Come, expand thy triune light;
   Flood my being with the essence
   Of the pink, blue, gold and white.

3. Holy lifeline to my Presence,
   Friend and brother ever dear,
   Let me keep thy holy vigil,
   Be thyself in action here.

And in full faith...

FOR YOUR JOURNAL

How Will *You* Answer Jesus' Call?

*"I call you to be those mighty electrodes of your
Holy Christ Self and your mighty I AM Presence
that the earth might receive the light."*

What does this Call mean to me?
What will I do to answer this Call?

The Chart of Your Divine Self

The Chart of Your Divine Self is a portrait of you and of the God within you. It is a diagram of you and your potential to become who you really are. It is an outline of your spiritual anatomy.

The upper figure is your "I AM Presence," the Presence of God that is individualized in each one of us. It is your personalized "I AM THAT I AM." Your I AM Presence is surrounded by seven concentric spheres of spiritual energy that make up what is called your "causal body." The spheres of pulsating energy contain the record of the good works you have performed since your very first incarnation on earth. They are like your cosmic bank account.

The middle figure in the chart represents the "Holy Christ Self," who is also called the Higher Self. You can think of your Holy Christ Self as your chief guardian angel and dearest friend, your inner teacher and voice of conscience. Just as the I AM Presence is the Presence of God that is individualized for each of us, so the Holy Christ Self is the Presence of the Universal Christ that is individualized for each of us. "The Christ" is actually a title given to those who have attained oneness with their Higher Self, or Christ Self. That's why Jesus was called "Jesus, the Christ."

What the Chart shows is that each of us has a Higher Self, or "inner Christ," and that each of us is destined to become one with that Higher Self—whether we call it the Christ, the Buddha, the Tao or the Atman. This "inner Christ" is what the Christian mystics sometimes refer to as the "inner man of the heart," and what the Upanishads mysteriously describe as a being the "size of a thumb" who "dwells deep within the heart."

We all have moments when we feel that connection with our Higher Self—when we are creative, loving, joyful. But there are other moments when we feel out of sync with our Higher Self—moments when we become angry, depressed, lost. What the spiritual path is all about is learning to sustain the connection to the higher part of ourselves so that we can make our greatest contribution to humanity.

The shaft of white light descending from the I AM Presence through the Holy Christ Self to the lower figure in the Chart is the crystal cord (sometimes called the silver cord). It is the "umbilical cord," the lifeline, that ties you to Spirit.

The Chart of Your Divine Self

Your crystal cord also nourishes that special, radiant flame of God that is ensconced in the secret chamber of your heart. It is called the threefold flame, or divine spark, because it is literally a spark of sacred fire that God has transmitted from his heart to yours. This flame is called "threefold" because it engenders the primary attributes of Spirit—power, wisdom and love.

The mystics of the world's religions have contacted the divine spark, describing it as the seed of divinity within. Buddhists, for instance, speak of the "germ of Buddhahood" that exists in every living being. In the Hindu tradition, the Katha Upanishad speaks of the "light of the Spirit" that is concealed in the "secret high place of the heart" of all beings.

Likewise, the fourteenth-century Christian theologian and mystic Meister Eckhart teaches of the divine spark when he says, "God's seed is within us."

When we decree, we meditate on the flame in the secret chamber of our heart. This secret chamber is your own private meditation room, your interior castle, as Teresa of Avila called it. In Hindu tradition, the devotee visualizes a jeweled island in his heart. There he sees himself before a beautiful altar, where he worships his teacher in deep meditation.

Jesus spoke of entering the secret chamber of the heart when he said: "When thou prayest, enter into thy closet, and when thou hast shut thy door, pray to thy Father which is in secret; and thy Father which seeth in secret shall reward thee openly."

The lower figure in the Chart of Your Divine Self represents you on the spiritual path, surrounded by the violet flame and the protective white light of God. The soul is the living potential of God—the part of you that is mortal but that can become immortal.

The purpose of your soul's evolution on earth is to grow in self-mastery, balance your karma and fulfill your mission on earth so that you can return to the spiritual dimensions that are your real home. When your soul at last takes flight and ascends back to God and the heaven-world, you will become an "ascended" master, free from the rounds of karma and rebirth. The high-frequency energy of the violet flame can help you reach that goal more quickly.

CHAPTER 19

*"The Call that you may make to me—as
the conclusion of the numerous Calls and
callings that I have given to you—is the
Call to walk the earth as my twin."*

Are You Ready for the Second Coming?
Walk the Earth as My Twin
Be an Example of the Aquarian-Age Christ

Keepers of the Flame of my father, Saint Germain, I pose you a question: Are you ready for the Second Coming?

["Yes!" (16-second standing ovation)]

Be seated, my beloved brothers and sisters.

I have heard and I have known, I have seen with my own eyes this dispensation of a cosmos delivered from the beginning to this conclusion of this retreat in Atlanta. And I tell you, beloved, that I desire to see a mighty conversion in your auras and hearts and beings and souls. And thus, my heart does open to you now.

For you see, beloved, you can experience the second coming of my Christ/your Christ within you. When you know yourself as worthy, as holy, as determined, as bearer of the honor flame that burns in your heart, even the threefold flame, I, then, would come to you in the fullness of the Holy Ghost for the quickening of your heart. I would enter your heart, for this is the true second coming of Christ in the earth, the first coming being my incarnation to inaugurate the Piscean age.

Thus, there have been saints along the way, beloved, and saints fifty thousand years ago who also knew me and knew me again in the quickening of Christ in their hearts.

Thus, beloved, I make known to you that when all is ready in your world and you feel the strength of balance in your body and in your spirit and you are ready for me to enter, the call that you may make to me—as the conclusion of the numerous calls and callings that I have given to you—is the call to walk the earth as my twin.

You understand the meaning of "the twin" from the Gospel of Thomas and its interpretation by the messenger and a number of scholars. Yes, beloved, your Christ/my Christ. There is indeed only one Christ, one begotten Son of the Father-Mother God, and it is the eternal light personified and manifest wherever the ray of light of a son or daughter of God has gone forth from the Central Sun. It is your calling, beloved.

I have given to you in my dictations of past years the steps and stages whereby you might seek that attainment and that oneness with me [as my twin]. I withhold nothing from you, beloved, but sometimes you do withhold yourselves and therefore forfeit all that you might receive from me.

It is my desire, with a deep desiring of God that fills all of my being—and my being that is manifest now, *filling* the Matter cosmos—it is my desire to walk and talk with you that your Christ might greet my Christ and we might embrace and that presence in the twain might be as one heart: thy heart/my heart.

Yes, beloved, I encourage you to seek me early. When you enter the body at dawn and begin to stretch and yawn and look around and say, "A new day is born!" remember that I am there and welcome me to your heart. Welcome your Holy Christ Self to descend into your temple and to be at home there.

My vision for you is that you might walk the earth as teachers, as anointed ones, as those holy ones of God, as angels or brother and sister who might impart such tender understanding, such support as the very support of my Presence and aura with you and of your own Presence, which is the Presence of God.

I would like to see you enjoy going about in the light of that Presence and the indwelling Christ *prior* to your ascension, that you may renew the days of long centuries ago when you had greater light (before you had made such karma) and you did walk the earth in that condition of the Christ with you and in you.

Think no longer, then, that your Holy Christ Self must only be above you, but think that your Holy Christ Self may be *in* you. But know also, beloved, that when the Christ does descend [into your temple], you can no longer be as human as you were before he descended, for some things must pass away to make room for the new day dawning of your personal Christhood.

Please note that most of you in some way or another practice a certain avoidance technique, avoiding the surrender of certain things to keep yourselves "humanly balanced." Little do you know that you close the door and do not answer when I knock lest you should have to receive me and I might enter and move the furniture around and change the hangings on the walls.

Yes, beloved, can you really have God and Mammon or Christ and Antichrist?

I think you know the answer. [You cannot. But forsaking Mammon and Antichrist] is a small price to pay to walk the earth as a shaft of light. But it is the ultimate price, for you not only have to set aside certain human-consciousness conditions but you must also know that some will be offended by the light and the Presence [and will rail against you].

You will have to choose your priorities. You will have to decide *how you want to spend the rest of your life.* You will give no less but much more to all whom you love and those who do not love you. But you will give it on certain terms—terms whereby you keep a level of the cosmic honor flame that you will not compromise because this or that one to whom you are attached insists on your being "more human."

Everyone has the human element until the hour of the ascension. Better, then, to be a good human being than not a human being at all, for people must be able to identify with you. And you can accomplish this and you will get very good at it, and that without even compromising the Christ flame in you.

Beloved hearts, [my call to you to walk the earth as my twin] is an open dispensation. It is the dispensation that you can call for [even as I have called you]. I do suggest that you run over the calls that I have given in the past dictations so that you may implement those calls as a foundation. I suggest you take your time, if you will, to decide. But know, beloved, that you are preparing for the bonding to my heart and I am preparing to receive you as my brides.

I therefore come in great love and devotion to you. And my

vision, as I have said, is to see you walk the earth before your ascension as masterful ones in the full dignity of the light that God has set upon you, even as he has set you apart as the I AM Race. All the things that you are are beautiful—and all of those things, beloved, are yours to manifest.

I see but a few causes of your separation from God. One is the world condemnation of the fallen ones and another is your failure to bind that condemnation and see that it is consumed by the violet flame.

Yes, the psyche must be mastered and made whole.

Yes, the violet flame can saturate.

Yes, my grace is sufficient for thee[1]—

thy grace is sufficient for me.

Let us, then, merge our graces, confess our Lord and show the whole wide world what is the profile of the Christ of Aquarius! Is it not the profile of the great adept with so many multiple talents—the great adept, my father, Saint Germain?

Oh, it is, beloved!

Think of the lives of Saint Germain and a thousand embodiments of his that you do not know of.

Think of all that he has done and can do!

Think of the multifaceted mind and personality and drive!

Think of Saint Germain and then you will know what a rich profile of the Christ he as the Hierarch of the Aquarian Age with blessed Portia bequeaths to you.

O blessed ones, what an age it can be! May you enjoy it to its fullest in all of the octaves of life. And may you be, beloved, to all people an example of the Aquarian-age Christ. Truly, such a gift is yours to give to this world and the universe.

I rejoice to be with you.

My offering is complete, for I never offer in part.

Do you desire the binding of the dweller-on-the-threshold? ["Yes!"]

I will contribute a part of the equation, but this is a work that *you* must work in your day. Better to accentuate the violet flame and then to deal with the dweller. If the dweller is bound yet there is a vacuum of non-Christhood because you have resisted your Holy Christ Self, well, then you shall be empty of both dweller and Christ. But, as I have taught, if you leave the house empty, other spirits will come to occupy it.[2]

Better call to me, then, to occupy your temple until you are ready for the full second coming, that at least I might displace something of your dweller-on-the-threshold as you do the [decree] work and angels obey your command in this regard. Better, then, to have a full cup than an empty cup and deliver yourself of the dweller day by day and point by point [instead of all at once].

I say, let there be the binding now by my very own angels, legions from the Father—the binding of fear and anxiety and doubt and the binding of deep-seated cleavages in your being and [conscious or unconscious] anger against the Godhead. These things will give way to Astrea and the violet flame, but you must have a very strong tie to God if you are going to go after these elements of the unconscious, so to speak, all at once.

Little by little and day by day these things can go.

And day by day the elements of Christhood may descend.

Yes, beloved, I AM your Divine Spouse. I long to embrace you and I shall embrace you fully when you shall have fully measured up to a certain level of this attainment. It is not necessary that you be wholly perfected to receive me in the second coming, but it is necessary that you have the strength and the balance to hold the position I bring and to defend it against the enemy within and without.

Let the wise ones proceed with caution and let them know that the Holy Spirit is always nigh to comfort, to teach, to enlighten, to rebuke and to set them straight, back on the path of life.

We have come, then, at the behest of the Lord Sanat Kumara. We join the Holy Kumaras and the Sponsors of Youth. We join the beloved Mary, my mother, Teresa of Avila, the Buddha of the Ruby Ray, Omri-Tas, the mighty archangels and all who have been a part of this conference.

So to the sweet ones of God, so to the mature ones, so to all who love, I AM your Jesus, Son of God, Son of man. I AM your twin on the road of life, and we shall walk and talk together until your victory is won.

I seal you now by my Sacred Heart. I place it over your heart, each one. Rejoice in my heart, beloved, but also know that the piercing of the heart is the initiation for the victory of the ascension.

I AM with you always, even unto the full flowering of the age of Aquarius and the end of the lower worlds of materialism.[3] For they shall not always be, *but the light-manifestation shall prevail!*

Pax vobiscum.

October 12, 1992
Voyages of Soul Discovery
Castlegate Hotel
Atlanta, Georgia

*Know, beloved, that you are approaching that stage when
I may call you brother and sister in the highest sense of the
word—in the sense of the word that you know your Christ as
my Christ and that I may see mirrored in you the fullness of the
only begotten Son of the Father-Mother God, who I AM.*

JESUS[4]

Jesus makes his final and most profound appeal to us in this
last dictation in his series of Calls. It is the culmination of the
path of discipleship that he has opened to us in all of his Calls:
that we walk the earth as his twin.

Jesus tells us that this is an open dispensation. There is no
time limit. He warns us of avoidance, and he has warned us a
number of times of the danger of procrastination. And yet he tells
us that our call should be made when we are ready: "When all is
ready in your world and you feel the strength of balance in your
body and in your spirit and you are ready for me to enter, the Call
that you may make to me—as the conclusion of the numerous
Calls and callings that I have given you—is the Call to walk the
earth as my twin."

What does it really mean to be Jesus' twin? We can trace this
concept to the earliest years of Christianity. We find it in the
Gospel of Thomas, a collection of sayings of Jesus that dates
from the same time as the four Gospels but was not included in
the New Testament. This writing is attributed to Judas Thomas,
who is called Jesus' "twin" in the text. Thomas is the Aramaic
word for "twin," and some have suggested that Thomas was literally Jesus' brother. However, the messenger explains the true
meaning of this as a spiritual relationship:

"Some people have mistakenly interpreted the concept of
Thomas as Jesus' twin as meaning a physical twin brother. But
the Gnostics understood that as we aspire to and become our
Real Self, we are becoming one with that Christ Self. The Christ

Self of us is also the Christ of Jesus. They are one and the same. So when we become like, or the reflection of, our Holy Christ Self, we also become the twin of Jesus. Jesus is our role model. When we fulfill his sayings and his Word and his light, our vibration, our countenance, our love should be like him. We should understand and know what Jesus would do and, therefore, also do those same works.

"Jesus was continually emphasizing in the Gnostic gospels that we should drink from the same source from which he had drunk and, therefore, become like him. Jesus stressed that God wanted the disciples to become like him, to become equal to him and a part of him, and then they would be one with the Father, the Father-Mother God, as he was one."[5]

Walking the earth as Jesus' twin in the full manifestation of our Christhood is truly what is meant by the Second Coming of Christ. The messenger explains what it really means to become the twin of Jesus:

"Scholar Elaine Pagels suggests that Gnostics may have attributed the *Gospel of Thomas* and the *Book of Thomas* to Jesus' 'twin brother' in order to 'suggest that "you, the reader, are Jesus' twin brother." Whoever comes to understand these books discovers, like Thomas, that Jesus is his "twin"—his spiritual "other self." '[6]

"This is a very profound meditation. Most Christians who have been taught that they are sinners and stamped with the concept of sin, that they can never rise again, and that they can be saved through Jesus Christ but not through their own path of individual attainment, should find it both astonishing and a cause for rejoicing that they can see themselves as a coequal with Jesus, as his twin brother or twin sister.

"Who else would we rather be like in the whole wide world than Jesus? I'm sure that all of us aspire to this, and I'm sure that all of us hear the demons condemn us, saying, 'You can never be like Jesus. And if you try, it is a sin, because it is a sin of pride.'

"Nothing could be farther from the truth, and this is the crux of the matter. This is the teaching of Jesus that has been lost. All other sayings and teachings in these four Gnostic gospels[7] and those you will find in *The Nag Hammadi Library*[8] are based upon this foundation: 'Become as I AM. I came down from heaven to show you the way. I AM that way, that truth and the life. He that will follow me will have everlasting life. Follow me in the works that I do, the words that I say, the consciousness that I AM.'

"These sayings from the Gospel of Thomas give the teachings whereby Jesus imparts to us the how-to—how to walk in his footsteps, how to understand the mysteries, how to probe these mysteries, how to become the embodiment of that mystery....

"We look at that Chart of Your Divine Self (see page 373), and we see the Holy Christ Self above us. That is the Christ that is the only begotten Son of God, the only begotten Son of the Father, full of grace and truth.[9] That Christ individualized for us becomes that very personal Holy Christ Self.

"Anyone who is one with that Christ, fully fused to that Christ, is also one with Jesus. Things equal to the same thing are equal to each other. Each Holy Christ Self is a crumb broken from the whole loaf of the Christ consciousness, or the Cosmic Christ of the cosmos.

"So there is one Universal Christ individualized for all of us. What is so special about Jesus is he has been the incarnation of that Word, that Christ, for aeons, and he has been chosen by the Father to save us, that our souls might be saved to become reunited with that same Christ-potential.

"Today we have that Christ as potential, and every day we hope we are becoming more of its manifestation. In Jesus, Christ lives and reigns as the fullness of that Christ manifestation in the tremendous glory of who he is and the service he has given for tens of thousands and hundreds of thousands of years to life-waves of this planet and many systems of worlds. Thus, he is truly our Lord and Saviour and our elder brother on the Path....

"You are intended to be the incarnation of God. And as you personalize and individualize that Christ, you will bring to the universe a unique manifestation of that Christ. Every ascended master is different and unique and yet is the embodiment of that same Christ-essence. So, to be the twin of Jesus does not mean to be the carbon copy of him. It means that we will assimilate his attributes and his actions and his teaching. We will be very much like him, but we will have the very unique expression that God has given to us in our unique blueprint."[10]

There have been saints throughout the ages who experienced this Second Coming of Christ within their hearts. Catherine of Siena was one such saint who recorded her experience of being Jesus' twin. Author Carol Flinders describes Catherine's experience:

"On another occasion, after Catherine had been praying 'for a clean heart,' the Lord appeared and removed her heart. In a few days he brought it back—except that it was his heart, not hers, and it beat a good deal more loudly than hers had! After this she felt herself to be loving others with Christ's own heart. The process that she would describe at the beginning of her *Dialogue* was well under way now. 'The soul is united with God, following in the footsteps of Christ crucified, and through desire and affection and the union of love he makes of her another himself.' "[11]

Jesus Holds a Vision for Us

Jesus has a beautiful vision he holds for us: "My vision for you is that you might walk the earth as teachers, as anointed ones, as those holy ones of God.... I would like to see you enjoy going about in the light of that Presence and the indwelling Christ *prior* to your ascension." He asks us to no longer think of our Holy Christ Self above us, but to think and feel that Christ is dwelling within our body temple.

Can you imagine embodying and sharing the fullness of Christ's love *before* you ascend? Walking the earth with his healing powers blessing all mankind?

Avoidance Techniques

In this dictation Jesus expresses his concern that many are practicing avoidance techniques that prevent them from becoming the fullness of their Christ Self. He says: "Please note that most of you in some way or another practice a certain avoidance technique, avoiding the surrender of certain things to keep yourselves 'humanly balanced.' " How do we do this? One way is by hanging onto certain human habits. Not letting go of these habits, Jesus says, may be the very thing that shuts him out of our lives. He knocks on the door of our hearts, and we don't hear him. He can't make contact with us.

Very often this decision is unconscious. Nevertheless, Jesus wants us to realize that we do have to choose. If we truly desire to answer his Call and walk the earth as his twin, he tells us, "You will have to choose your priorities. You have to decide how you want to spend the rest of your life." This will mean letting go of certain human attachments and activities that keep us from receiving the fullness of Christ. These may be things that we know are not in keeping with the cosmic honor flame and that compromise the Christ flame in our hearts, or they may be the preoccupations and enjoyments of the world that are not harmful but simply do not leave time or space in our lives for meditation, devotion and drawing down the light of God.

There are reasons we sometimes avoid the higher path, the higher truth. The messenger gives us an understanding of why this is so: "We have the promise of Jesus that he will send us the Comforter and the Holy Spirit,[12] that we will find the truth and that when we find it, the truth will make us free.

"Why are we disturbed when we find the truth? Because we are comfortable in our untruths, our illusions, our accommodations, our human consciousness, the things we desire to be ignorant about, because if we had knowledge in those things, then we would have to change our lifestyle.

"The truth is disturbing because it is alchemical. It is a living flame. We are not simply finding some intellectual treatise when we find the truth of the living God. We are finding the power of that living Word, and when that Word comes into us, it is sweet in the mouth and bitter in the belly,[13] because it works change within us. We will become disturbed. Our lives will be rearranged. The sword will descend that Jesus said he came to bring,[14] dividing households, dividing our own individual members, dividing the Real from the Unreal.

"If you seek the truth of Jesus Christ, expect to find it. If you expect to find it, expect to be disturbed. Be willing to change. Be willing to walk up and down the earth until you are remade in the likeness of God through trial, through adversity, through love, through communion, through whatever the Saviour brings you.

"You will be amazed at what is the Truth by contrast to the error you have lived with. And when you have that truth, you will reign over all. You will reign over yourself, over your body, over your organs, over your health, over your life, your emotions, your mind. You will become the master of yourself and therefore be sought after as a leader of men and women. But first and always and foremost, you must be a follower of Jesus Christ....

"[In *The Gospel of Thomas,* we read:] 'Jesus said... "There will be days you will seek me but will not find me." '[15] Why do we not find Jesus? It is karma, the blindness of karma, the out-of-alignment state, the state of dryness when Jesus wants us to prime the pump, to increase the light, to supply the light whereby and wherewith we can see him. When Jesus appears to us, he is supplying the light. He is opening our vision. He is enabling us to see him.

"On the days that we do not find him, these are the days when he wants us to find the Christ in ourselves and to bring him the lawful gift of our Christhood.... There is a rhythm of cycles. There come the days when you do not feel the outpouring of light. These are the days when you must give light to God."[16]

When we don't feel the Presence and light of God, it may be because we are bearing an extra burden of darkness in our bodies. Whether it is personal or planetary doesn't really matter. What matters is that we accelerate and intensify our calls and push on through the density that is covering (for a time) the light within our hearts. Consider what Jesus has to say about the cause of our feeling of separation and determine to make the call for your victory:

"I see but a few causes of your separation from God. One is

the world condemnation of the fallen ones, and another is your failure to bind that condemnation and see that it is consumed by the violet flame. "

SPIRITUAL EXERCISES

Prayer to Walk the Earth as Jesus' Twin

Beloved mighty I AM Presence, beloved Jesus, seal me in your Sacred Heart and let your heart be my heart. Let me find that perfect balance whereby I can walk the earth as your twin. No joy would be greater than to walk the earth in the fullness of my Christhood, your Christhood. Therefore, open my eyes, O Lord, that I might truly see thee face-to-face.

Meditation on Surrender

Spend some time in meditation with a picture of the Master Jesus in front of you.

Center in your heart, commune with Jesus and ask him to place his Electronic Presence over you. Ask him to place his Sacred Heart over your heart. Open your heart to the Master, and let him know you desire to be one with him. Ask him to show you those things in your life that are blocks to his entering in more fully, things he would have you personally surrender. You may wish to give the following prayer:

Dear Jesus, I desire to physically embody the fullness of my Holy Christ Self and to walk the earth as your twin. Please show me what I am holding onto that I think I need to keep me 'humanly balanced,' but in reality is an avoidance technique and is blocking my communion with your heart. Show me what it is that I can surrender that will open the door to you and allow you to bring me into congruence with my Real Self, and into oneness with your Sacred Heart.

Then say three times: Let that mind be in me that was also in Christ Jesus.

Now, sit quietly for the next few minutes meditating upon his picture and his Sacred Heart. Listen and be receptive and open to the promptings of the still, small voice within.

Give the Surrender Rosary

Mother Mary tells us: "Surrender! Surrender to this law within all that which is anti-Mother, anti-God, anti-the-Real-Self—all of these schisms and divisions that are fabricated within the subconscious. Let go of everything! Give everything to God, and understand that it is like carrying your dirty wash to the laundromat. You put it in, it comes out clean. You give to God everything that you are, and he gives back to you everything cleaned and purified."[17]

Mother Mary has given us a rosary that is a ritual for surrender. By reciting "The Fourteenth Rosary: The Mystery of Surrender,"[18] we can enter into the heart of the flame and into the heart of the Blessed Mother and engage in the process of consciously surrendering to God. If we find it difficult to surrender to God, we can enter into this ritual and ask Jesus and Mother Mary to help us give up those elements of self that resist the surrender to a higher love.

FOR YOUR JOURNAL

How Will *You* Answer Jesus' Call?

"The Call that you may make to me—as the conclusion of the numerous Calls and callings that I have given to you—is the Call to walk the earth as my twin."

What does this Call mean to me?
What will I do to answer this Call?

The Christ of Aquarius

As Jesus concludes the cycle of his Calls, he offers us a vision of what it can mean for the world if we answer his Calls and become the fullness of all he desires for us.

Two thousand years ago Jesus came to inaugurate the age of Pisces. He called his disciples to leave their nets. He called them to a path of Christhood. He told them, "Verily, verily, I say unto you, He that believeth on me, the works that I do shall he do also; and greater works than these shall he do; because I go unto my Father."[1] The Call, ultimately, was to walk in his footsteps and to become the Christ. The Christhood of Jesus would multiply our own, and we would then be able to manifest the greater works he promised.

For two thousand years we have had the opportunity, and the world has had the opportunity, to answer that Call. There should be many Christed ones in the world today. We should be at the dawn of a golden age.

If we have procrastinated and not answered the Call, Jesus comes now at the end of the age to tell us, "It is not too late." The door is still open. If we enter in and become that Christ, we may yet fulfill the destiny of Pisces. The culmination of the age of Pisces should be the Christ consciousness embodied in many sons and daughters of God, and this should be the foundation of Aquarius. This is what Jesus speaks of near the conclusion of this cycle: the profile of the Christ of Aquarius.

Each age builds on the foundation of the previous one. Jesus' mission in Pisces was built on the foundation of Abraham, Moses and the dispensations of the Age of Aries. In the same way,

Saint Germain's mission as the Hierarch of the Aquarian Age (as Jesus held that office for Pisces) is being built on the foundation of Pisces.

Jesus shares his vision of Aquarius as a golden age, and he opens a door for us to enter in. It is the door of his heart, his life given to us. As we enter in and fulfill all that Jesus calls us to do, we can lay the foundation for discipleship in the New Age.

The Calls of Jesus

1. "Come, leave your nets! I will make you fishers of men."

2. "Take up the sword of the Spirit and fight for my sheep ere they are lost to the clutches of the drug peddlers and the peddlers of deceit and annihilation."

3. The call to the path of the ascension.

4. "I call to you to be world teachers."

5. The call for ten thousand Keepers of the Flame.

6. "I call you to be my disciples."

7. "I ask that you renew your commitment to giving my Watch, my 'Vigil of the Hours.' "

8. "Become that Christ!... It is time for you to be true shepherds and ministers."

9. The call to be true shepherds of the children of God.

10. "I call you to the House of the LORD, your mighty I AM Presence."

11. "I *command* you to allow that Christ to descend into your temple."

12. "Take back unto yourself the karma I have borne for you these two thousand years."

13. "I call you to a life of the Holy Ghost."

14. "I call you to my temple of initiation."

15. "Above and beyond all to which I have called you,...may you become all love."

16. "Become agents of the Cosmic Christ...that the children of the light might enter in to this sheepfold."

17. "I call you to...the perfecting of the soul as my apostle."

18. "I have come to call you to be my shepherds."

19. "Drink this cup of my Christhood.... Be the instruments of my light...to the youth of the entire world, to children bruised and battered."

20. "See the great calling...to embody that light, that I AM THAT I AM, that portion of Christos that is yours to claim."

21. "Save the homeless and the street people from that sense of abject self-negation.... Be converted to serve those who sense they are the poor in spirit."

22. The call to "espouse the higher calling in God" and "to stand in defense of life."

23. "I call you to repentance."

24. "The call of love"—the "outreaching of your heart, your hand and your speaking of my Truth...to all who have been a part of me and my life."

25. The call to prepare for the initiation of the descent into hell.

26. "I call you to the heart of God."

27. "I call you to be those mighty electrodes of your Holy Christ Self and of your mighty I AM Presence that the earth might receive the light."

28. "I make known to you that when all is ready in your world and you feel the strength of balance in your body and in your spirit and you are ready for me to enter, the call that you may make to me—as the conclusion of the numerous calls and callings that I have given to you—is the call to walk the earth as my twin."

Notes

N.B.: Throughout the dictations in this book, bracketed material denotes words unspoken yet implicit in the dictation, added by the Messenger under Jesus' direction for clarity in the written word.

Books listed here are published by Summit University Press, Corwin Springs, Montana, unless otherwise noted.

INTRODUCTION
1. John 14:12.
2. 2 Cor. 1:11-19.
3. John 15:1-8.

CHAPTER 1
This dictation by Jesus the Christ is published in its entirety in *Pearls of Wisdom,* vol. 27 no. 59, December 16, 1984. As a preface to the dictation, the messenger read Exodus 33 and 34.

1. Matt. 5:18.
2. Saint Germain is the seventh angel prophesied in Revelation 10:7 who comes to sponsor the finishing of the mystery of God "as he hath declared to his servants the prophets."
3. Rev. 3:12.
4. Ps. 61:2.
5. Matt. 4:4.
6. Deut. 5:9.
7. John 14:23.
8. Matt. 28:20.
9. Matt. 11:28, 30.
10. Matt. 4:18-20.
11. Elizabeth Clare Prophet, Summit University lecture, "The Purpose of the Coming of Maitreya," March 16, 1985.
12. Matt. 8:22.
13. Elizabeth Clare Prophet, John the Beloved Seminar, Lecture #1, July 6, 1982.
14. Gautama Buddha, "The Planetary Initiation of the Ruby Ray," *Pearls of Wisdom,* vol. 33, no. 17, May 6, 1990.

15. Isa. 1:18.
16. Exod. 3:14.
17. Elizabeth Clare Prophet, *Inner Perspectives* (Corwin Springs, Mont.: The Summit Lighthouse Library, 2001), pp. 26-28.
18. Helios, "The Power of the Call," *Pearls of Wisdom,* vol. 34, no. 11, March 17, 1991.
19. Matt. 10:5-6.
20. This prayer is adapted from a dictation by Gautama Buddha and Saint Germain, "The Teaching Is for the Many," *Pearls of Wisdom,* vol. 29, no. 21, May 25, 1986.

CHAPTER 2

This dictation by Jesus the Christ is published in its entirely in *Pearls of Wisdom,* vol. 30 no. 18, May 3, 1987.

1. Mark 15:39.
2. 1 Pet. 2:5.
3. 2 Tim. 2:15.
4. Matt. 10:34.
5. John 4:35.
6. Rev. 19:9.
7. John 21:15-17.
8. Matt. 10:34 New Jerusalem Bible.
9. And God said, Let us make man in our image, after our likeness: and let them have dominion over the fish of the sea, and over the fowl of the air, and over the cattle, and over all the earth, and over every creeping thing that creepeth upon the earth.—Gen. 1:26.
10. Astrea, "I Enlist Your Help," *Pearls of Wisdom,* vol. 34, no. 13, March 31, 1991.
11. Archangel Michael, "Charge! Charge! Charge! And Let Victory Be Proclaimed!" *Pearls of Wisdom,* vol. 17, no. 15, April 14, 1974.
12. Mark L. Prophet and Elizabeth Clare Prophet, *The Lost Teachings of Jesus,* 4 vols.
13. Jesus, "The Coming of the Divine Teacher," *Pearls of Wisdom,* vol. 29, no. 78, December 23, 1986.
14. Jesus and Kuthumi, *Prayer and Meditation.*
15. Jesus, "The Point of Dazzling Joy," *Pearls of Wisdom,* vol. 35, no. 69, December 29, 1992.
16. Jesus, "The Overcoming Victory of the Light," *Pearls of Wisdom,* vol. 31, no. 48, August 6, 1988.

CHAPTER 3

This dictation by Jesus the Christ is published in its entirety in *Pearls of Wisdom,* vol. 30, no. 27, July 5, 1987.

1. Matt. 28:20.
2. Rom. 13:10.
3. John 15:13.
4. Gal. 6:5.
5. John 9:5.
6. John 15:13.
7. 1 Cor. 11:24.
8. Archangel Gabriel, "Called to an Unusual Sacrifice," *Pearls of Wisdom,* vol. 30, no. 55, November 22, 1987.
9. Matt. 28:18.
10. The ascended master Paul the Venetian was embodied as Paolo Veronese, one of the major artists of the 16th-century Venetian school. Paolo Veronese ascended on April 19, 1588. As the ascended master Paul the Venetian, he is the chohan (lord) of the third ray of love. His devotion is to beauty, the perfection of the soul through compassion, patience, understanding, self-discipline and the development of the intuitive and creative faculties of the heart by the alchemy of self-sacrifice, selflessness and surrender.
    His retreat, the Château de Liberté, is located in the etheric plane over southern France on the Rhône River. (Its physical counterpart is a château now owned by a private French family.) At the etheric level it contains classrooms with paintings and artwork of every kind from all ages and races and cultures, as well as workshops for musicians, writers, sculptors and students of voice. Here the masters introduce new techniques in every field of art.
11. Gautama Buddha, "The Teaching is for the Many," *Pearls of Wisdom,* vol. 29, no. 21, May 25, 1986.
12. 1 Cor. 15:31.
13. Lanello, "How to Ascend," *Pearls of Wisdom,* vol. 35, no. 10, March 8, 1992.
14. Matt. 6:33; Luke 12:31.
15. Lanello, "How to Ascend."
16. Serapis Bey, "Motivation," *Pearls of Wisdom,* vol. 33, no. 3, January 21, 1990.
17. Mark L. Prophet and Elizabeth Clare Prophet, *The Masters and the Spiritual Path,* pp. 93-94. For further teaching on the ascension, see *The Masters and the Spiritual Path,* ch. 2, and Annice Booth, *The Path to Your Ascension.*

18. John 21:15-17.
19. Archangels Jophiel and Uriel, "Qualifying World Teachers to Dispense the Illumination of the New Age," *Pearls of Wisdom,* vol. 28, no. 5, February 3, 1985.
20. Goddess Sarasvati, "We Do Work!" *Pearls of Wisdom,* vol. 35, no. 39, September 29, 1992.
21. Lanello, "Through the Heart of the One Sent—the Reigniting of the Flame," *Pearls of Wisdom,* vol. 24, no. 62, April 1981.
22. Jesus, July 20, 1979, unpublished.
23. 1 Pet. 2:5.
24. John 8:32.
25. El Morya, *The Chela and the Path,* pp. 102-104.
26. Elizabeth Clare Prophet, "The Practical Art of Living a Spiritual Life," April 12, 1997.
27. Excerpted from: Elizabeth Clare Prophet, Summit University lecture, September 21, 1973.

CHAPTER 4

The complete dictation by Jesus is published in the *Pearls of Wisdom,* vol. 30, no. 56, November 25, 1987.

"Watch With Me" Jesus' Vigil of the Hours released by Elizabeth Clare Prophet is a worldwide service of prayers, affirmations and hymns, which in 1964 the Master called upon Keepers of the Flame to keep individually or in groups. The service was dictated by the ascended master Jesus Christ for the protection of the Christ consciousness in every son and daughter of God and in commemoration of the vigil the Master kept alone in the Garden of Gethsemane when he said: "Could ye not watch with me one hour?" Available in 44-page booklet and on 90-min. audiocassette B87096.

1. Rev. 21:2-27; 22:1-7.
2. On Jesus' retreat and his tutoring of the apostle Paul, see *Lords of the Seven Rays,* Book One, pp. 183-88, 199-203, 225.
3. Matt. 5:14.
4. Jer. 23:5, 6; 33:15, 16.
5. The Maha Chohan, the "Great Lord" who presides over the seven chohans of the rays, holds the office in the hierarchy of the Great White Brotherhood of Representative of the Holy Spirit.
6. John 8:31.
7. Eccles. 1:9.
8. James 1:12; Rev. 2:10.
9. 1 John 5:6-8.

10. Prov. 4:7.
11. John 15:12.
12. Ps. 91:1.
13. John 15:13; 10:17; Rom. 16:4; 1 John 3:16.
14. Prior to the dictation the messenger delivered a lecture on the Lost Years and the Lost Teachings of Jesus in which she read the Gnostic poem "The Hymn of the Pearl" and the commentary on it from *Gnostic Scriptures Interpreted,* by G. A. Gaskell. The poem, thought to have been composed by the apostle Thomas, portrays the soul's descent from the highest spiritual plane into the planes of illusion with loss of memory of her origin. There she faces the trial and tribulation of the lower life until she responds to the Call from Home, which eventuates in her ascent culminating in her union with the Divine.
15. John 20:17.
16. Matt. 15:8; Jer. 6:13, 14; 14:13-15; 23:1, 2, 9-40; 27:9, 10, 14, 15; 28; 29:8, 9, 21-32.
17. The messenger Mark L. Prophet who founded The Summit Lighthouse in 1958, called by El Morya to deliver the Lost Teachings of Jesus and the prophecy of Saint Germain as they would be dictated to him by the ascended masters.
18. Job 19:26; John 14:12; Rom. 8:14-17, 29; Gal. 4:6, 7; 1 John 3:2.
19. Luke 19:13.
20. 2 Tim. 2:15.
21. Kuthumi and Djwal Kul, *The Human Aura,* pp. 372-373.
22. Ibid.
23. El Morya, *The Chela and the Path,* pp. 19-20.
24. Isa. 6:8.
25. Jesus and Kuthumi, *Corona Class Lessons,* ch. 25.
26. Elizabeth Clare Prophet, July 13, 1979.
27. John 10:30.
28. Jesus, "Christhood," *Pearls of Wisdom,* vol. 31, no. 21, May 22, 1988.
29. John 12: 44, 45, 49, 50.
30. John 1:9.
31. Mark L. Prophet and Elizabeth Clare Prophet, *Pearls of Wisdom,* vol. 27, Book I, Introduction, pp. 3-4.
32. John 10:30, 38; 14:9-11, 20; 17:21-23.
33. John 20:17.
34. John 14:13.
35. *Pearls of Wisdom,* vol. 27, Book I, Introduction, pp. 6-7.

36. Ancient Buddhist scriptures reveal that Jesus traveled to India and the Himalayas between the ages of 13 and 30 in preparation for his Galilean mission. See Elizabeth Clare Prophet, *The Lost Years of Jesus.*
37. Lord Maitreya, "The Mission of Jesus Christ," *Pearls of Wisdom,* vol. 27, no. 47A, September 26, 1984.
38. There is another retreat associated with Jesus' Arabian Retreat that is not in use at this time. It is in a subterranean complex of buildings, which the masters hermetically sealed before a cataclysm covered the complex with desert sands. Nearly 400 feet beneath the surface is a huge chamber with 50-foot high columns decorated with hieroglyphs. Other stylized paintings in purple and gold line the walls. In an adjoining council chamber the cosmic symbols of the twelve houses of the sun are inlaid in the floor. The building style and interior design of this subterranean city resemble ancient Greek and Roman architecture.
39. 2 Cor. 12:4.
40. Elizabeth Clare Prophet, lecture on healing and the medical profession, July 3, 1986.
41. Elizabeth Clare Prophet, *Inner Perspectives* (Corwin Springs, Mont.: Summit University, 1991) pp. 391-92.
42. Matt. 26:40; Mark 14:37.
43. Elizabeth Clare Prophet, memo to Summit Lighthouse staff, December 6, 1989.
44. Ibid.
45. Jesus, "I Love You," *Pearls of Wisdom,* vol. 34, no. 41, August 25, 1991.

CHAPTER 5

This dictation by Jesus the Christ is published in its entirety in *Pearls of Wisdom,* vol. 30, no. 74, December 13, 1987.

1. Jesus' dictation commenced at 3:13 pm, CST.
2. See "The Hound of Heaven," a poem by the English poet Francis Thompson (1859-1907).
3. Luke 18:1-8.
4. Elizabeth Clare Prophet, "Teaching on *A Dweller on Two Planets,*" part 16, August 10, 1990.
5. The science of the cosmic clock, taught by Mother Mary to the messenger Elizabeth Clare Prophet, is a new-age astrology that provides the scientific means of understanding and charting the cycles of personal and planetary karma that return to us daily as the tests and trials of the path of initiation. For further study

on the cosmic clock, see "The Cosmic Clock: Psychology for the Aquarian Man and Woman," in Elizabeth Clare Prophet, *The Great White Brotherhood in the Culture, History, and Religion of America,* pp. 173-206.

6. Elizabeth Clare Prophet, "Teachings of Jesus Christ on Your Path of Personal Christhood," June 27, 1993.

7. Matt. 22:1-14.

8. Portia, "The Mother of Aquarius Steps Down from Cosmic Levels," *Pearls of Wisdom,* vol. 31, no. 41, July 18, 1988.

9. El Morya, "Chela—Christed One—Guru: Offices on the Path of the Individualization of the God Flame," *Pearls of Wisdom,* vol. 28, no. 11, March 17, 1985.

10. Elizabeth Clare Prophet, "Teachings of Jesus Christ on Your Path of Personal Christhood," June 27, 1993.

11. Archangel Jophiel and Archeia Hope, "Is Anything Too Hard for the LORD?" *Pearls of Wisdom,* vol. 32, no. 36, September 3, 1989.

12. John 14:15.

13. See p. 8.

14. Elizabeth Clare Prophet, "Teachings of Jesus Christ on Your Path of Personal Christhood," June 27, 1993.

15. Elizabeth Clare Prophet, Summit University lecture, November 6, 1975.

16. Elizabeth Clare Prophet, Summit University lecture, March 21, 1979.

17. Jesus and Kuthumi, *Corona Class Lessons,* p. 220.

CHAPTER 6

This dictation is published in its entirety in *Pearls of Wisdom,* vol. 31, no. 38, July 10, 1988.

1. In Catholic theology the Church Militant is the Church on earth whose function is to engage in constant warfare against its enemies, the powers of evil, in contrast to the Church Triumphant, the Church in heaven whose members have achieved union with God.

2. This statement of the Lord does not imply that there are no saints within the Church. It is rather a generalization because the percentages left within the Church are very small by comparison to those who are without. In this case the exceptions prove the rule.

3. Matt. 21:12, 13; Mark 11:15-17; Luke 19:45, 46; John 2:13-17.

4. There were traditions in the first to third centuries of a long

interval between the resurrection and ascension. The Church Father Irenaeus wrote, "From the fortieth and fiftieth year a man begins to decline towards old age, which our Lord possessed while He still fulfilled the office of a Teacher, even as the Gospel and all the elders testify; those who were conversant in Asia with John, the disciple of the Lord, [affirming] that John conveyed to them that information" (Against Heresies, c. 180). The third-century Gnostic text Pistis Sophia (1:1) states: "It came to pass, when Jesus had risen from the dead, that he passed 11 years discoursing with his disciples and instructing them." See *The Lost Years of Jesus*, pp. 4-5; *The Lost Teachings of Jesus 1*, pp. 240-41.
5. Matt. 7:15.
6. In the Gospel of Thomas, Jesus is recorded as instructing his disciples: "I am not your master. Because you have drunk, you have become drunk from the bubbling stream which I have measured out.... He who will drink from my mouth will become as I am: I myself shall become he, and the things that are hidden will be revealed to him.... The Kingdom is inside of you, and it is outside of you. When you come to know yourselves, then you will be known, and you will realize that you are the sons of the living Father" (logia 13, 108, 3). The Gnostic Gospel of Philip describes the devotee of Christ who no longer calls himself a Christian "but a Christ": "You saw the Spirit, you became Spirit. You saw Christ, you became Christ. You saw [the Father, you] shall become Father. So [in this place] you see everything and [do] not [see] yourself, but [in that place] you do see yourself—and what you see you shall [become]" (67:26, 27; 61:29-35, in The Nag Hammadi Library in English [San Francisco: Harper & Row, 1977], pp. 140, 137).
7. John 9:4.
8. Ray-O-Light, "Keep Moving," *Pearls of Wisdom*, vol. 25, no. 29, July 18, 1982.
9. Jesus Christ, "I Love You," *Pearls of Wisdom*, vol. 34, no. 41, August 25, 1991.
10. Elizabeth Clare Prophet, "Krishna, the Divine Lover and Healer of Your Soul," July 1, 1993.
11. Jesus Christ, "I Love You."
12. "Krishna, the Divine Lover and Healer of Your Soul."
13. Jesus Christ, "I Love You."
14. *Krishna: The Maha Mantra and Bhajans*, audiocassette B92070, available from The Summit Lighthouse.

15. Elizabeth Clare Prophet, "Beams of Essential Light," *Pearls of Wisdom,* vol. 24, no. 22, May 31, 1981.

CHAPTER 7

This dictation by Jesus the Christ is published in its entirety in *Pearls of Wisdom,* vol. 31, no. 83, December 4, 1988.

1. Mal. 3:1; Matt. 11:10; Mark 1:2; Luke 1:76; 7:27.
2. Hab. 1:13.
3. Therefore the office of the messenger is the shield protecting the eyes of the people from the direct gaze of the I AM THAT I AM. Thus, the messenger goes before the face of the Presence, even as scripture declares that God sends his messenger, the Holy Christ Self, before the face of the people that they might commune with the Son who is the Divine Mediator between the Absolute and the relative states of existence.
4. Isa. 40:31.
5. Ps. 69:9; John 2:17; Isa. 9:7; 59:17.
6. Luke 23:34.
7. Luke 24:49.
8. Rev. 9:1-12; 11:7; 17:8; 20:1-3.
9. Rev. 21:23.
10. John 9:4, 5; 12:35.
11. Matt. 22:29; Mark 12:24.
12. Judg. 7:16-22 (Matt. 9:16, 17; Mark 2:21, 22; Luke 5:36-38).
13. John 14:2.
14. John 8:58.
15. El Morya, "A Special Report from the Chief of the Darjeeling Council," *Pearls of Wisdom,* vol. 37, no. 1, January 2, 1994.
16. John 6:53.
17. Elizabeth Clare Prophet, "On the Bonding to the Heart of the Guru," August 9, 1991.
18. Matt. 25:1-13.
19. *Pearls of Wisdom,* vol. 31, no. 80, November 26, 1988, note 14. For other teachings by the messenger on the dark night, including readings and commentary on the writings of Saint John of the Cross, see Elizabeth Clare Prophet, *Living Flame of Love,* 8-audiocassette album, 12-1/2 hrs., A85044; "The Dark Night of the Soul," April 12, 1974. See also Archangel Gabriel, *Mysteries of the Holy Grail,* pp. 173, 368-69.
20. Elizabeth Clare Prophet, "The Dark Night of the Soul," April 12, 1974.
21. Mark 15:34; Matt. 27:46.

22. Elizabeth Clare Prophet, "Roots of Christian Mysticism," part 2, June 28, 1992.
23. Durga, "The Power of Confrontation," *Pearls of Wisdom,* vol. 35, no. 5, February 2, 1992.
24. *The Living Flame of Love,* 8-audiotape album, #A85044.

CHAPTER 8

This dictation by Jesus the Christ is published in its entirety in *Pearls of Wisdom,* vol. 32, no. 60, December 10, 1989.

1. Jesus' Second Coming foretold. Matt. 24:27-31; Mark 13:24-26; Luke 21:25-28; 1 Thess. 4:16, 17; Rev. 1:7.
2. Matt. 26:26; Mark 14:22; Luke 22:19; 1 Cor. 11:24.
3. John 5:25.
4. Matt. 8:11, 12; 22:8-14; 25:30.
5. Second death. Rev. 2:11; 20:6.
6. Rev. 12:12.
7. Matt. 7:15; Luke 11:39.
8. Matt. 13:24-30, 36-43.
9. Rev. 1:7.
10. Ps. 19:14.
11. Ps. 69:9; John 2:17; Isa. 9:7; 59:17.
12. Gen. 5:21, 22, 24; Heb. 11:5.
13. John 21:15-17.
14. Jer. 4:31; Mic. 4:9, 10; John 16:21.
15. Matt. 24:40, 41; Luke 17:34-36.
16. "As for man, his days are as grass." Ps. 103:15, 16.
17. "The ungodly are like chaff." Ps. 1:4.
18. John 4:34; 5:30, 36; 9:4; 17:4.
19. "He which is filthy": Rev. 22:11. "Knowest not thou art naked": Rev. 3:16, 17.
20. In the novel *The Strange Case of Dr. Jekyll and Mr. Hyde* by Robert Louis Stevenson, Dr. Jekyll is a respectable and virtuous citizen who is fascinated by the idea of isolating the good and evil in human nature. He develops a drug to periodically transform himself into Mr. Hyde, a separate personality through whom he gives vent to evil impulses. When he commits murder, Dr. Jekyll realizes his creation has overpowered his own instincts for good. No longer able to restore his original personality at will, Dr. Jekyll takes his own life just before he is to be arrested. On November 26, 1987, the messenger gave teaching on the confrontation with the dweller-on-the-threshold in which she commented on the story of Dr. Jekyll and Mr. Hyde,

describing Mr. Hyde as the embodiment of Dr. Jekyll's dweller-on-the-threshold. See Elizabeth Clare Prophet, "The Lost Teachings of Jesus: On the Enemy Within," on two 90-min. audiocassettes, A87097.

21. Jesus, "The Path of the Builders," *Pearls of Wisdom,* vol. 36, no. 36, September 1, 1993.
22. Saint Germain, October 11, 1970.
23. John 12:35.
24. Kuthumi, "The 'Second Coming' of the Saints," *Pearls of Wisdom,* vol. 32, no. 61, December 13, 1989.
25. Elizabeth Clare Prophet, "On the Defense of Freedom," July 1, 1987.
26. Rev. 3:11.
27. Gautama Buddha, *Quietly Comes the Buddha,* (Corwin Springs, Mont.: Summit University Press, 2000), ch. 11.
28. Serapis Bey, "The Mobilization of Spiritual Forces," *Pearls of Wisdom,* vol. 25, no. 60.
29. El Morya, "Reinforcements of Reality," October 27, 1974.
30. Rom. 7:19, 20.
31. Acts 7:58-60; 8:1-3; 9:1 31; 13-28.
32. Rom. 8:6, 7.
33. 1 Tim. 5:24.
34. Elizabeth Clare Prophet, "Christ and the Dweller," *Pearls of Wisdom,* vol. 26, no. 38, Sept. 18, 1983.
35. Jesus Christ, "The Sanctification of the Heart," *Pearls of Wisdom,* vol. 31, no. 88, December 26, 1988.
36. Elizabeth Clare Prophet, "The Path of Twin Flames," *Pearls of Wisdom,* vol. 29, no. 25, June 10, 1986.

CHAPTER 9

This dictation was published in its entirety in *Pearls of Wisdom,* vol. 32, no. 65, December 31, 1989.

1. Luke 19:13.
2. Ps. 82:6; John 10:34; see the Jerusalem Bible.
3. John 10:1-16, 27, 28.
4. Matt. 18:11-14; Luke 15:3-7.
5. See Hercules, "We Shall Carry Your Burden," *Pearls of Wisdom,* vol. 32, no. 47, November 3, 1989.
6. See chapter 12.
7. Matt. 19:28; Luke 22:30; 1 Cor. 6:3.
8. Isa. 1:18.
9. Rom. 6:6; Eph. 4:22; Col. 3:9.

10. James 1:12.
11. Elizabeth Clare Prophet, "Lesson Two from the Holy Spirit: The Prerequisites to a Master-Disciple Relationship with the Holy Spirit," June 28, 1994.
12. Rev. 1:4, 8.
13. Jesus Christ, "The Gift of Resurrection's Flame," *Pearls of Wisdom,* vol. 33, no. 33, August 26, 1990.
14. Jesus Christ, September 1, 1993.
15. Matt. 11:28-30.
16. 1984 *Pearls of Wisdom, Book II,* Introduction II, p. 63.
17. Matt. 13:24-30.
18. Omri-Tas, "Saturate the Earth with Violet Flame!" *Pearls of Wisdom,* vol. 27, no. 50A, October 17, 1984.

CHAPTER 10

This dictation by Jesus the Christ is published in its entirety in *Pearls of Wisdom,* vol. 33, no. 16, April 29, 1990.

1. See Spiritual Exercises.
2. El Morya, "Bonded to the Lord of the First Ray," *Pearls of Wisdom,* vol. 33, no. 13, April 8, 1990.
3. Stigmata: the scientifically inexplicable reproduction of the wounds of the Passion of Christ on the body. The stigmata may be invisible, wherein pain is experienced without any physical signs, or visible, wherein open wounds or scars are seen on the hands, feet, near the heart, on the head, shoulders or back. These wounds may bleed either continuously or periodically, usually on Fridays or during Lent. Saint Francis of Assisi is the first known to have received the stigmata.
4. James 1:21.
5. Ps. 42:1.
6. Matt. 20:16; 22:14.
7. Mark 16:14.
8. Rom. 13:8-10; Gal. 5:14.
9. Matt. 6:24-34; Luke 12:22-31.
10. Rev. 12:10.
11. Matt. 24:36-41; Luke 17:34-36.
12. Isa. 40:4; Luke 3:5.
13. Luke 23:46.
14. Matt. 18:2, 3; Mark 10:15; Luke 18:17.
15. See chapter 8.
16. Rev. 12:17; 19:10.
17. Ezek. 1:4.

18. Exod. 28:36; 39:30; Jer. 2:3; Zech. 14:20.
19. Matt. 15:25-28; Mark 7:27-29.
20. Luke 12:42-48.
21. See Spiritual Exercises.
22. See Spiritual Exercises.
23. Rose of Light, "The Opening of the Rose of Light," *Pearls of Wisdom,* vol. 32, no. 52, November 8, 1989.
24. See Spiritual Exercises.
25. Gautama Buddha, "The Initiation of the Heart," *Pearls of Wisdom,* vol. 31 no. 84, December 10, 1988. See also Helena Roerich, *Heart* (New York: Agni Yoga Society, 1975), nos. 15, 105, 113, 206, 254, 350, 415, 423, 453, 547-48.
26. Agni yoga is the yoga of fire.
27. Ezek. 1:4.
28. Rose of Light, "The Opening of the Rose of Light."
29. The nine gifts of the Holy Spirit are described by Saint Paul in his first letter to the Corinthians: "For to one is given by the Spirit the word of wisdom; to another the word of knowledge by the same Spirit; to another faith by the same Spirit; to another the gifts of healing by the same Spirit; to another the working of miracles; to another prophecy; to another discerning of spirits; to another divers kinds of tongues; to another the interpretation of tongues." [1 Cor. 12:8-10]
30. Matt. 6:19-30.
31. Luke 12:42-48; 16:1-13; 1 Cor. 4:1, 2; 1 Pet. 4:10.
32. Matt. 28:18.
33. The Maha Chohan, "The Desiring of the Soul That Must Exceed All Other Desiring," *Pearls of Wisdom,* vol. 33, no. 19, May 20, 1990.
34. Matt. 28:18.
35. Saint Germain, "Freedom Is Imperiled This Day," *Pearls of Wisdom,* vol. 34, no. 38, August 4, 1991.
36. The Maha Chohan, "The Mandate of the Holy Spirit," *Pearls of Wisdom,* vol. 31, no. 29, June 19, 1988.
37. See Elizabeth Clare Prophet, Introduction I, "Lord Maitreya: The Coming Buddha Who Has Come," in 1984 *Pearls of Wisdom, Book I,* pp. 52-53.
38. The Maha Chohan, July 2, 1962.

CHAPTER 11

This dictation by Jesus the Christ is published in its entirety in *Pearls of Wisdom,* vol. 33, no. 49, December 16, 1990.

1. John 10:16.
2. Frequently, English usage of past centuries comes into play in ascended master dictations. Here the master chooses to use the phrase "things of which you desire to be delivered." Although in current usage, the words *from which* would normally be used (in the sense that one is "delivered from" something), *The Oxford English Dictionary* shows the "of which" form as obsolete. In former times, the phrase *delivered of* was often used to mean "to be set free from, released from, rescued from."
3. Isa. 6:5-8.
4. Rev. 20:4-6.
5. Jesus once appeared to Catherine of Siena as she was praying and said: "Do you know, daughter, who you are and who I am? If you knew these two things, you would be blessed. You are that which is not; I am He who is. If you have this knowledge in your soul, the enemy can never deceive you; you will escape all his snares; you will never consent to anything contrary to my commandments; and without difficulty you will acquire every grace, every truth, every light." Biographer Igino Giordani records that "with that lesson Catherine became fundamentally learned: she was founded upon a rock; there were no more shadows. I, nothing; God, All. I, nonbeing; God, Being." See Igino Giordani, *Saint Catherine of Siena—Doctor of the Church*, trans. Thomas J. Tobin (Boston: Daughters of St. Paul, St. Paul Editions, 1975), pp. 35, 36.
6. Luke 7:37-48.
7. Matt. 19:24; Mark 10:25; Luke 18:25.
8. Gen. 4:1-7.
9. The Ascended Master El Morya was embodied as Melchior, one of the three wise men who journeyed to give adoration to the Christ Child. These three adepts from the East charted the exact time and place of Jesus' birth by astrology. "We have seen his star in the East and are come to worship him" (see Matt. 2:1-12).
10. Luke 14:23.
11. Matt. 24:15-18; Mark 13:14-16.
12. Isa. 2:10-22; 13:6-16; 34:8; 61:2; 63:4-6; Jer. 46:10; Ezek. 30:3; Joel 1:15; 2:1, 2, 11, 31, 32; Zeph. 1:7-10, 14-18; Zech. 14:1; Mal. 4; 1 Thess. 5:2, 3; 2 Pet. 3:10-12; Rev. 1:10; 19:11-21; Matt. 24:15-31; Mark 13:14-27.
13. At the conclusion of his New Year's Eve Address, December 31, 1989, Gautama Buddha announced: "Blessed ones, may I present to you as I take my leave of you the Lord Buddha Jesus Christ, the Lord Buddha Kuthumi, who stand before you fully

arrayed in their Buddhahood and [fully capable of] taking you
on the long, long yet very short journey to your own Buddhahood" (*Pearls of Wisdom,* vol. 33, no. 22, January 14, 1990).
The messenger writes in her Introduction to the 1984 *Pearls of
Wisdom:* "Christic initiation is a prerequisite to Buddhic initiation. And Jesus is our Saviour who, with Kuthumi, has saved
our souls so that we may enter the highest path, following
their example all the way to the gate of the City of Light. But
look again, for these beloved World Teachers have also attained
to their Buddhahood and thus they are fully empowered to take
us all the way to the throne of Shamballa, East and West"
(1984 *Pearls of Wisdom, Book I,* Introduction I, p. 40).
14. The word *virya* (Sanskrit) is variously translated as "vigor,"
    "energy," "strength," "manliness," "zeal," "power," "dili-
    gence." In Buddhist teachings, *virya* is one of the ten *paramitas*
    ("perfect virtues") that one must practice and perfect as a pre-
    requisite to the attainment of Bodhisattvahood.
15. Prov. 16:32; 25:28.
16. John 21:15-17.
17. *avatar* [Sanskrit *avatara* 'descent', from *avatarati* 'he descends',
    from *ava-* 'away' + *tarati* 'he crosses over']: a divine incarnation.
18. Every soul of light has a destined day of victory. If one fulfills
    all things required of him by God, he will achieve his victory on
    that day. If not, that day will find him unprepared and will pass
    like any other day.
19. John 9:5.
20. Matt. 7:29.
21. 2 Kings 2:13-14.
22. Hilarion, "The Challenges of Apostleship: The Call, the Con-
    version, the Working of the Works of the Lord," *Pearls of Wis-
    dom,* vol. 20, no. 16, April 17, 1977.
23. Hilarion, "A Campaign on Behalf of the Children of the
    World," *Pearls of Wisdom,* vol. 38, no. 7, February 12, 1995.
24. Matt. 24:14; Mark 13:10.
25. Hilarion, "Preach the Gospel of Salvation in Every Nation,"
    Pearls of Wisdom, vol. 33, no. 39, October 7, 1990.
26. Gautama Buddha, "The Resurrection May Not Be Postponed,"
    Pearls of Wisdom, vol. 33, no. 2, January 14, 1990.
27. Jesus Christ, "Close Communion," *Pearls of Wisdom,* vol. 37,
    no. 45, November 6, 1994.

CHAPTER 12

This dictation by Jesus with Magda is published in its entirety in

Pearls of Wisdom, vol. 34, no. 8, February 24, 1991.
1. Exod. 26:31-35; 40:1-3, 21; Lev. 16:2, 12, 15; 21:23; Matt. 27:51; Heb. 6:19; 9:1-12; 10:19, 20.
2. Gen. 32:30; Exod. 33:11; Num. 14:14; Deut. 5:4; 34:10; Ezek. 20:33-35.
3. See Mother Mary, "The Lost Teachings of Jesus on Women's Rights," *Pearls of Wisdom,* vol. 33, no. 41, October 21, 1990.
4. Rev. 21:1, 2.
5. Rev. 1:8, 11; 21:6; 22:13.
6. Gen. 1:11, 12.
7. 1 Cor. 15:51, 52.
8. Matt. 5:16.
9. John 8:31.
10. Matt. 26:26-28.
11. John 16:33
12. John 11:38-44.
13. Matt. 18:11-14; Luke 15:3-7; 19:10.
14. John 8:12; 9:5.
15. Matt. 5:14.
16. Matt. 18:20.
17. Sanat Kumara, "The Message of the I AM Presence Defeats the Shrinking Man Syndrome," *Pearls of Wisdom,* vol. 42, no. 15, April 11, 1999.
18. Mother Mary, "The Fusion of Your Heart with My Own," *Pearls of Wisdom,* vol. 33, no. 48, December 9, 1990.
19. Patricia Kirmond, *Messages from Heaven,* p. 103.
20. Astrea, "I Enlist Your Help," *Pearls of Wisdom,* vol. 34, no. 13, March 31, 1991.
21. Elizabeth Clare Prophet, "Teachings of Jesus Christ on Your Path of Personal Christhood," June 27, 1993.
22. Saint Germain, "Preparing for the Seventh Root Race and the Golden Age," *Pearls of Wisdom,* vol. 39, no. 14, April 7, 1996.
23. Astrea, in *Keepers of the Flame Lesson* 23, p. 39.
24. Astrea, "I Enlist Your Help," *Pearls of Wisdom,* vol. 34, no. 13, March 31, 1991.
25. El Morya, "The Mission of Twin Flames Today," *Pearls of Wisdom,* vol. 28, no. 33, August 18, 1985.
26. Eph. 6:12.
27. Mother Mary, "To Prick the Conscience of the Nations," *Pearls of Wisdom,* vol. 27, no. 48, September 30, 1984.
28. Saint Germain, "The Opening of the Seventh Seal," *Pearls of Wisdom,* vol. 30, no. 37, September 13, 1987.
29. Patricia Kirmond, *Messages from Heaven,* p. 105.

CHAPTER 13

This dictation by Jesus is published in its entirety in *Pearls of Wisdom*, vol. 34, no. 18, May 5, 1991. The Messenger's scriptural reading prior to Jesus' dictation was John 21.

A recommended resource on the subject of abortion is "What Women Need to Know about the Soul when Faced with Tough Decisions" (Minneapolis: Mystic Paths Publishing, 2001). For copies, go to www.soulchoice.org, or call 1-888-TheSoul.

1. Rev. 19:11-16.
2. John 20:16.
3. On January 22, 1973, the Supreme Court issued its decision in the case of Roe v. Wade, which legalized abortion nationwide. The decision was based on an implied constitutional right to privacy. The court also ruled that the unborn child is not included in the definition of a "person" as protected under the Constitution. From 1973 to the time of Jesus' dictation in 1991, over 25 million abortions had been performed in the United States. By 2001 the total was more than 40 million. An estimated 40 million to 60 million abortions each year had been performed worldwide from 1973 to 1991, making a total of between 730 million and 1.1 billion.
4. Acts 2.
5. Matt. 21:12, 13; Mark 11:15-17; Luke 19:45, 46.
6. John 21:15-17.
7. James 1:21. See also Jesus Christ, December 25, 1985, and Lord Maitreya, January 1, 1986, in 1986 *Pearls of Wisdom*, Book I, pp. 112-15, 206-12.
8. John 5:39.
9. On March 30, 1991, the messenger conducted an all-day seminar, "Life Begets Life," on the right to life and the ascended masters' teachings on abortion.
10. In a dictation given October 3, 1965, the Goddess of Liberty stated the position of the Karmic Board on family planning: "You ought not to bring forth more children than you are able to care for and for whom you may adequately express your love."

Those in the pro-choice movement say that a woman should be able to choose whether or not to have a child. As the messenger stated in her "Life Begets Life" seminar, March 30, 1991, "We all agree but we also must state that she makes her choice before conception—not after. We have better and better birth-control methods. And the time to decide whether you are going to participate in the creative process is never after conception. Abortion is not a birth-control method."

11. The third-century Christian theologian Origen of Alexandria, an embodiment of the messenger Mark L. Prophet, taught the doctrine of the preexistence of the soul. See *Origen, On First Principles,* 2.9.5-8, trans. G. W. Butterworth (Gloucester, Mass.: Peter Smith, 1973), pp. 133-37; Elizabeth Clare Prophet with Erin L. Prophet, *Reincarnation: The Missing Link in Christianity,* ch. 16.

12. John 5:25.

13. 1 John 4:17, 18.

14. Luke 24:13-35.

15. Luke 19:13.

16. *Gospel of Thomas,* logia 13, 108, in James M. Robinson, ed., *The Nag Hammadi Library in English,* 3d ed., rev. (New York: HarperCollins Publishers, 1990), pp. 127, 137, paperback.

17. Elizabeth Clare Prophet, *The Astrology of the Four Horsemen,* p. 125.

18. Mark L. Prophet and Elizabeth Clare Prophet, *Saint Germain on Alchemy,* p. 293.

19. Gal. 6:7.

20. *Saint Germain on Alchemy,* pp. 65-66.

21. Mother Mary, "Planetary Judgment," *Pearls of Wisdom,* vol. 40, no. 53, December 29, 1997.

22. Saint Germain, "A Line of Sacred Fire: I Have Drawn It with My Life," *Pearls of Wisdom,* vol. 25, no. 15, April 11, 1982.

23. The Blessed Mother, "I Stand By You: Champion the Cause of the Child!" *Pearls of Wisdom,* vol. 36, no. 16, April 18, 1993.

24. The Great Divine Director, "Arrest the Cycles," *Pearls of Wisdom,* vol. 26, no. 36, September 4, 1983.

25. Adapted from Lanello, "How to Ascend," *Pearls of Wisdom,* vol. 35, no. 10, March 8, 1992.

26. Kuan Yin, "The Gift of Good Friday," *Pearls of Wisdom,* vol. 36, no. 24, June 13, 1993.

27. Adapted from an invocation by Elizabeth Clare Prophet, May 3, 1980.

CHAPTER 14

This dictation by Jesus the Christ is published in its entirety in *Pearls of Wisdom,* vol. 34, no. 23, June 9, 1991.

1. Jer. 31:33, 34.

2. Matt. 24:22; Mark 13:20.

3. Num. 13:21; 14:28-35; 20:1; 27:14; Deut. 32:51, 52.

4. Mal. 3:1-3.
5. Rev. 3:11.
6. Rom. 12:19; Heb. 10:30; Deut. 32:35, 36.
7. Matt. 27:16-26; Mark 15:7-15; Luke 23:13-26; John 18:38-40.
8. Adapted and excerpted from Elizabeth Clare Prophet, "The Golden Age of Jesus Christ on Atlantis," April 28, 1991.
9. Prov. 14:12.
10. El Morya, "Give Me Your God-Controlled Attention," *Pearls of Wisdom,* vol. 35, no. 19, May 10, 1992.
11. John 10:1-10; Rev. 3:8.
12. "The Golden Age of Jesus Christ on Atlantis."
13. Saint Patrick, "I Call the Living Saints," *Pearls of Wisdom,* vol. 28, no. 16, April 21, 1985.
14. El Morya, "The Light and the Beautiful," *Pearls of Wisdom,* vol. 31, no. 77, November 13, 1988.
15. John 8:11.
16. Matt. 18:21-35.
17. Kuan Yin, "Forgive and Be Forgiven," *Pearls of Wisdom,* vol. 34, no. 58, November 17, 1991.

CHAPTER 15

This dictation by Jesus the Christ is published in its entirety in *Pearls of Wisdom,* vol. 34, no. 66, December 22, 1991.

1. Matt. 22:1-14.
2. See 1991 *Pearls of Wisdom,* pp. 348-49, 355-56, 739-50. For Omri-Tas' dispensation to multiply your violet flame decrees, see pages 178-79.
3. See Igino Giordani, *Saint Catherine of Siena—Doctor of the Church,* trans. Thomas J. Tobin (Boston: Daughters of St. Paul, St. Paul Editions, 1975), pp. 35, 36.
4. See Og Mandino, *The Greatest Salesman in the World* (New York: Bantam Books, 1968).
5. Goddess of Light, "Weaving the Wedding Garment with Crystal Fires and Emerald Rays," July 3, 1974.
6. Gautama Buddha, "Once Upon a Footstep," *Pearls of Wisdom,* vol. 31, no. 2, January 10, 1988.
7. The Maha Chohan, "Communion of the Holy Spirit with the Souls of Mankind," April 11, 1974.
8. Mark L. Prophet and Elizabeth Clare Prophet, *Climb the Highest Mountain: The Path of the Higher Self,* pp. 8-9.
9. Elizabeth Clare Prophet, "On the Soul," *Pearls of Wisdom,* vol. 38, no. 29, July 2, 1995.
10. The Goddess of Wisdom, "A Page in the Mother's Book of

Healing," *Pearls of Wisdom,* vol. 20, no. 9, February 27, 1977.

11. Saint Germain, "Seize the Torch of Aquarius and Run with It!" *Pearls of Wisdom,* vol. 39, no. 30, July 28, 1996.
12. Matt. 19:19.
13. Excerpted from Elizabeth Clare Prophet, "How to Give and Receive More Love," May 4, 1997.
14. Djwal Kul, December 28, 1996.
15. Gal. 4:19; 2:20.
16. Elizabeth Clare Prophet, "Roots of Christian Mysticism," June 27, 1992.

CHAPTER 16

1. Matt. 25:1-13.
2. Jesus' dictation commenced at 7:55 pm.
3. Heb. 12:2.
4. Matt. 19:29-30; Mark 10:29-31.
5. Rev. 22:11.
6. The qualities of God-harmony, God-gratitude and God-justice are charted on the 6, 7, and 8 o'clock lines of the cosmic clock, comprising the emotional quadrant. For more information on the cosmic clock, see Elizabeth Clare Prophet, *The Great White Brotherhood in the Culture, History and Religion of America,* ch. 15.
7. The story of Phylos the Tibetan is found in his book *A Dweller on Two Planets* (Borden Publishing Company). Phylos recounts his embodiment as Zailm Numinos on the continent of Atlantis, his experiences in the afterlife, and his next incarnation in nineteenth century America. In that embodiment he faced the karma he had made twelve thousand years earlier on Atlantis. Phylos says, "The state after the grave…is the condition of harvest, where no one acts….Earthly conditions begun on earth…must be finished on earth. So karma decrees" (p. 238). Elizabeth Clare Prophet has given commentary on Phylos' teachings in a series of lectures, available through The Summit Lighthouse.
8. Heb. 11:35.
9. 1 Pet. 3:19.
10. Heros and Amora, *Pearls of Wisdom,* vol. 32, no. 20, May 14, 1989.
11. Elizabeth Clare Prophet, "On Dealing with Death, Discarnates and Malevolent Spirits," Part III, August 22, 1991.
12. Ibid.

13. *Pearls of Wisdom,* vol. 31, no. 46, July 30, 1988, note 2.
14. Archangel Michael, "The Summoning: Straight Talk and a Sword from the Hierarch of Banff," *Pearls of Wisdom,* vol. 28, no. 10, March 10, 1985.
15. Saint Germain, "Put in a Good Word for Me!" *Pearls of Wisdom,* vol. 40, no. 31, August 3, 1997.
16. Lanello, "Points of Darkness," *Pearls of Wisdom,* vol. 36, no. 2, January 10, 1993.
17. Ibid.
18. *Pearls of Wisdom,* vol. 38, no. 38, September 3, 1995, note 26.

CHAPTER 17

This dictation by Jesus the Christ is published in its entirety in *Pearls of Wisdom,* vol. 34, no. 67, December 29, 1991.

1. Rev. 21:1, 23-25; 22:5.
2. 1 John 4:1.
3. Rev. 22:12.
4. Jesus, "Christhood Is the Call," *Pearls of Wisdom,* vol. 37, no. 48, November 27, 1994.
5. Lanello, "The Covenant of Compassion," *Pearls of Wisdom,* vol. 27, no. 35, July 1, 1984.
6. Mother Mary, "A Trilogy of the Mother III: The Initiation of the Fusion of Solar Energies," *Pearls of Wisdom,* vol. 17, no. 52, December 29, 1974.
7. Elizabeth Clare Prophet, *Saint Germain's Prophecy for the New Millennium,* pp. 343-44.
8. Kuthumi, "Remember the Ancient Encounter," *Pearls of Wisdom,* vol. 28, no. 9, March 3, 1985.
9. Mother Mary, "The Re-Creation of Self," *Pearls of Wisdom,* vol. 32, no. 44, October 29, 1989.
10. Elizabeth Clare Prophet, "Messenger's Meditation on God in your Heart," *Pearls of Wisdom,* vol. 27, no. 58, December 9, 1984.
11. *Saint Germain's Prophecy for the New Millennium,* pp. 344-45.

CHAPTER 18

This dictation by Jesus the Christ is published in its entirety in *Pearls of Wisdom,* vol. 35, no. 18, May 3, 1992.

1. John 6.
2. See chapter 7.

3. John 2:1-11.
4. See Elizabeth Clare Prophet, *The Lost Years of Jesus.*
5. Matt. 11:28.
6. "Lo, here! Lo, there!" Matt. 24:23-26; Mark 13:21, 22; Luke 17:20, 21.
7. "Abba, Father." Mark 14:36; Rom. 8:14-17; Gal. 4:6, 7.
8. Archangel Raphael, "Golden Pearls from the Heart of the Earth," *Pearls of Wisdom,* vol. 35, no. 2, January 12, 1992.
9. John 7:38.
10. Mother Mary, "Marriage in the Church Universal and Triumphant II," *Pearls of Wisdom,* vol. 27, no. 2, January 8, 1984.
11. Matt. 24:27.
12. Saint Germain, "Choose You This Day Whom Ye Will Serve," *Pearls of Wisdom,* vol. 18, no. 31, August 3, 1975.
13. Ps. 42:1.
14. Serapis Bey, "Motivation," *Pearls of Wisdom,* vol. 33, no. 3, January 21, 1990.
15. Prov. 4:23.
16. Elizabeth Clare Prophet, "The Science of the Sacred Heart," Part 1, *Pearls of Wisdom,* vol. 44, no. 13, April 1, 2001.
17. Jesus, "Must We Have Only a Remnant?" *Pearls of Wisdom,* vol. 29, no. 74, December 14, 1986.
18. Elizabeth Clare Prophet, "A Special Meditation on the Mother Flame," July 2, 1978.

CHAPTER 19

This dictation by Jesus the Christ is published in *Pearls of Wisdom,* vol. 35, no. 66, December 16, 1992.

1. 2 Cor. 12:9.
2. Matt. 12:43-45; Luke 11:24-26.
3. Matt. 28:20.
4. Jesus, "The Igniting of Joy," *Pearls of Wisdom,* vol. 35, no. 67, December 20, 1992.
5. Elizabeth Clare Prophet, "The Lost Teachings of Jesus on the Gospel of Thomas," October 13, 1991.
6. Elaine Pagels, *The Gnostic Gospels* (New York: Random House, Vintage Books, 1981), p. 22.
7. The messenger is referring to *The Secret Book of James, The Gospel of Thomas, The Book of Thomas* and *The Secret Book of John,* four Gnostic texts found in Marvin W. Meyer, trans., *The Secret Teachings of Jesus: Four Gnostic Gospels* (New

York: Random House, Vintage Books, 1986).
8. *The Nag Hammadi Library in English* (San Francisco: Harper & Row, 1981).
9. John 1:14.
10. Elizabeth Clare Prophet, "The Lost Teachings of Jesus on the Gospel of Thomas."
11. Carol Lee Flinders, *Enduring Grace: Living Portraits of Seven Women Mystics,* (San Francisco: HarperSanFrancisco, 1993), p. 114.
12. John 14:16, 26.
13. Rev. 10:9.
14. Matt. 10:34.
15. *The Secret Teachings of Jesus: Four Gnostic Gospels,* The Gospel of Thomas, Saying 38, p. 26.
16. Elizabeth Clare Prophet, "The Lost Teachings of Jesus on the Gospel of Thomas."
17. Elizabeth Clare Prophet, *Inner Perspectives* (Corwin Springs, Mont.: The Summit Lighthouse Library, 2001) p. 324.
18. Elizabeth Clare Prophet, *The Fourteenth Rosary: The Mystery of Surrender,* double-cassette album, A91143. Booklet of same title with all the words of the prayers, devotions and scriptural readings is included or available separately from The Summit Lighthouse.

CONCLUSION
1. John 14:12.

Pocket Guides to Practical Spirituality Series:
Alchemy of the Heart
Your Seven Energy Centers
Soul Mates and Twin Flames
Violet Flame to Heal Body, Mind and Soul
The Art of Practical Spirituality
How to Work with Angels
Creative Abundance
Access the Power of Your Higher Self
The Creative Power of Sound

TITLES FROM
THE SUMMIT LIGHTHOUSE LIBRARY®
The Opening of the Seventh Seal
Inner Perspectives
Morya I
Community
Wanting to Be Born: The Cry of the Soul
Walking with the Master: Answering the Call of Jesus
Afra: Brother of Light

FOR MORE INFORMATION
For more information about Summit University Press or
The Summit Lighthouse Library, to place an order or to receive
a free catalog of our books and products, please contact us at:

Summit University Press
PO Box 5000, Corwin Springs, MT 59030-5000 USA
Tel: 1-800-245-5445 or 406-848-9500
Fax: 1-800-221-8307 or 406-848-9555
www.summituniversitypress.com

Mark L. Prophet and Elizabeth Clare Prophet are pioneers of modern spirituality and internationally renowned authors. For more than 40 years the Prophets have published the teachings of the immortal saints and sages of East and West known as the ascended masters. Together they have given the world a new understanding of the ancient wisdom as well as a path of practical mysticism.

Their books, available in fine bookstores worldwide, have been translated into more than 20 languages and are sold throughout the world.